Banana Pro Blueprints

Leverage the capabilities of Banana Pro with exciting real-world projects

Ruediger Follmann

Tony Zhang

BIRMINGHAM - MUMBAI

Banana Pro Blueprints

First published: December 2015

Production reference: 1211215

Published by Packt Publishing Ltd.
Livery Place
35 Livery Street
Birmingham B3 2PB, UK.

ISBN 978-1-78355-238-2

www.packtpub.com

Credits

Authors
Ruediger Follmann
Tony Zhang

Reviewers
Lalith Gallage
Nikolaos Margaris
Paul Mundt
Rob Seder

Commissioning Editor
Edward Bowkett

Acquisition Editor
Meeta Rajani

Content Development Editor
Anish Sukumaran

Technical Editor
Chinmay S. Puranik

Copy Editor
Sonia Michelle Cheema

Project Coordinator
Izzat Contractor

Proofreader
Safis Editing

Indexer
Hemangini Bari

Graphics
Disha Haria

Production Coordinator
Conidon Miranda

Cover Work
Conidon Miranda

About the Authors

Ruediger Follmann was born in 1968 in Germany. He studied electrical engineering at RWTH Aachen, Germany, and received his PhD from the University of Duisburg-Essen, Germany. He has worked for IMST GmbH, Germany, for more than 20 years, where he heads the RF circuits and system integration department. IMST is a design and development company with more than 170 employees. He uses embedded boards in many different projects, for example, in order to control MMICs or hybrid electronics. Follmann is the author of many technical articles as well as *Das Raspberry Pi Kompendium*, *Springer*.

Tony Zhang was born in 1990 in China. He studied control science and engineering at HIT, China, and received his master's degree in 2015. Since 2014, Tony has been working with LeMaker community, where he is the cofounder and is heading the R&D department.

About the Reviewers

Lalith Gallage is a charted IT professional with more than 12 years of experience in information communication technology, including embedded control designing, industrial automation, and CMS (SharePoint Server, Joomla, sensenet, Umbraco, and Odoo) customization. He has published several articles on the CodeProject website (http://www.codeproject.com/) and enjoys writing in his free time.

He is currently working at Sri Lanka Telecom and is a guest lecturer at many leading institutes in Sri Lanka in the fields of microcontroller and C# programming. In his free time, he likes to relax in his aquaponic garden.

He has expertise in several known languages, such as C++, C#, Python, PLSQL, PHP, and ASP.NET. He is also proficient in certain hardware platforms such as Arduino, Raspberry Pi, Banana Pi, Rabbit, and PIC.

His professional qualifications include a masters degree in IT from Cardiff Metropolitan University, UK, BIT from the University of Colombo, Sri Lanka, national diploma in engineering sciences (electronics and telecommunication) from Sri Lanka, and CITP from the UK.

Nikolaos Margaris currently works as a senior frontend developer on a collaboration and communication software that uses AngularJS and NodeJS. He enjoys clean and performant JavaScript code and tests it too. In his spare time, he likes reading about new technologies and wandering through the IoT world. Good music and some retro PC/console games have always added flavor to his life. Reviewing this book was an enjoyable experience for him, and he hopes to come across more opportunities like this one. You can find out more about him at http://www.nikolaosmargaris.gr/.

> All thanks to my soul mate, Vaya. Her love and patience gives meaning to my life.

Paul Mundt is the founder and managing director of Adaptant Solutions AG, a software and solutions company focused on providing adaptable technologies and solutions needed to enable cross-sectorial data utilization and exploration in an evolving data regulation and compliance landscape.

Previously, Paul was the CTO of OS & Virtualization, and director of the system software department at Huawei's European Research Center, leading an R&D department responsible for the future OS and virtualization strategy and architecture, focusing on the areas of heterogeneous systems, convergence of Cloud and HPC, and the future data center architectures.

Earlier, at Renesas, he was responsible for establishing both the initial open source strategy and vision, while leading the organization to consistently become one among the top 10 contributors to the Linux kernel, resulting in wide-reaching system software and IP consolidation across a diverse MPU/MCU product portfolio.

He has more than 15 years of experience in both Linux kernel development and technology management across a diverse range of domains (HPC, embedded, enterprise, and carrier grade). He has also previously worked for Nokia, TimeSys, and MontaVista in various technical and leadership positions.

Rob Seder has been involved in information technology for over 20 years. He has been a technophile and geek from an early age. His day job primarily involves working on Microsoft .NET technologies, but he also invests heavily in Linux, Mac, IoT, automation, 3D printing, and other interesting infrastructures or development technologies. Rob has mostly worked in financial and insurance industries over the years, and he enjoys keeping himself up to date with the most current technologies that are available.

You can find Rob's blog at `http://blog.robseder.com` or contact him at `@RobSeder` on Twitter.

www.PacktPub.com

Support files, eBooks, discount offers, and more

For support files and downloads related to your book, please visit www.PacktPub.com.

Did you know that Packt offers eBook versions of every book published, with PDF and ePub files available? You can upgrade to the eBook version at www.PacktPub.com and as a print book customer, you are entitled to a discount on the eBook copy. Get in touch with us at service@packtpub.com for more details.

At www.PacktPub.com, you can also read a collection of free technical articles, sign up for a range of free newsletters and receive exclusive discounts and offers on Packt books and eBooks.

https://www2.packtpub.com/books/subscription/packtlib

Do you need instant solutions to your IT questions? PacktLib is Packt's online digital book library. Here, you can search, access, and read Packt's entire library of books.

Why subscribe?

- Fully searchable across every book published by Packt
- Copy and paste, print, and bookmark content
- On demand and accessible via a web browser

Free access for Packt account holders

If you have an account with Packt at www.PacktPub.com, you can use this to access PacktLib today and view 9 entirely free books. Simply use your login credentials for immediate access.

Table of Contents

Preface	**ix**
Chapter 1: Introduction to Banana Pro	**1**
Banana Pro	**2**
Specifications of Banana Pro	3
Banana Pro onboard LEDs	9
Getting started	**9**
The first boot	12
Available operating systems for Banana Pro	**13**
Android	14
Linux	15
The FEX file	18
Transferring an OS to a hard disk	23
Add-ons	**27**
The LCD module	27
The 7-inch LCD step-by-step guide	28
The camera module	33
A step-by-step guide to the camera module	34
Cases	36
GPIO add-ons	38
An onboard microphone	39
Summary	**40**
Chapter 2: Programming Languages	**41**
Basic principles	**42**
Remote connections	42
Secure Shell	42
Using xrdp for remote desktop connection	43
Basic requirements for programming Banana Pro	44
Editors	45

Shell programming	**47**
Checking the Banana Pro temperature	47
Controlling Banana Pro's LEDs from SSH	48
Programming GPIOs from SSH	50
Another shell example	52
WiringBP	53
Python	**55**
The basics	56
A simple web server	57
Using Python for GPIO	58
Setting LEDs in Python	60
A Python window example	62
C/C++	**64**
The WiringBP C code example	66
C access to onboard LEDs	67
Debugger	73
Scratch	**76**
Hello world – example for Scratch	77
Using LN Digital with Scratch	78
New kernels	**81**
Compiling on Banana Pro	82
Cross-compilation	83
Summary	**85**
Chapter 3: Wireless Projects	**87**
OpenVPN	**88**
Connecting from Android	93
WLAN	**95**
Setting up WLAN	95
Setting up an access point mode	96
On air	**100**
The AirPlay protocol	101
AirPrint	104
Printing from Android and iOS	111
Serving web pages	**112**
Installing PHP and MySQL	113
Installing contao	116
A measurement server	**125**
The FTDI/SPI control of devices	126
A web server	129
Explanations	131
Summary	**132**

Chapter 4: An Arcade Cabinet — **133**

Implementing hardware accelerations — **134**
  Installing dependencies — 134
    Installing modules — 134
    Installing packages — 135
    Installing a directory — 135
  Installing libdri2 — 135
  Installing libump — 136
  Installing the sunxi-mali driver — 136
    The X11 version of the sunxi-mali driver — 137
    The framebuffer version of the sunxi-mali driver — 137
  Installing xf86-video-fbturbo — 137
  Getting device permission — 138
  Testing hardware acceleration — 139

Implementing libretro emulators — **142**
  Installing dependent packages — 142
  Installing libretro frontend - RetroArch — 142
    The X11 version of RetroArch — 143
    The framebuffer version of RetroArch — 143
  Installing libretro cores — 144
    Installing iMAM4ALL libretro core — 144
    Installing the SNES libretro core — 144
  Configuration — 145
  Playing games — 146
    Playing a game directly with a command line — 146
    Playing a game from the RetroArch menu interface — 147
  Testing games — 149

Building PCSX — **149**
  Installing dependent packages — 149
  Installing PCSX — 149
    Downloading PCSX ReARMed — 150
    Patching — 150
    Compiling and installing — 150
    Playing PCSX games — 151
  Configuration — 151
  Testing PCSX games — 152

Making an arcade cabinet for Banana Pro — **152**
  Preparing the materials — 152
    A suitcase — 152
    A joystick — 153
    A micro USB extended line — 154
    A USB hub — 154
    An LCD display — 155
    An audio extended line — 155
    A mini keyboard — 156

Designing a frame 156
Assembling 157
Assembling a base frame 158
Assembling Banana Pro and a joystick 158
Mounting an LCD 159
Assembling a top frame 160
Playing the Banana Pro arcade cabinet **161**
Configuring output to an LCD 161
Configuring a joystick controller 164
Playing the game on the arcade cabinet 166
Summary **167**
Chapter 5: A Multimedia Center **169**
Kernel preparation **170**
Adding the I2S audio device 170
Setting the graphics memory to maximum 172
Deactivating display driver kernel logging 173
Activating IR driver key repetition 174
Activating the sunxi lirc driver 174
Correcting display driver brightness 175
Adding the DVB-SKY S960 USB box 176
Installing the accelerated mali driver 176
Video Disk Recorder (VDR) **178**
Setting display settings 178
Setting locales 179
Adding (non-free) Debian multimedia packages 180
Loading required modules 180
A network address 180
Editing the FEX file 181
Installing required packages 182
Installing and patching VDPAU 183
Compiling VDR 185
Defining a sound device 188
Adding a default sound device 188
Using an electrical SPDIF with Banana Pro 189
Configuring a remote control 190
irexec 196
Adding a USB DVB stick 196
The DVB kernel driver 196
The DVB userspace driver 200
VDR scripts 201

Adding plugins to VDR   204
  Watching DVDs   205
  Listening to audio CDs   206
  Watching teletext   207
  Changing VDR's skin   208
  Streaming TV to mobile devices   210
  Switching to external players   211
  Additional plugins   212
Remote controlling the VDR   212
Troubleshooting   213
  Device permissions   213
  Changing libvdpau version   214
The Xbox Multimedia Center (XBMC) installation   **214**
Summary   **217**
Chapter 6: Remote Controlling a Smart Monitor Car   **219**
Implementing the IP camera   **220**
Installing ffmpeg   220
Instaling nginx   221
Configuring the nginx server   222
  Starting the nginx server   222
  Accessing the nginx server   223
  Autostarting the nginx server at system boot 224
Setting up a camera   226
  Camera specifications   226
  Connecting the camera module   228
  Testing the camera module on Banana Pro   231
Streaming a video via the Internet   232
Setting up the hardware of a smart monitor car   **234**
Preparing the materials   234
  A car suite   235
  The L289N motor drive board   236
  Battery   236
  A 5 inch LCD   237
Assembly   237
Configuring the display output for the 5 inch LCD   240
Controlling a smart monitor car using a remote   **240**
Webiopi for Banana Pro   240
  Installing webiopi for Banana Pro   240
  Testing webiopi on Banana Pro   241
Using webiopi to control the car   245
  The control logic   246
  Writing the webiopi controlling code   246
Adding the car controls to the IP camera web page   254
Summary   **256**

Chapter 7: A Laser Engraver — **257**

Setting up the frame for laser engraving — **258**
Preparing materials — 258
Setting up the laser engraving machine hardware — 262

Configuring software on Banana Pro — **264**
Installing dependencies — 264
Installing the GrblController software — 264

Installing software on a PC — **267**
Installing Inkscape — 267
Installing Arduino — 268

Loading a program into the laser CPU — **269**
Loading bootloader — 269
Loading the driving code — 270

How to use a laser engraver — **273**
Generate the G code — 273
Beginning the engraving process — 278

Summary — **279**

Chapter 8: Scratch – Building a Smart House — **281**

Configuring LeScratch — **282**
Installing the prerequisites — 282
Setting up the system — 283
Setting up Scratch Mesh — 284
Running LeScratch — 284

Controlling the LeScratch peripherals — **286**
General Purpose Input Output (GPIO) — 287
Instructions — 287
Example: The GPIO board — 287
Inter-Integrated Circuit — 291
Instructions — 291
Example – a LN-HUB-32IO USB hub — 292
Serial Peripheral Interface (SPI) — 294
Instructions — 295
Example – LN digital or SPI general — 296
Example: LN Digital (the LNDI commands) — 297
The step motor — 298
Technical specifications — 299
Example – the step motor — 300
Real-time clock — 302
Technical specifications — 303
Example – RTC — 303
The ultrasonic sensor — 305
Technical specifications — 305
Example – the ultrasonic sensor — 306

The humidity and temperature sensor   307
    Technical specifications   307
    Example – the DHT sensor   308
The sound detect sensor   309
    Technical specifications   310
    Example – the sound detect sensor   310
The AD/DA converter   312
    Technical specifications   312
    Example – the AD/DA convertor   313
Photoresistor   315
    Technical specifications   315
    Example – a photoresistor   316
The touch sensor   318
    Technical specifications   318
    Example – the touch sensor   318
The tilt sensor   319
    Technical specifications   319
    Example – the tilt sensor   320
The LCD1602 display   321
    Technical specifications   322
    Example – the LCD1602 display   322
Building the LeScratch smart house   **324**
Summary   **331**
Index   **333**

Preface

The book mainly focuses on some popular applications and projects using Banana Pro. It first introduces the basic usage of Banana Pro, including its hardware and software, and then some applications, such as a multimedia center and laser engraver. The sole purpose of this book will be to show what you can do with Banana Pro through a number of projects, ranging from home automation projects, cameras around the house, and robotics.

This book follows a tactical plan that will guide you through the implementation of Banana Pro and its configurations. You will then learn the various programming languages used with Banana Pi with the help of in-depth examples.

What this book covers

Chapter 1, *Introduction to Banana Pro*, introduces the Banana Pro single board computer. It explains all its available interfaces as well as the installation of the Linux OS, which will be used in this book.

Chapter 2, *Programming Languages*, explains several programming languages, such as Python, C/C++, and Scratch. In several examples, the usage of these programming languages is shown through a step-by-step approach.

Chapter 3, *Wireless Projects*, introduces wireless projects. It shows how Banana Pro can be used as a wireless hotspot or print server. Additionally, the serving of web pages is explained in combination with content management systems. Finally, a measurement server is set up in order to control an electronic circuit.

Chapter 4, An Arcade Cabinet, describes how to turn Banana Pro into an arcade cabinet. A step-by-step approach shows you how to install and configure different game emulations. This chapter also describes the steps required to set up a cabinet house with the help of a joystick and an LCD display for Banana Pro.

Chapter 5, A Multimedia Center, introduces the usage of Banana Pro as a multimedia center. You will be shown how a DVB receiver is set up through a series of steps. This receiver allows the recording of TV transmissions, watching DVDs, and listening to audio CDs.

Chapter 6, Remote Controlling a Smart Monitor Car, teaches you how to make a small mobile car with the remote monitor function. It describes how to realize the IP camera function on Banana Pro. It also shows you how to set up a small mobile car. Finally, you will see how a web page can be used to control the car and view the video of the camera in the car.

Chapter 7, A Laser Engraver, shows the laser engraver made by Banana Pro along with a laser CPU. You will learn how to design the frame of the laser engraver and use different kinds of software on the Banana Pro. The laser CPU and PC can be used together to engrave patterns on some special types of material such as cardboard.

Chapter 8, Scratch – Building a Smart House, describes how to use Scratch and some other GPIO libraries together to control different sensors. Then, you will learn how to combine all the sensors together in a virtual small house to simulate the smart house.

What you need for this book

You would need Banana Pro, an SD card (a minimum of 4 GB is recommended), an AC plug, a hard disk drive, and a USB DVB receiver (optional).

Who this book is for

This book is for all embedded board enthusiasts who want to use their credit-card-sized computer boards for extraordinary projects. An example of LeMaker's Banana Pro computer as a home entertainment center or a arcade cabinet is described in a step-by-step approach. Get the most out of your embedded board using it in your daily lives or for challenging projects. This book is the perfect guide for these purposes.

Conventions

In this book, you will find a number of text styles that distinguish between different kinds of information. Here are some examples of these styles and an explanation of their meaning.

Code words in text, database table names, folder names, filenames, file extensions, pathnames, dummy URLs, user input, and Twitter handles are shown as follows: "On a wired connection, it can be read from the `eth0` section by typing the `sudo ifconfig` command in a shell."

A block of code is set as follows:

```
#include <stdio.h>
double div(double a, double b)
{
    return(a/b);
}

int main(void)
{
int a;

    for (a=4; a>0; a--)
printf("10:%d = %lf\n", a, div(10,a));
    return 0;
}
```

When we wish to draw your attention to a particular part of a code block, the relevant lines or items are set in bold:

```
ARCH = arm
PLATFORM = generic
BUILTIN_GPU = unai
SOUND_DRIVERS = sdl
PLUGINS = plugins/spunull/spunull.so plugins/dfxvideo/gpu_peops.so
plugins/gpu_unai/gpu_unai.so plugins/gpu-gles/gpu_gles.so
HAVE_TSLIB = 1
HAVE_GLES = 1
CFLAGS_GLES =
```

Any command-line input or output is written as follows:

```
sudo /etc/init.d/ssh start

sudo /etc/init.d/ssh stop
```

New terms and **important words** are shown in bold. Words that you see on the screen, for example, in menus or dialog boxes, appear in the text like this: "Go to **Scratch-UI-Panes | ScratchFrameMorph | menu/button actions | addServerCommandTo**."

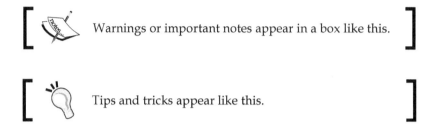

[Warnings or important notes appear in a box like this.]

[Tips and tricks appear like this.]

Reader feedback

Feedback from our readers is always welcome. Let us know what you think about this book—what you liked or disliked. Reader feedback is important for us as it helps us develop titles that you will really get the most out of.

To send us general feedback, simply e-mail feedback@packtpub.com, and mention the book's title in the subject of your message.

If there is a topic that you have expertise in and you are interested in either writing or contributing to a book, see our author guide at www.packtpub.com/authors.

Customer support

Now that you are the proud owner of a Packt book, we have a number of things to help you to get the most from your purchase.

Downloading the example code

You can download the example code files from your account at http://www.packtpub.com for all the Packt Publishing books you have purchased. If you purchased this book elsewhere, you can visit http://www.packtpub.com/support and register to have the files e-mailed directly to you.

Downloading the color images of this book

We also provide you with a PDF file that has color images of the screenshots/ diagrams used in this book. The color images will help you better understand the changes in the output. You can download this file from: `http://www.packtpub. com/sites/default/files/downloads/BananaPiBlueprints_ColorImages.pdf`.

Errata

Although we have taken every care to ensure the accuracy of our content, mistakes do happen. If you find a mistake in one of our books — maybe a mistake in the text or the code — we would be grateful if you could report this to us. By doing so, you can save other readers from frustration and help us improve subsequent versions of this book. If you find any errata, please report them by visiting `http://www.packtpub. com/submit-errata`, selecting your book, clicking on the **Errata Submission Form** link, and entering the details of your errata. Once your errata are verified, your submission will be accepted and the errata will be uploaded to our website or added to any list of existing errata under the Errata section of that title.

To view the previously submitted errata, go to `https://www.packtpub.com/books/ content/support` and enter the name of the book in the search field. The required information will appear under the **Errata** section.

Piracy

Piracy of copyrighted material on the Internet is an ongoing problem across all media. At Packt, we take the protection of our copyright and licenses very seriously. If you come across any illegal copies of our works in any form on the Internet, please provide us with the location address or website name immediately so that we can pursue a remedy.

Please contact us at `copyright@packtpub.com` with a link to the suspected pirated material.

We appreciate your help in protecting our authors and our ability to bring you valuable content.

Questions

If you have a problem with any aspect of this book, you can contact us at `questions@packtpub.com`, and we will do our best to address the problem.

1
Introduction to Banana Pro

Embedded boards are part of our lives. We use them daily, and sometimes even without recognizing or knowing about them. They are included in mobile phones, washing machines, or implemented in our televisions. These little computers work in the background and consume very little power.

This chapter introduces Banana Pro. Banana Pro is an updated version of Banana Pi that's been designed by the LeMaker team (`http://www.lemaker.org`) from China. LeMaker is a charitable organization and aims to provide educational services by selling its Banana boards and building a community around this technology, similar to what the Raspberry Pi foundation in the UK has done.

Banana Pro is the current flagship of LeMaker. It is compatible with many Linux-based operating systems including Android. In this chapter, Banana Pro is introduced to you along with its connection possibilities. The most popular operating systems in the market today are explained here and the principal installation as well as the boot process is described.

There are already many add-ons available for Banana Pro, such as LCD modules in various sizes, a camera module, or modules that connect to GPIO pins. Sections of this chapter deal with the detailed installation of an LCD module, describing the step-by-step installation and operation of a camera module and provide background information on additional add-ons.

In particular, this chapter includes the following sections:

- Banana Pro
- Getting started
- Operating systems
- Add-ons

Banana Pro

Since Raspberry Pi was born, a lot of new embedded boards have seen the light of day. A very popular one is Banana Pro. It came into the market in late 2014, is affordable ($45 USD), and offers many interfaces (*Figure 1*).

Banana Pro is the size of a credit card (92 mm x 60 mm and 48 g) and uses an Allwinner A20 system on chip. This includes a dual core CPU (ARM Cortex-A7, 1 GHz), a Mali 400 MP2 GPU, and a 1 GB SDRAM. Additionally, there is also a AP6181 Wi-Fi module onboard. Banana Pro makes use of the AXP209 **Power Management Unit** (**PMU**), which is very power efficient and allows power monitoring.

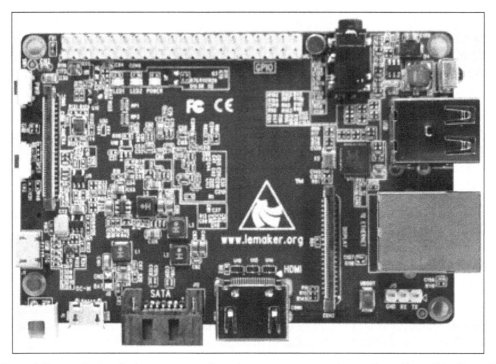

Figure 1: Banana Pro is a dual core computer featuring many connectors (source: http://en.wikipedia.org/wiki/Banana_Pro).

Specifications of Banana Pro

Table 1 summarizes the Banana Pro specifications. Everything is available to build a complete computer system, including a hard disk or connection to a television or computer screen. Both the Gb LAN and WLAN guarantee easy integration into networks and fast operation, for example, as NAS. USB sockets allow the usage of a keyboard, mouse, or even DVB receivers (refer to *Chapter 4*, *An Arcade Cabinet*). The 40-pin **General Purpose Input Output (GPIO)** header allows arbitrary experiments that feature different bus systems, such as **CAN (Controller Area Network)** or **SPI (Serial Peripheral Interface)**. Different LEDs provide board statuses; **CSI (Camera Serial Interface)** and **LVDS (Low Voltage Differential Signaling)** interfaces are also available. The CSI interface can be used in order to connect a camera and LVDS interface that can be used for display connection purposes. Even an onboard microphone is implemented. The following are the Banana Pro specifications:

Components	Specification
System on chip	Allwinner A20, SATA 2, two USBs, and one Micro-USB
CPU	1 GHz Cortex-A7 dual-core
GPU	Mali 400 MP2, OpenGL 2.0/1.1 (hardware accelerated)
Memory	1 GB DDR3 SDRAM
Power	5V/2A using Micro-USB (DC and/or USB OTG)
PMU	AXP209
USB	Two USBs of the 2.0 version and one USB 2.0 OTG
Low level connectors	A 40-pin GPIO header, including UART, I2C, SPI, PWM, CAN, I2S, and SPDIF
Storage	A Micro-SD card, SATA 2.0, and a 2.5 inch hard disk power supply onboard
Network	10/100/1000 Ethernet RJ 45 and 150 Mbps Wi-Fi 802.11 b/g/n
Display	HDMI-A 1.4, a composite video (PAL and NTSC) (via 3.5 mm TRRS jack shared with an audio output), and LVDS/RGB/CPU display interface (DSI) for raw LCD panels. 11 HDMI resolutions from 640×480 to 1920×1080 plus various PAL and NTSC standards
Video	An HD H.264 2160p video decoding. A multiformat FHD video decoding, including Mpeg1/2, Mpeg4, H.263, H.264, and so on. An H.264 high-profile 1080p@30fps or 720p@60fps encoding
Camera	An 8-bit parallel camera interface
Audio outputs	HDMI, analog audio (via a 3.5 mm TRRS jack that's shared with composite video out), I2S audio (also potentially for audio input), and an electrical SPDIF audio output
Audio input	An onboard microphone

Components	Specification
Buttons	A reset button, power button, and a U-boot button
LEDs	A power status LED (red), Ethernet status LED (blue), and a user-defined LED (green)
Other	An onboard IR receiver
Dimensions	92 mm x 60 mm and 48 gm

Table 1: Banana Pro specifications

Contrary to many other embedded boards, Banana Pro offers a SATA connector for the direct connection to a 2.5 inch hard disk connection. Moreover, for SSDs or a 2.5 inch hard disk, a power connector is onboard.

Note the correct polarity of the SATA/DC power connector. Compared to CubieBoard or Cubietruck, Banana Pro uses the concept of changed polarity. Therefore, when ordering a Banana Pro SATA/DC cable, be sure of the DC polarity (*Figure 2*).

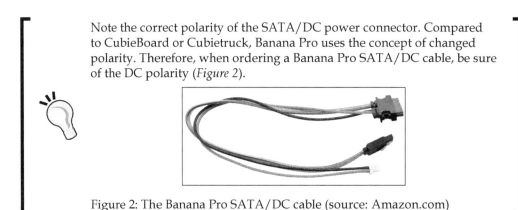

Figure 2: The Banana Pro SATA/DC cable (source: Amazon.com)

All the connectors of Banana Pro are explained in *Figure 3*. These are as follows:

- **Debug TTL UART**: This interface can be used in order to connect to a serial console PC/laptop via a serial USB cable for debugging purposes.

- **Display interface**: Use this connector to connect to an LCD. LeMaker offers three different sizes of LCDs that are up to 7 inches in size.

- **HDMI**: Using an HDMI (type A) or an HDMI (type A) cable (HDMI 1.4), this socket allows the connection to a monitor or television. In addition to this, digital audio can be transferred through this connector.

- **SATA 2.0 interface and SATA/DC 5V**: Banana Pro has a SATA 2.0 connector onboard. Furthermore, the DC for SSDs or 2.5 inch hard disks can be directly supplied (*Figure 2*).

- **The micro USB power**: Connect your 5V micro USB power supply to this connector in order to boot Banana Pro. While the 1.2A power supply may be sufficient to boot the board without a hard disk, I recommend at least a 2A power supply when the hard disk is connected to the board. Also, keep in mind that a 7 inch LCD connected to the board will consume an additional 750mA.

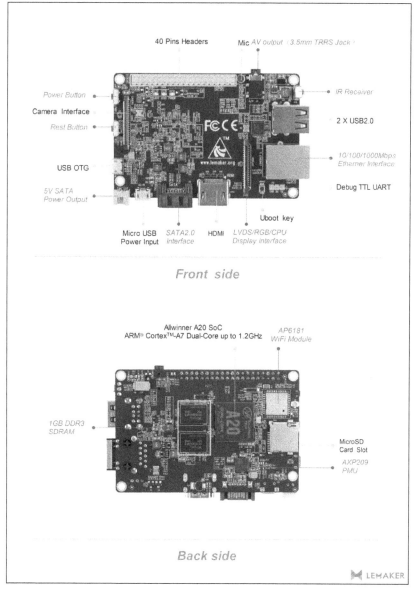

Figure 3: Connectors of Banana Pro

- **USB OTG**: This allows for switching between a host and target mode. When in host mode, power will be drawn from Banana Pro to a drive or USB device that's connected. Many OTG implementations are currently limited and do not enable the powering of all devices.

Figure 4: The USB OTG to USB adapter (source: Amazon.com)

[Using an adapter cable (*Figure 4*), USB devices can be connected to this port.]

- **Reset button**: Pushing this button will reboot Banana Pro. Note that pushing this button during an operation may result in data corruption. It is recommended that you always shut down Banana Pro using the `sudo halt -p` command when using Linux.

- **Camera interface**: This connector allows the usage of the LeMaker camera.

- **Power button**: This button will boot Banana Pro after shutdown.

- **40-pin GPIO header**: This header provides different signals, such as SPI, CAN, I2S, I2C, UART, or SPDIF.

- **Microphone**: The microphone can be used for recordings (mono).

- **AV output**: This connector combines analog videos and analog audio in a so-called TRRS jack (*Figure 5*):

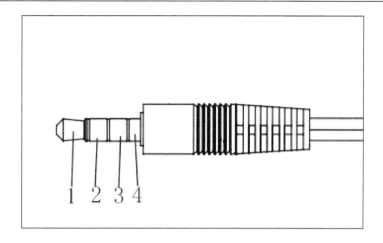

Figure 5: The TRRS connector for Banana Pro. Pin 1 is audio left, pin 2 is audio right, pin 3 is video out and pin 4 is ground.

 There are adapter cables available that separate audio and videos (*Figure 6*):

Figure 6: The TRRS splitter for audio and videos

- **IR Receiver**: Banana Pro features an onboard IR receiver that receives remote control signals.

- **2 x USB**: Connect your USB devices here.

- **Ethernet interface**: Banana Pro provides a 1 Gb Ethernet interfaces that offers a true GB speed.

- **The microSD card slot**: Banana Pro boots from a microSD card since a direct boot from a hard disk is not possible. However, a root filesystem can be directed to the hard disk once it's booted from the microSD card.

- **FEL button**: FEL is a low-level subroutine that's contained in the BootROM on Allwinner devices. It is used for the initial programming and recovery of devices using a USB.

In addition to the preceding connectors, Banana Pro offers a WLAN module that can also work as an access point. Banana Pro does not supply a **real-time clock** (**RTC**). However, there are RTC add-on boards available at `http://www.wvshare.com/product/PCF8563-RTC-Board.htm`.

Figure 7: The RTC add-on board for Banana Pro. Source: http://www.wvshare.com.

Banana Pro onboard LEDs

Banana Pro features several LEDs onboard. The red LED lights up as soon as DC power is supplied to the board. The blue LED shows Ethernet activity. The green and blue LEDs can be set individually. *Chapter 2, Programming Languages*, will show you how these LEDs can be programmed.

Getting started

LeMaker offers several predefined images for download. These can be found at `http://www.lemaker.org/resources/9-38/image_files.html`. Simply download the image file you want and copy it to a microSD card. The minimum required SD card size is 4 GB.

When using the Windows OS, WIN32 Disk Imager (`http://sourceforge.net/projects/win32diskimager`) can be used in order to transfer an image to an SD card. However, make sure that you select the correct drive for the Win32 Disk Imager. An incorrect drive may result in loss of data.

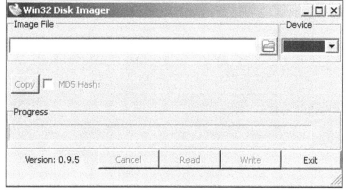

Figure 8: Win32 Disk Imager can be used in order to transfer Banana Pro image files to a microSD card (source: SourceForge.net)

Using Linux, image files can be transferred to a Micro SD card using the following command:

```
sudo dd bs=4M of=/dev/sdX if=/path/to/banana_pro.img
```

For uncompressed images, use the following command

```
gzip -dc /home/your_username/image.gz | sudo dd bs=4M of=/dev/sdX
```

For compressed images, replace /dev/sdX with your SD card. Note that the block size is set to 4M and will work most of the time. If it doesn't, try 1M, although this will take a considerably longer to complete.

There is one exception for Banana Pro using the Android operating system. Using *Win32 Disk Imager* or the dd command of Linux will not work here. Special software called *PhoenixCard* will be required. PhoenixCard for Windows can be downloaded from https://drive.google.com/file/d/0B_VynIqhAcB7NTg2UkRDdHRWX2s/ edit. Before you do this, the SD card should be formatted by clicking on **Format to Normal** (*Figure 9*):

Figure 9: Copying Android to an SD card for Banana Pro by first formatting the SD card to normal

It is mandatory to select the **Startup** from the **Write Mode**. After formatting the card, click on the **OK** button in the Information window. In a second step, the Android image can be burned to the SD card (*Figure 10*). This step will take a few minutes to complete.

After writing any image to the microSD card, put the SD card into Banana Pro SD card slot and connect the DC power supply afterwards. This will boot your image. Currently, Banana Pro supports Android 4.4. Version 4.4 is available from this forum at `http://www.bananapi.com/index.php/forum/adroid/117-android-4-4-for-banana-pi-beta-1-release-note`.

Figure 10: Copying the Android OS to an SD card for Banana Pro by burning an image to an SD card

Set up your Banana Pro according to Figure 11 after you've copied the image to the SD card.

The first boot

Depending on the chosen image, the first boot will take 20 to 30 seconds. The first boot on Android will take much longer, so be patient.

 Some Android versions may require two micro USB power connectors at the same time. One must be supplied to the micro USB DC before boot, and the other one to the micro USB OTG. During my experiments with Android 4.2, one power supply connection was sufficient.

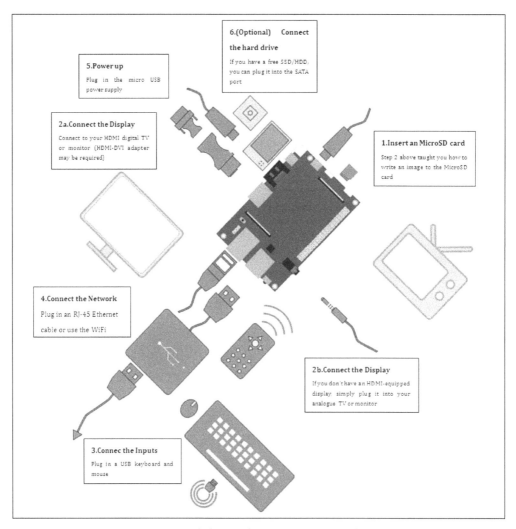

Figure 11: Setting up Banana Pro before the first boot (source: http://www.lemaker.org/cn/product-bananapro-guide.html)

Available operating systems for Banana Pro

This section presents some of the available operating systems for Banana Pro. Here, Android has briefly described some of the most important Linux distributions:

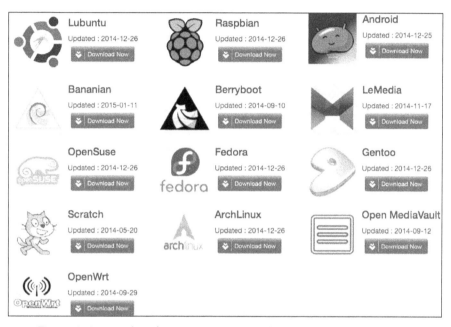

Figure 12: A screenshot of operating systems available on the LeMaker web page

LeMaker offers image versions for both Banana Pi and Banana Pro. However, be sure to download the correct image.

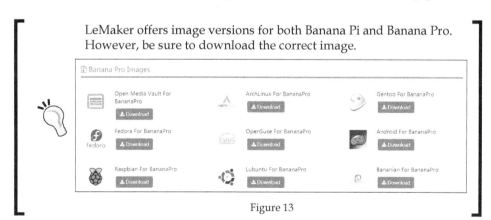

Figure 13

Android

Although Android is based on Linux, both architectures are quite different. This can be seen even in the example of low-level C language routines, which Google exchanged for Android. In addition to this, Google prohibits all code that's licensed under GPL (GNU Public License). For this reason, Android only implements a rudimentary shell featuring only a few shell commands. Due to the C-library incompatibilities, normal Linux code, even if it's especially compiled for the ARM architecture, will not run under Android. Nevertheless, Android is a very popular **operating system** (**OS**) that's used by many phones and tablets. It fully supports graphic hardware in terms of accelerated video and 3D graphics. For this reason, the first Banana Pro version of **Kodi** (formerly known as **XBMC** and **Xbox** Media Centre) made use of an accelerated Android graphics library (refer to *Chapter 4*, *An Arcade Cabinet*).

Applications for Android can be developed using a special **software development kit (SDK)** and Java itself as most Android applications are based in Java. Although this book concentrates on Linux projects rather than Android projects, we will take a short look at Android on Banana Pro.

LeMaker provides three different Android images: one for a 5 inch TFT, the second for a 7 inch TFT, and the third using the HDMI cable as a video output. To install an Android OS, simply download the required version. You most probably want to start with the HDMI enabled version. Use PhoenixCard (as seen in the previous section) in order to write the image to an SD card. Insert this SD card and boot Android. After a while, the start screen of Android will be visible.

Figure 14: This is Android 4.4 running on Banana Pi/Pro (http://www.bananapi-kaufen.de/wp-content/uploads/2014/07/800px-Android_v2.jpg)

Android can be controlled by using a keyboard and mouse. Bluetooth and WLAN will work out of the box and some applications are already preinstalled.

Figure 15: Android 4.4 running on Banana Pro (source: bananapi.com)

Linux

There are a variety of Linux distributions available on the LeMaker download site (*Figure 13*). The most famous operating systems are *Raspbian, Bananian, Lubuntu,* and *Gentoo. LeMedia,* a special Linux distribution that provides the Xbox media center, Kodi (formerly known as XBMC), is not available on the official LeMaker download website. We will later on compile and install XBMC for other operating systems such as a Debian distribution. No matter which Linux OS you decide on incorporating, the procedure is always the same: Copy the image to an SD card and boot the card within Banana Pro.

After copying the image, the SD card will contain a directory called /boot. This directory contains the Linux kernel (called uImage; refer to *Chapter 2, Programming Languages,* for this), a file called uEnv.txt, and a binary file (usually script.bin or bananapro.bin). The uEnv.txt file contains kernel parameters, such as screen resolutions, and the binary file contains the complete settings for Banana Pro with respect to all connectors.

My `uEnv.txt` file looks like this:

```
console=tty1
root=/dev/mmcblk0p1 rootwait
extraargs=rootfstype=ext4 sunxi_ve_mem_reserve=190 sunxi_g2d_mem_
reserve=16
sunxi_fb_mem_reserve=32 hdmi.audio=EDID:1 disp.screen0_output_
mode=1920x1080p50 panic=10 consoleblank=0
script=bananapro.bin
kernel=uImage
```

It defines `/dev/tty1` as a console terminal, uses the first partition of an SD card as a root device (`/dev/mmcblk0p1`), and provides some additional kernel parameters. The video output mode is completely HD progressive (`1920x1080p50`). The binary file is called `bananapro.bin` in my case, and the kernel is `uImage` within the `/boot` directory. The function of the binary file is described in the next section (the FEX file).

For my experiments, I've used a Banana Pi Linux image of Igor Pečovnik (`http://www.igorpecovnik.com/2014/09/07/banana-pi-debian-sd-image/`), which I adapted to Banana Pro. In the meantime, the Banana Pi image is compatible with Banana Pro.

I recommend that you download the Debian Wheezy version that comes with kernel 3.4. Although this kernel is not up to date, it enables all the hardware features of Banana Pro as opposed to kernel 4.2, which, for example, neither has an audio driver nor an accelerated video output.

The image itself is based on Debian Wheezy and comes with kernel 3.4. Similar to *Bananian*, this distribution does not come with any X11 server or display manager. Therefore, I've installed the MATE Windows manager and the `slim` login manager. Similar to the X11 framebuffer driver, I've used sources from `https://github.com/ssvb/xf86-video-fbturbo`. This driver requires a number of packages to be installed first as follows:

```
sudo apt-get install git build-essential xorg-dev xutils-dev x11proto-
dri2-dev
sudo apt-get install libltdl-dev libtool automake libdrm-dev autoconf
```

Now, acquire the sources of xf86-video-fbturbo, compile them, and then install them as follows:

```
sudo su
cd /usr/local/src
```

```
git clone https://github.com/ssvb/xf86-video-fbturbo.git
cd xf86-video-fbturbo
autoreconf -vi
./configure --prefix=/usr
make
make install
```

Afterwards, copy the default `xorg.conf` file to the location of your `xorg.conf` like this:

```
sudo cp xorg.conf /etc/X11/xorg.conf
```

Do not forget to back up any existing `xorg.conf` files first. In *Chapter 4*, *An Arcade Cabinet*, we will install accelerated Mali drivers for a desktop in addition to a framebuffer turbo driver.

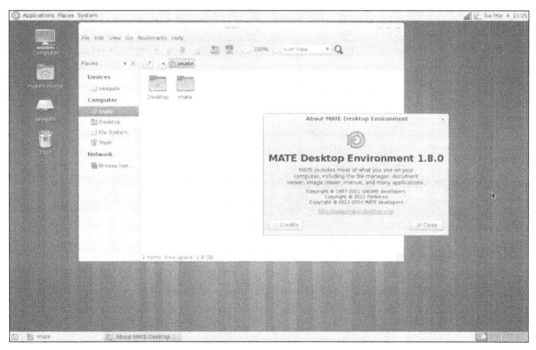

Figure 16: The MATE desktop environment (source: mate-desktop.org)

MATE needs to be installed from the Debian Wheezy backports. Add `deb http://http.debian.net/debian wheezy-backports main` to the `/etc/apt/sources.list` file. This can be done using this command:

```
sudo nano /etc/apt/sources.list
```

Afterwards, run the following shell commands:

```
sudo apt-get update
sudo apt-get upgrade
apt-get install mate-desktop-environment mate-desktop-environment-extras
sudo apt-get install slim
```

In order to install the MATE desktop and *slim*, a configuration can be done in the `/etc/slim.conf` file. I've added/changed the following lines:

```
sessionstart_cmd xhost + && xset s noblank && xset s off && xset -dpms
default_user pi
auto_login yes
```

The first line disables access control to the X-windows server. This is needed later on in *Chapter 4*, *An Arcade Cabinet*. In addition to this, screensavers and power management for the X-server are switched off. The second line sets the default user as the `pi` user. The last line allows the `pi` user to automatically log in without providing a password.

This user `pi` can be added to the system using this shell command:

```
sudo adduser
```

You need to answer all the questions prompted by the system and use the `pi` as a username.. Most Linux distributions provide an already secure shell access (`ssh`). If not, simply install the `openssh` server by typing the following command that will enable a remote login with `ssh` on port `22`:

```
sudo apt-get install openssh-server
```

The FEX file

Banana Pro reads interface settings from a binary file called `script.bin` or `bananapro.bin` that is located in the `/boot` directory. This file defines video output, GPIO selection, and much more. Each value consists of a `key = value` pair combination under a `[sectionheader]`. All three entries are case-sensitive. A complete selection of all possible entries can be found at `http://linux-sunxi.org/Fex_Guide`.

The FEX files can be compiled into a binary file (and recompiled into an ASCII FEX file) using the `fex2bin` or `bin2fex` commands. These tools are available on GitHub (`sunxi-tools` is available at `https://github.com/linux-sunxi/sunxi-tools`). The `sunxi-tools` require `libusb` as a prerequisite.

Additionally, `git` will be installed. Git can be used in order to clone a directory that's available on the Internet on a local SD card or hard disk using this command:

```
sudo apt-get install libusb-1.0-0-dev git
```

Afterwards, clone the `sunxi-tools` repository and then build and install the tools:

```
git clone https://github.com/linux-sunxi/sunxi-tools
cd sunxi-toolsmake
sudo make install
```

The syntax of `fex2bin` and `bin2fex` is easy. Simply provide two filenames (the original and the converted one, respectively). Take a look at the following example:

```
sudo fex2bin /boot/script.fex /boot/script.bin
```

This will generate a new `script.bin` binary file that's based on the `script.fex` ASCII file in the `/boot` directory.

 If `uEnv.txt` redefines, for example, display settings as compared to `script.bin`, this file will be preferred over `script.bin`.

A typical display section in the FEX file looks like this:

```
[disp_init]
disp_init_enable = 1
disp_mode = 0
screen0_output_type = 3
screen0_output_mode = 4
screen1_output_type = 2
screen1_output_mode = 11
fb0_framebuffer_num = 2
fb0_format = 10
fb0_pixel_sequence = 0
fb0_scaler_mode_enable = 0
fb1_framebuffer_num = 2
fb1_format = 10
fb1_pixel_sequence = 0
fb1_scaler_mode_enable = 0
```

```
lcd0_backlight = 197
lcd1_backlight = 197
lcd0_bright = 50
lcd0_contrast = 50
lcd0_saturation = 57
lcd0_hue = 50
lcd1_bright = 50
lcd1_contrast = 50
lcd1_saturation = 57
lcd1_hue = 50
```

The section header of the FEX file is `[disp_init]`.`disp_init_enable`, the value of which can be either `1` (enabled display output) or `0` (disabled display output). The display mode is a value between `0` and `4` according to the following table:

Mode	Display mode
0	`screen0 (screen0, fb0)`
1	`screen1 (screen1, fb0)`
2	`dualhead (screen0, screen1, fb0, fb1)` (two screens and two framebuffers)
3	`xinerama (screen0, screen1, fb0)` (two screens and one big framebuffer)
4	`clone (screen0, screen1, fb0)` (two screens and one standard framebuffer)

Table 2: The display modes for Banana Pro

The `screen0_out_color_range` mode defines the output color for HDMI. It applies to both `screen0` and `screen1`. Therefore, there is no `screen1_out_color_range`. The output color range can be set according to the following table:

Type	Output color range
0	16-255 is the default limited range
1	0-255 is the full range (PC level)
2	16-235 is the limited range (video level)

Table 3: The output color range for Banana Pro

The `screen0_output_type` mode sets the output type for `screen0` according to the following table. Therefore, use `screen0_output_type` accordingly:

Type	Output type
0	None
1	LCD
2	TV
3	HDMI
4	Analog video

Table 4: The output types for Banana Pro

The following screen output modes (`screen0_output_mode` and `screen1_output_mode`) can be defined for `screen0` and `screen1`:

Mode	Used for the TV/HDMI output	Used for analog video output
0	480i	1680 x 1050
1	576i	1440 x 900
2	480p	1360 x 768
3	576p	1280 x 1024
4	720p50	1024 x 768
5	720p60	800 x 600
6	1080i50	640 x 480
7	1080i60	
8	1080p24	
9	1080p50	
10	1080p60	1920 x 1080
11	PAL	1280 x 720
14	NTSC	

Table 5: The screen output modes for Banana Pro

The `fb0_framebuffer_num` value is the number of framebuffers to be used for the `0` framebuffer. It can be set to `2` for double buffering. Use `fb1_framebuffer_num` accordingly. The pixel format for both framebuffers can be defined as `fb0_format` or `fb1_format` according to this table:

Format	fb0_format
4	RGB655
5	RGB565
6	RGB556
7	ARGB1555
8	RGBA5551
9	RGB888
10	ARGB8888
12	ARGB4444

Table 6: The framebuffer format for Banana Pro

The framebuffer pixel sequences (`fb0_pixel_sequency` and `fb1_pixel_sequence`) must be set to `0` for Linux and `2` for Android operating systems (refer to this table):

Sequence	fb0_pixel_sequence or fb1_pixel_sequence
0	ARGB
2	BGRA

Table 7: The framebuffer pixel sequence for Banana Pro

The `Framebufferscaler` mode can be enabled or disabled for both framebuffers (`fb0_scaler_mode_enable` and `fb1_scaler_mode_enable`). Use a value of `0` to disable the `scaler` mode and a value of `1` to enable the `scaler` mode. The `Scaler` mode may improve the picture quality of some settings. The `lcd0_backlight` is a value between `0` and `240` and sets the PWM rate on a selected PWM GPIO. The same is true for `lcd1_backlight`. All the remaining settings are self-explanatory.

LeMaker provides special configuration files that can be used with LCD screens (refer to *The LCD module* section).

Transferring an OS to a hard disk

Banana Pro cannot boot directly from a hard disk. This section will show you how the Linux operating system can be copied from a microSD card to a hard disk and how a system can boot into the OS of the hard disk.

First, boot your Banana Pro with a connected hard disk (SATA and DC). The kernel messages will show the SATA device (usually /dev/sda). In order to get a filesystem overview, the lsblk command can be used. This command will list the complete filesystem including the attached hard disk.

Verify the contents of the hard disk using the following command:

```
fdisk -l /dev/sda
```

Principally, the available hard disk space must be equal to or larger than the size of the SD card in order to host the OS. The fdisk command can be used to partition the disk in terms of erasing or adding hard disk partitions. Use this program with care as it can delete everything that exists on your hard disk. The following steps assume an empty hard disk or a hard disk whose content is not needed any more.

The hard disk can be partitioned using the fdisk command:

```
sudo fdisk /dev/sda
```

The p (print) command will print partition table:

```
Command (m for help): p
```

Existing partitions can be removed using the d (delete) command:

```
Command (m for help): d
Partition number (1-6): 1
```

New partitions can be added using the n (new) command:

```
Command (m for help): n
Partition type:
   p   primary (0 primary, 0 extended, 4 free)
   e   extended
Select (default p): p
Partition number (1-4, default 1): 1
```

The w (write) command writes all changes to the disk:

```
Command (m for help): w
The partition table has been altered!
```

After this, the fdisk write command will automatically quit. If no other partitions (for example, swap) are required, you can press RETURN when prompted for the first and last sectors. In its simplest sense, a swap partition serves as an overflow to Banana Pro's memory (RAM). It might be useful when compiling huge software packages such as Kodi (formerly known as XBMC). As an alternative, a file on a hard disk or SD card can be used for swapping. A swap partition itself has the 82 partition ID, which can be changed using the t (toggle) command followed by the ID. Swap partitions can be formatted using the following command:

```
mkswap /dev/sdaX,
```

X represents the swap partition (for example, 6). Swap partitions will be activated as follows:

```
swapon /dev/sdaX
```

New (empty) partitions must be formatted before usage. The following command formats the first partition (sda1) with the .ext4 filesystem and labels it as rootfs. In doing so, all existing data on this partition will be erased. Therefore, use this command with caution and only format empty partitions or partitions whose content is not needed any more:

```
sudo mke2fs -t ext4 -L rootfs /dev/sda1
```

In this step, the complete data from the microSD card will be copied to the hard disk. In our example, the first partition of the hard disk will be mounted into the /mnt directory; rsync will be used to transfer all data to the directory:

```
sudo mount /dev/sda1 /mnt
sudo rsync -ax / /mnt
```

The complete copy process will take a while. In the last step, the boot parameters of the uEnv.txt file will be adjusted to use the hard drive. Change root=/dev/mmcblk0p1 in the /boot/uEnv.txt file to this:

root=/dev/sda1

This can be done using the nano editor by typing this:

sudo nano /boot/uEnv.txt

Finally, restart Banana Pro with the following command:

sudo reboot

The system should be redirected from the microSD card to the hard disk right now. A df -h command on my system delivers the following (320 GB of free hard disk space):

```
Filesystem        Size   Used  Avail  Use%  Mounted on
rootfs            289G   157G  118G   57%   /
/dev/root         289G   157G  118G   57%   /
devtmpfs          380M      0  380M    0%   /dev
tmpfs             128M   280K  128M    1%   /run
tmpfs             5,0M      0  5,0M    0%   /run/lock
tmpfs             128M   2,3M  126M    2%   /run/shm
tmpfs             1,0G   4,0K  1,0G    1%   /tmp
/dev/mmcblk0p1     14G    11G  2,4G   83%   /media/lime-next
```

If you want to make any changes to uEnv.txt after booting to the hard disk, you will need to mount the SD card first, change into the SD card boot directory, and edit uEnv.txt accordingly:

sudo mount /dev/mmcblk0p1 /mnt

cd /mnt/boot

sudo nano uEnv.txt

The same applies to the installation of a new kernel (refer to *Chapter 2, Programming Languages*).

The gparted software is a graphical frontend for fdisk and other tools. It is very useful to add, delete, or even resize partitions. It may later be required for backups, where it can be used to shrink a partition, for example, on an SD card in order to use windisk32imager to copy the contents of the SD card to the backup medium.

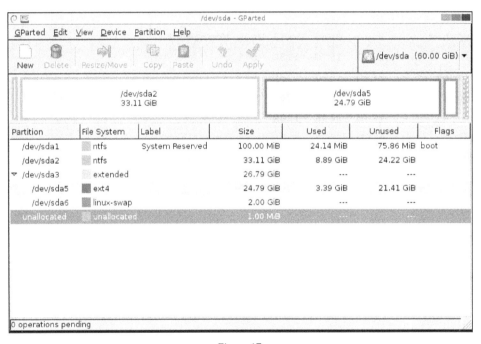

Figure 17

Add-ons

There are a lot of add-ons available for Banana Pro. LeMaker offers LCD modules in three different sizes from 3.5 inches up to 7 inches. Moreover, LeMaker offers a camera board that can be directly connected to Banana Pro. Last but not least, several cases are available that allow the mounting of an WLAN antenna, while others even provide a hard disk housing.

The LCD module

This table shows the resolution of LeMaker LCDs depending on their panel size:

LCD panel size	Resolution
3 to 5 inches	320 x 240 pixels
5 inches	640 x 480 pixels
7 inches	1024 x 600 pixels

Table 8: The LeMaker LCD panel size resolutions.

In dependence of the LCD panel size, LeMaker offers three different binary files that can be used in order to initialize the LCDs while booting (`script.bin`). The files are available from GitHub (`https://github.com/LeMaker/fex_configuration`). This GitHub tree provides both FEX files and compiled FEX files (`bin` files). Be sure to download the ones for Banana Pro as Banana Pi files are also available. Banana Pro files are named `banana_pro_Xlcd.bin`, whereas, `X` represents the LCD panel size (3 to 5, 5, or 7 inches, respectively). Copy this file to the first partition of your microSD card and rename it as `script.bin` (or whatever your `bin` file is called).

Do not overwrite bin files without creating a backup first. There are a lot of settings included in these files, and once the files are lost, changes must be applied step by step again manually.

When operating the LCD display, be sure that your power supply can deliver enough current. While a 2A supply may be sufficient to operate Banana Pro and a 2.5 inch hard disk, the display will draw another 750mA. In this case, a 5V/3A supply is required.

The 7 inch LCD module data is summarized in the following table:

Specifications for the 7 inch LCD module	
LCD size	7.0 inch(diagonal)
Interface	Parallel LVDS of 8-bits
Resolution	024 x 3(RGB) x 600
Driver element	a-Si TFT active matrix
Dot pitch	0.05(W) × 0.15(H) mm
Connections to Banana Pro	40-pin FPC to the Display Sensor Interface (DSI)
Surface treatment	Glare
Color arrangement	RGB-stripe
View direction	6 o'clock
Power	5V/550mA
Active area	153.6(W) × 90.0(H) mm
Dimensions	165.75(W) ×105.39(H) × 2.45(D) mm
Weight	300 g

Table 9: The LeMaker 7 inch LCD module specifications

The 7-inch LCD step-by-step guide

In the following section, the installation and operation of a 7 inch LeMaker LCD is described. In the first step, the system will be updated:

```
sudo apt-get update
sudo apt-get upgrade
```

Let's look at the software part afterwards. Replace the /boot/bananapro.bin directory with your boot directory and script.bin with your binary startup file:

```
git clone http://github.com/LeMaker/fex_configuration
cd fex_configuration/
sudo cp bin/banana_pro_7lcd.bin /boot/bananapro/script.bin
```

Afterwards, edit the /etc/modules file and add the lcd module to it. If the lcd module is already available and commented out using #, simply remove the hash sign as shown in the following screenshot:

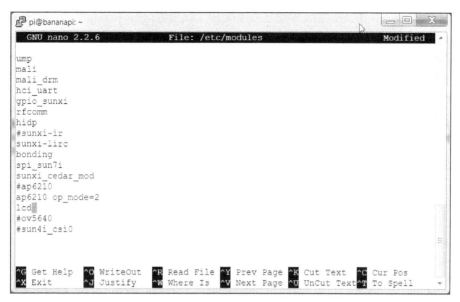

Figure 18

After this, power off Banana Pro before installing a cable for the 7 inch LCD. The 7 inch display comes together with a 100 mm and 0.5 mm spacing **flexible printed circuit (FPC)** cable.

Figure 19: The LeMaker 7 inch LCD with the FPC cable and Banana Pro

Turn the LCD around carefully and gently pull out the brown cable clamp from both ends:

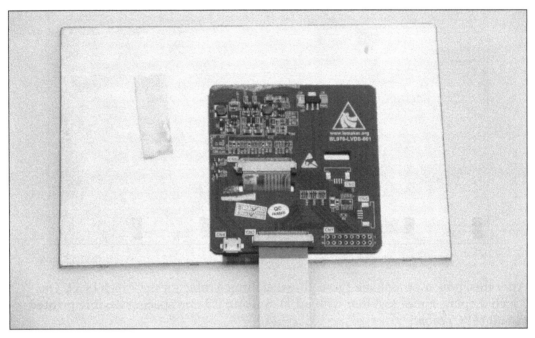

Figure 20

Push the flexible cable carefully. Make sure it is straight and the silver conductive end faces downwards toward the blue circuit board, and blue tape faces upwards (*Figure 18*). After the cable has been inserted completely, push down on both sides of the cable clamp at the same time.

Installing a cable on Banana Pro is pretty much the same as installing the cable on the preceding LCD module. The cable connects to the CON2 connector of Banana Pro board. Do not use the CON1 camera connector. Again, pull out the cable clamps at both sides and push the cable in from the top. The blue protective tape must face the Ethernet jack, while the conductive fingers at the end of the cable face Banana Pro board (*Figure 21*):

Figure 21: Connecting the LCD to Banana Pro

After the cable is inserted completely, push down on both sides of the clamp and boot your Banana Pro. You should now see this booting screen on the LCD (refer to *Figure 22*).

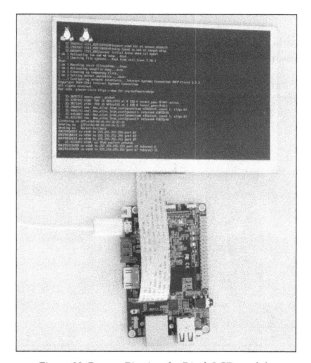

Figure 22: Banana Pi using the 7 inch LCD module

The flex cable that's provided is quite short (100 mm only). If you want a larger cable, you may search the Internet for `FPC cable 40 0.5 mm`. The LCD is capable of showing the X11 desktop (refer to *Figure 23*) as well as high-resolution videos in full HD.

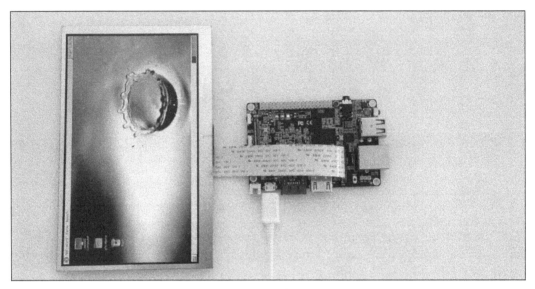

Figure 23

Banana Pro shows an H264 video on a 7 inch LCD using `mplayer`. This will look similar to what is shown in the following image:

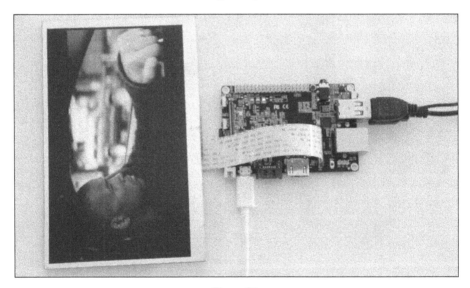

Figure 24

The camera module

Banana Pro camera module (*Figure 25*) uses an **Omnivision 5640 CMOS** image sensor in an autofocus module and with an integral IR filter. The camera module connects to Banana Pi board via the CSI (CON1). It fulfils the specifications provided in *Table 10*.

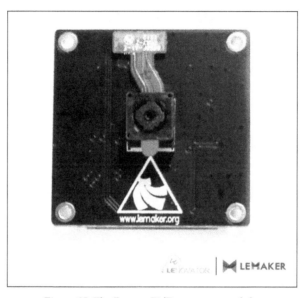

Figure 25: The Banana Pi/Pro camera module.

The following are the specifications for the LeMaker Banana Pro camera module:

Specification type	Requirements
Image sensor	An omnivision 5640 CMOS image sensor in an autofocus module with an integral IR filter (650±10nm)
Resolution	5 megapixels
Active array size	2592 x 1944
Maximum frame rate	1080p 30fps@24Mhz
Picture formats	JPEG PNG YUV420 RGB888
Video formats	Raw h.264
Connection to Banana Pro	A 40-pin FPC to the **CSI-0 (Camera Sensor Interface)**

Specification type	Requirements
Image control functions	• **Automatic exposure control (AEC)** • **Automatic white balance (AWB)** • **Automatic black-level calibration (ABLC)** • Automatic band filters • Mirror and flip functions
Temperature range	For an OS: -30 °C to 70 °C For a stable image: 0 °C to 50 °C
Lens size	1/4" (quarter inch)
Dimensions	36 x 32 x 10 mm
Weight	5 g

Table 10

A step-by-step guide to the camera module

The installation of a camera module is as easy as the installation of an LCD module. Firstly, required kernel modules will be inserted and are specifically used by this component:

```
sudo modprobe ov5640
sudo modprobe sun4i_csi0
```

The preceding commands load the Omnivision camera kernel driver and the CSI driver. In order to load these drivers permanently, add the ov5640 and sun4i_csi0 modules to /etc/modules using this command:

```
sudo nano /etc/modules
```

 If your Linux OS does not have a module called sun4i_csi0, try sun4i_csi instead.

Before installing the hardware to your Banana Pro, make sure it is shut down and disconnected from any power supply. Similar to the LCD module cable, remember to also not touch the silver ends of the camera module flexible cable. The cable, again, is quite short (about 6 cm in length).

The Banana Pro camera module connector is shown in *Figure 24*. Open the connector and insert the flexible cable carefully (*Figure 25*).

The connector in Banana Pro is called CON1. Do not use CON2 instead as this is the LCD connector (refer to *The LCD module* section). Using the wrong connector can cause serious damage to your Banana Pro or the extension board because the pin definitions are completely different.

Open the CON1 connector and put the free end of the camera flexible cable into this connector as shown in *Figure 26*. Finally, confirm that both ends of the flexible cable are sitting correctly in their sockets. Before using the camera, peel off the plastic foil that covers the lens. The complete arrangement can be seen in the following figure:

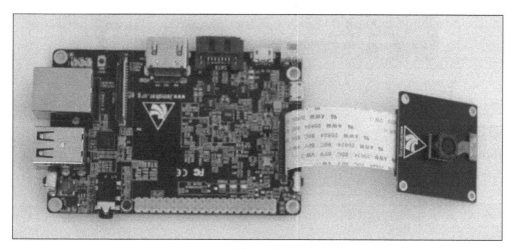

Figure 26

The mplayer software can be used in order to test the camera:

```
sudo apt-get install mplayer
sudo mplayer tv://
```

On a television, the result would look like what is shown in the following image:

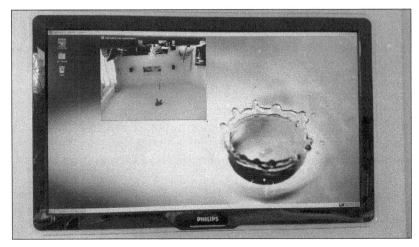

Figure 27

Cases

Although Banana Pro has been available since the end of 2014, there are already a few cases available. Most cases are acrylic cases (refer to this image):

Figure 28: The Banana Pro acrylic case (source: Amazon.com)

Lenovator offers a case that can integrate both Banana Pro and a 2.5 inch hard disk drive (*Figure 29*). The case allows the mounting of the original LeMaker Wi-Fi antenna that's provided together with Banana Pro.

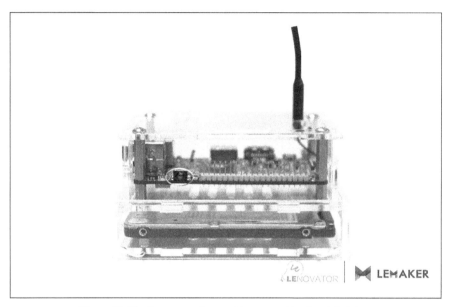

Figure 29: The Lenovator Banana Pro case with a hard disk bay

Banana Pro uses an onboard **U.FL** connector (refer to *Figure 30*). The female U.FL connectors are not designed with reconnection in mind, and they are only rated for a few reconnects before replacement is needed.

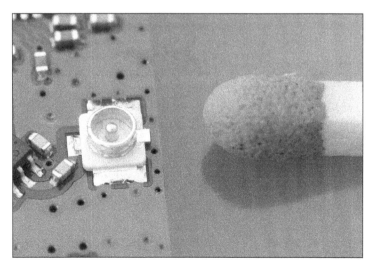

Figure 30: Banana Pro onboard the UFL antenna connector (source: Wikipedia)

For those of you who do not want to integrate a hard disk into a case, the acrylic case of Allnet may be a good choice. The case comes with an R-SMA 5 dBi omnidirectional antenna and adapter cable from U.FL to R-SMA.

Figure 31: The Banana Pro acrylic case with the 5 dBi antenna and R-SMA connector (source: the Allnet shop)

GPIO add-ons

Lenovator provides a general purpose input/output (GPIO) interface called LN digital. LN digital is designed to plug in Banana Pro's GPIO header

GPIO can be used for input (such as reading sensor information) and output (such as controlling relays and motors). So, the peripherals you buy are typically either input or output devices for GPIO. This extends the basic functionality that are offer from the GPIO on the Pi. The board offers the following:

- 8 open-collector outputs
- 8 LED indicators
- 8 digital outputs
- 4 tactile switches
- 2 changeover relays

It can be plugged directly into Banana Pro GPIO socket and programmed in Python, Scratch, or C (refer to *Chapter 2*, *Programming Languages*).

Figure 32: The LN digital interface board for Banana Pro

An onboard microphone

Banana Pro provides an onboard microphone. Recordings can be made using this command:

```
sox -t alsa default output.wav
```

The preceding command requires sox to be installed. If sox is not available, it can be installed using this command:

```
sudo apt-get install sox
```

Press *Ctrl* + *C* to stop the recording. The recording will be saved as output.wav in the current directory. Recordings can be listened to using this command:

```
mplayer output.wav
```

The microphone sensitivity can be set using the following command:

```
alsamixer
```

The complete audio installation and settings will be explained in detail in *Chapter 4, An Arcade Cabinet.*

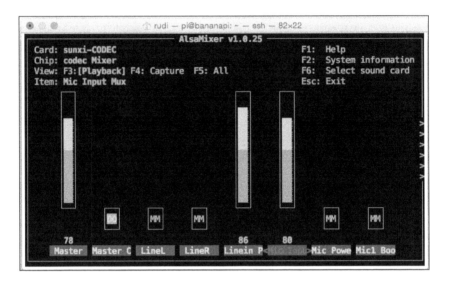

Figure 33: Setting the microphone sensitivity using alsamixer

Summary

This was the first chapter of this book in which Banana Pro was introduced. All the connectors of the board were described in detail. Different operating systems were introduced. You learned how to transfer an operating system from an SD card to a hard disk. Moreover, FEX and bin files were introduced, allowing the configuring of Banana Pro hardware. In addition to this, you learned how add-ons, such as LCDs or a camera module, could be used with Banana Pro.

The next chapter will deal with three different programming languages: Scratch, Python, and C/C++. Additionally, the installation of your own kernel will be explained.

2
Programming Languages

This chapter deals with programming languages. A single chapter, of course, cannot replace complete books that are dedicated to certain programming languages. However, when compiling or executing programs from the Internet, basic knowledge of programming languages may help to debug functionality and finally get things working as expected.

In this chapter, some basic principles, such as remote connections and editors, are explained. Afterwards, you will learn something about shell programming. This programming will be required later, for example, within *Chapter 5*, *A Multimedia Center*.

Python is a scripting language, which is interpreted on the fly. You will learn the basics of Python and a data visualization example is also provided.

Most program sources from the Internet are C/C++ programs. You will learn the basics of C using the GNU C-compiler, makefiles, and a debugger.

Another section deals with Scratch. Scratch is a graphical programming language for children aged 8 and upward. Each programming section contains an example of how to deal with external interfaces using GPIO or other buses.

The last section of this chapter deals with compiling and installing new kernels from a source. This is often needed in order to add certain functionality to a system. The following sections are covered in detail:

- Basic principles
- Bash
- Python
- C/C++
- Scratch
- New kernels

Basic principles

The first section of this chapter deals with basic principles that are required for programming. A programmer is not always sitting in front of Banana Pro. Remote connections to Banana Pro will allow remote programming. Furthermore, another section in this chapter will describe principal programming tools, such as editors, compilers, or debuggers.

Remote connections

This section explains the first possible remote connections to Banana Pro, such as `ssh` or `remote desktop`. These tools allow the development of programs without sitting in front of Banana Pro.

Secure Shell

A **Secure Shell** (**SSH**) login allows the remote login to Banana Pro from any other computer. For Windows operating systems, `Putty` can be used for remote connections (`http://www.putty.org`). For a Linux operating system, remote connections to Banana Pro can be initiated using this command:

```
ssh user@ip-address -pport
```

Replace `ip-address` with the IP address or hostname of your Banana Pro and port with the port number that `openssh-server` is running on. Refer to *Chapter 3, Wireless Projects*, for instructions on the installation of `openssh-server`. The port number is usually `22`. While this works well for computers that are connected to an internal net only, port forwarding may be required when using computers outside the internal net. Port forwarding is a feature of an Internet router. The `openssh-server` runs as a service under Linux operating systems. It can be started or stopped by using these commands:

```
sudo /etc/init.d/ssh start
sudo /etc/init.d/ssh stop
```

Usually, services will be automatically started during a system boot. While `ssh` is perfectly suited for some programming without any IDE, the next section describes the installation of the X11 remote desktop protocol, which allows viewing the Banana Pro desktop on a remote computer.

The IP address of Banana Pro within my home network is `192.168.178.86`. On a wired connection, it can be read from the `eth0` section by typing the `sudo ifconfig` command in a shell.

The IP address is provided by the `dhcp` server. For network settings, refer to *Chapter 3, Wireless Projects*. Now, I'll call the following command:

ssh pi@192.168.78.86

My `ssh` connection to Banana Pro on the MAC OS is as follows:

```
● ○ ●                    ⚙ rudi — pi@bananapi: ~ — ssh — 80×15
mbair:~ rudi$ ssh pi@192.168.178.86
pi@192.168.178.86's password:



    |-) -----  ------   ------  --------|---
    |=) ------ ------   ------  --------|--
    |_) ------ |_|  |_| |_| |_|  --------|--


Last login: Sun Feb  8 12:34:39 2015 from mbair.fritz.box

Load: 1,00, 1,01, 1,05 - Board: 44.2°C - Memory: 677Mb

pi@bananapi:~$ ▒
```

Figure 1: The SSH remote connection to my Banana Pro that's initiated from the MAC OS

> X11 programs, such as XBMC, can be started from a remote shell.
> However, the `DISPLAY` variable must be set correctly and the X11 access
> control must be disabled (refer to *Chapter 4, An Arcade Cabinet*, for a more
> detailed explanation):
>
> **DISPLAY=:0.0 /allwinner/xbmc-pvr-binhf/lib/xbmc/xbmc.bin**
>
> X-windows programs can be passed to other X-servers that append `-X`
> to the SSH call:
>
> **ssh pi@ip-address -pport -X**

Using xrdp for remote desktop connection

The `xrdp` is a server for the **Remote Desktop Protocol (RDP)**. On Banana Pro, it can be easily installed using this command:

sudo apt-get install xrdp

It will also run as a service (/etc/init.d/xrdp). On the MAC OS, the CoRD freeware can be used to connect remotely to the Banana Pro X-windows. *Figure 2* shows the Banana Pro desktop on my MAC computer using CoRD. Windows provides Remote Desktop for the same purpose. In Windows, after launching the **Remote Desktop Connection** from **Start** or running the %windir%\system32\mstsc.exe command in the command prompt, you will be prompted for credentials. Enter pi/bananapi as credentials and you will see the X11 desktop within the Remote Desktop window.

Figure 2: The Banana Pro X11 desktop in the Mac OS uses xrdp and CoRD

Note that CoRD & Co. do not support the OpenGL ES extension. Thus, MALI-accelerated programs, such as es2gears, will not start within CoRD.

Basic requirements for programming Banana Pro

There are a few minimum requirements for programming, such as an editor, compiler, or debugger. There are also several IDEs available that integrate all of the preceding tools.

Editors

While editors, such as vi, have a steep learning curve, a more simple-to-use editor is **nano**. The nano editor is full-featured, available on every platform, and is obvious/intuitive to learn. It also has full syntax and keyword highlights for most programming languages.

This editor is invoked by the following command:

```
nano filename
```

The filename is the name of the file to be edited. For those of you who like their editors to be convenient, I can recommend cream. The cream editor is a fusion between a GUI editor and vi. It can be installed using this command:

```
sudo apt-get install cream
```

Here is a screenshot of cream. It handles syntax highlighting for different source code types:

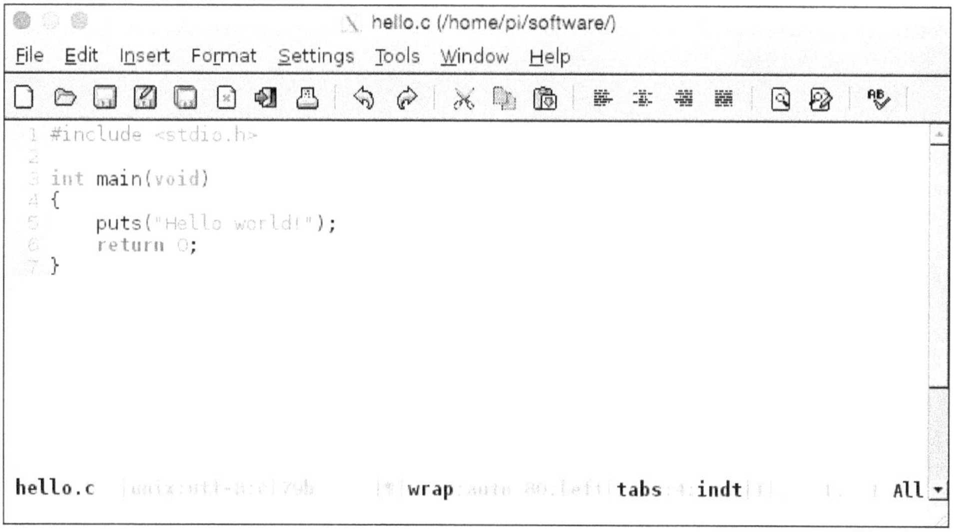

Figure 3: The cream GUI editor showing the 'hello world' C code example

If you feel that a compiler, debugger, and more should be available from the GUI, Eclipse (*Figure 4*) is worth looking at. The Eclipse editor is mainly programmed in Java and comes with many add-ons. Guess how it is installed? Correct, simply call the following command:

```
sudo apt-get install eclipse
```

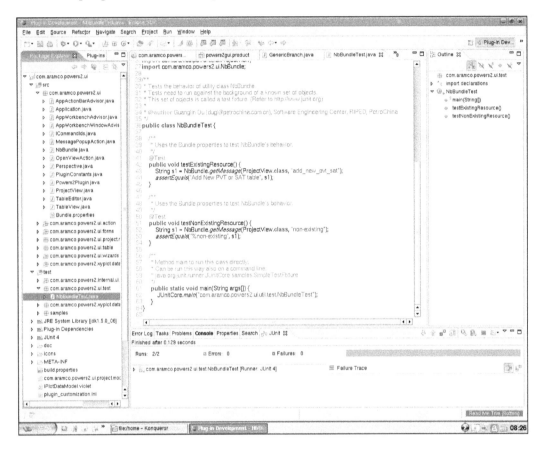

Figure 4: Eclipse is a complete IDE software development tool (source: eclipse.org)

Shell programming

A Linux shell is a command line interpreter that provides a user interface for a system itself. It can be used to install programs (`apt-get install`) or even for some programming, including conditions, logic, or loops. Linux provides many different shells. Very often, the Bourne shell is used, which was developed in the 70s by Stephen R. Bourne. This shell provides input and output redirection, pipes, background processes, and much more. For all Linux systems, a Bourne-compatible shell in the `/bin/sh` directory is available.

Checking the Banana Pro temperature

Let's start our first shell program using these steps:

1. Edit a file called temperature and place the following content in it:

   ```
   #!/bin/sh
   cat /sys/devices/platform/sunxi-i2c.0/i2c-0/0-0034/temp1_input
   ```

2. Save the file afterwards and make it executable:

   ```
   chmod 775 temperature
   ```

3. Execute this file by typing this:

   ```
   ./temperature
   ```

My output shows 36200, which is the Banana Pro temperature multiplied by 1,000. The first line of the `temperature` file source code instructs the system to use `/bin/sh` as a shell. The second line prints the temperature sensor value of Banana Pro. The `awk` scripting language can be used in order to format the output. You can install `awk` using the following command:

```
sudo apt-get install gawk
```

The temperature file is changed to the following content:

```
#!/bin/sh
cat /sys/devices/platform/sunxi-i2c.0/i2c-0/0-0034/temp1_input | awk '{
printf ("CPU temperature is = %0.1f°C\n",$1/1000); }'
```

The output is now as follows:

```
CPU temperature is = 36.2°C
```

The `awk` is an interpreted language that can be used in order to format text outputs. In the second line of the preceding file, the temperature output (`36200`) is piped to `awk`. The `awk` command prints the first (and only) argument ($1) as a float value with one digit after the decimal point ($0.1) followed by a carriage return (\n). In addition to this, the argument is divided by 1,000 ($1/1000) and the `CPU temperature is =` text is added.

Controlling Banana Pro's LEDs from SSH

Shell scripts can also be used in order to control the Banana Pro's LEDs. Banana Pro features three LEDs. The green and blue LEDs can be controlled by user software. The red LED lights up as soon as power supply is connected to Banana Pro.

The green LED can be switched on and off from a root-shell with this command:

```
echo default-on > /sys/class/leds/green\:ph24\:led1/trigger
echo none > /sys/class/leds/green\:ph24\:led1/trigger
```

For non-root shells, the command is as follows:

```
echo none | sudo tee /sys/class/leds/green\:ph24\:led1/trigger
```

The blue LED is available at `/sys/class/leds/blue\:pg02\:led2`.

The following command shows all the possibilities to set the onboard Banana Pro's LEDs:

```
cat /sys/class/leds/green\:ph24\:led1/trigger
```

```
[none] battery-charging-or-full battery-charging battery-full battery-charging-blink-full-solid ac-online usb-online mmc0 mmc1 timer heartbeat backlight gpio cpu0 cpu1 default-on rfkill0 rfkill1
```

```
pi@bananapi: ~
pi@bananapi:~$ cat /sys/class/leds/green\:ph24\:led1/trigger
[none] battery-charging-or-full battery-charging battery-full battery-charging-b
link-full-solid ac-online usb-online mmc0 mmc1 timer heartbeat backlight gpio cp
u0 cpu1 default-on rfkill0 rfkill1
pi@bananapi:~$
```

Figure 5

The value, which is currently set, is shown in brackets (for example, [none]). Later on, we will have a closer look at the gpio trigger. We will now write a shell script that will make the green LED blink in a second time rhythm:

```
nano ./blink-leds
```

```
#!/bin/sh
```

```
echo none > /sys/class/leds/green\:ph24\:led1/trigger
```

```
while true; do
```

```
echo default-on > /sys/class/leds/green\:ph24\:led1/trigger
```

```
sleep 1
```

```
echo none > /sys/class/leds/green\:ph24\:led1/trigger
```

```
sleep 1
```

```
done
```

 The preceding script will run forever (while true; do). After switching on the green LED, the script will sleep for one second (sleep 1), switch the LED off, sleep for another second, and so on. The script must be run as a root and can be stopped by pressing *Ctrl + C*.

Make the program executable like this:

```
$ chmod +x ./blink-leds
```

Then, to run the new program, execute the following:

```
$ sudo ./blink-leds
```

Programming GPIOs from SSH

Banana Pro features a 40-pin header (*Figure 6*).

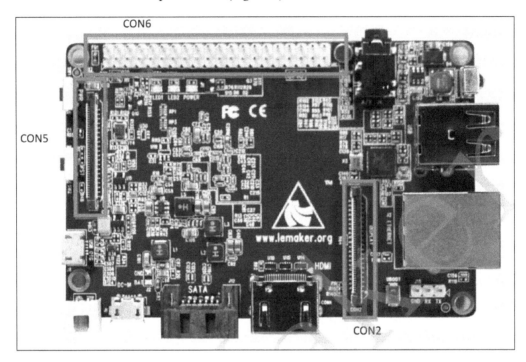

Figure 6

The following image shows the description of GPIO pins:

Figure 7: Banana Pro GPIO pins and meaning

 Banana Pro GPIO pins are not 5V-resistant. The maximum allowed input voltage is 3.3V. Using 5V on a 3.3V input pin may permanently damage Banana Pro.

In the next example, we define the GPIO pin 23 as an output pin, and set its voltage to high. From a root shell (sudo su), we define GPIO 23 first:

```
echo 23 > /sys/class/gpio/export
```

Afterwards, the kernel generates the directory:

```
/sys/class/gpio/gpio23
```

We assign GPIO 23 pin as an output pin:

```
echo out >/sys/class/gpio/gpio23/direction
```

We then set this pin to high (+3.3 V):

```
echo 1 >/sys/class/gpio/gpio23/value
```

A logical *low* corresponds to:

```
echo 0 >/sys/class/gpio/gpio23/value
```

Onboard LEDs can also be used as a GPIO indicator for input pins. The following example will triggers a green LED once voltage is provided to GPIO pin 23:

```
echo 23 > /sys/class/gpio/export
echo gpio > /sys/class/leds/green\:ph24\:led1/trigger
echo 23 > /sys/class/leds/green\:ph24\:led1/gpio
```

After providing the preceding commands, the green onboard LED will light up as soon as an external +3.3 V is connected to the GPIO pin 23. The A20 SOC provides internal pull-down resistors. Activating these resistors will result in a more sensitive interrupt and therefore a faster interrupt. Internal pull-downs can be activated as follows:

```
echo 23 > /sys/class/gpio/export
echo falling > /sys/class/gpio/gpio23/edge
echo down > /sys/class/gpio/gpio23/pull
echo gpio > /sys/class/leds/green\:ph24\:led1/trigger
echo 23 > /sys/class/leds/green\:ph24\:led1/gpio
```

The GPIO pin 23 can be freed again using this command:

```
echo 23 > /sys/class/gpio/unexport
```

Another shell example

With the preceding knowledge and an additional condition, we can now program a little shell script that will light up the green LED if the WLAN connection is available. Create a new script file like this:

```
#!/bin/bash
if [[ `cat /sys/class/net/wlan0/operstate` == "up" ]]
then
    echo default-on > '/sys/class/leds/green:ph24:led1/trigger'
else
    echo none > '/sys/class/leds/green:ph24:led1/trigger'
fi
```

Now, mark it as executable and run this script:

```
chmod +x ./wifi-leds
```

```
sudo ./wifi-leds
```

The /sys/class/net/wlan0/operstate function can have two states: *down* or *up*. In the *up* state, the green LED is switched on, and in the *down* state, it is switched off. If wlan0 is not configured, the preceding script will not work correctly. In this case, eth0 could be used instead of wlan0 in order to monitor the Ethernet connection.

> LED functions can also be set in the FEX file (refer to *Chapter 1, Introduction to Banana Pro*). An example of this is as follows:.
>
> ```
> [leds_para]
> leds_used = 1
> leds_num = 2
> leds_pin_1 = port:PH20<1><default><default><0>
> leds_name_1 = "ph20:green:led1"
> leds_trigger_1 = "heartbeat"
> leds_pin_2 = port:PH21<1><default><default><0>
> leds_name_2 = "ph21:blue:led2"
> leds_trigger_2 = "cpu0"
> ```
>
> Remember to compile the FEX file to the bin file using the fex2bin command.

WiringBP

Working with the sys class requires long paths to be typed. The LeMaker GitHub provides a software similar to WiringPi called WiringBP, which eases the handling of GPIO ports.

WiringBP (for Banana Pro) can be cloned from GitHub:

```
git clone -b bananapro https://github.com/LeMaker/WiringBP.git
cd WiringBP
chmod +x ./build
sudo ./build
```

This will generate the complete WiringBP library so that it can be installed together with associated programs. For testing purposes, we start the gpio program with the readall parameter in order to read the status of all Banana Pro GPIO pins:

```
cd gpio
sudo ./gpio readall
```

The output would look similar to what is shown in the following screenshot. The middle columns represent physical rows of pins and the columns on the left-hand side and right-hand side represent the various settings/names for each pin.

```
●  ●  ●                rudi — pi@bananapro: ~/WiringBP/gpio — ssh — 85×28
pi@bananapro:~/WiringBP/gpio$ sudo ./gpio readall
+-----+-----+---------+------+---+--Banana Pro--+---+------+---------+-----+-----+
| BCM | wPi |   Name  | Mode | V | Physical | V | Mode | Name    | wPi | BCM |
+-----+-----+---------+------+---+----++----+---+------+---------+-----+-----+
|     |     |    3.3v |      |   |  1 || 2  |   |      | 5v      |     |     |
|   2 |   8 |   SDA.1 | ALT5 | 1 |  3 || 4  |   |      | 5V      |     |     |
|   3 |   9 |   SCL.1 | ALT5 | 1 |  5 || 6  |   |      | 0v      |     |     |
|   4 |   7 |  GPIO. 7|  IN  | 0 |  7 || 8  | 0 | ALT0 | TxD     | 15  | 14  |
|     |     |      0v |      |   |  9 || 10 | 0 | ALT0 | RxD     | 16  | 15  |
|  17 |   0 |  GPIO. 0| ALT4 | 0 | 11 || 12 | 0 | IN   | GPIO. 1 | 1   | 18  |
|  27 |   2 |  GPIO. 2| ALT4 | 0 | 13 || 14 |   |      | 0v      |     |     |
|  22 |   3 |  GPIO. 3| ALT4 | 0 | 15 || 16 | 0 | IN   | GPIO. 4 | 4   | 23  |
|     |     |    3.3v |      |   | 17 || 18 | 0 | IN   | GPIO. 5 | 5   | 24  |
|  10 |  12 |    MOSI | ALT5 | 0 | 19 || 20 |   |      | 0v      |     |     |
|   9 |  13 |    MISO | ALT5 | 0 | 21 || 22 | 0 | ALT4 | GPIO. 6 | 6   | 25  |
|  11 |  14 |    SCLK | ALT5 | 0 | 23 || 24 | 0 | ALT5 | CE0     | 10  | 8   |
|     |     |      0v |      |   | 25 || 26 | 0 | ALT5 | CE1     | 11  | 7   |
|   0 |  30 |   SDA.0 | ALT4 | 0 | 27 || 28 | 0 | ALT4 | SCL.0   | 31  | 1   |
|   5 |  21 | GPIO.21 |  IN  | 0 | 29 || 30 |   |      | 0v      |     |     |
|   6 |  22 | GPIO.22 | ALT4 | 0 | 31 || 32 | 0 | ALT4 | GPIO.26 | 26  | 12  |
|  13 |  23 | GPIO.23 | ALT0 | 0 | 33 || 34 |   |      | 0v      |     |     |
|  19 |  24 | GPIO.24 | ALT5 | 0 | 35 || 36 | 0 | ALT5 | GPIO.27 | 27  | 16  |
|  26 |  25 | GPIO.25 | ALT5 | 0 | 37 || 38 | 0 | ALT5 | GPIO.28 | 28  | 20  |
|     |     |      0v |      |   | 39 || 40 | 0 | ALT5 | GPIO.29 | 29  | 21  |
+-----+-----+---------+------+---+----++----+---+------+---------+-----+-----+
| BCM | wPi |   Name  | Mode | V | Physical | V | Mode | Name    | wPi | BCM |
+-----+-----+---------+------+---+----+--Banana Pro--+------+---------+-----+-----+
pi@bananapro:~/WiringBP/gpio$ ▊
```

Figure 8: The gpio readall output on my Banana Pro

Let's set GPIO.25 as an output pin:

```
sudo ./gpio mode 25 out
```

The `sudo ./gpio readall` command shows that GPIO 25 is now an output pin (*Figure 9*). For GPIO 25, the mode is changed from ALT5 to OUT:

```
●  ●  ●                rudi — pi@bananapro: ~/WiringBP/gpio — ssh — 85×6
|  26 |  25 | GPIO.25 | OUT  | 0 | 37 || 38 | 0 | ALT5 | GPIO.28 | 28  | 20  |
|     |     |      0v |      |   | 39 || 40 | 0 | ALT5 | GPIO.29 | 29  | 21  |
+-----+-----+---------+------+---+----++----+---+------+---------+-----+-----+
| BCM | wPi |   Name  | Mode | V | Physical | V | Mode | Name    | wPi | BCM |
+-----+-----+---------+------+---+----+--Banana Pro--+------+---------+-----+-----+
pi@bananapro:~/WiringBP/gpio$ ▊
```

Figure 9: The Gpio readall output on my Banana Pro after defining GPIO 25 as the output pin

In a next step, we will set the output voltage of GPIO.25 to high (3.3V):

```
sudo ./gpio write 25 1
```

A quick `gpio readall` shows that GPIO pin 25 is now high, and the voltage for pin 25 has changed from `0` to `1`:

```
● ○ ○              ⌂ rudi — pi@bananapro: ~/WiringBP/gpio — ssh — 85×7
|  19 |  24 | GPIO.24 | ALT5 | 0 | 35 || 36 | 0 | ALT5 | GPIO.27 | 27 | 16 |
|  26 |  25 | GPIO.25 |  OUT | 1 | 37 || 38 | 0 | ALT5 | GPIO.28 | 28 | 20 |
|     |     |     0v  |      |   | 39 || 40 | 0 | ALT5 | GPIO.29 | 29 | 21 |
+-----+-----+---------+------+---+----++----+---+------+---------+----+-----+
| BCM | wPi |  Name   | Mode | V | Physical | V | Mode | Name    | wPi | BCM |
+-----+-----+---------+------+---+---+--Banana Pro--+---+------+---------+----+-----+
pi@bananapro:~/WiringBP/gpio$ ▊
```

Figure 10: The Gpio readall output on my Banana Pro after setting GPIO 25 to high

With the help of multimeter, the voltage of GPIO pin 25 could be measured.

WiringBP does not only provide shell tools, such as GPIO, it also provides a library and header file for your own C/C++ code developments.

There are different numbering schemes for the Banana Pro GPIO header as follows:

BCM_GPIO stands for **Broadcom SOC channel**. This numbering is related to Raspberry Pi and is also available on Banana Pro. The `gpio` software can use this numbering scheme by providing the `-g` parameter, for example, `gpio -g mode 26 out`

The optional `-1` flag causes pin numbers to be interpreted as hardware pin numbers, for example, `gpio -1 mode 37 out`.

Python

"Python is a programming language that lets you work quickly and integrate systems more effectively."

- Python website (`http://www.python.org`)

It is true that nearly no other interpreter language is as popular as Python. Additionally, there are a bunch of add-ons for Python that are available, ranging from a simple web server to complex graphics libraries. In this section, the reader will learn some basics of Python. We will use Python in order to program GPIO pins. We will look at a more complex example that will deal with graphical output in a window.

The basics

Before Python can be used, Python itself and the associated developer packages need to be installed:

```
sudo apt-get install python python-dev
```

For my examples, I've used 2.7.x version of Python. Python 3.x is not needed in order to execute the examples.

Since Python is an interpreter, there are two possibilities of executing a *Hello world!* program. The first option is to invoke Python in a terminal by typing `python`.

This will start the interpreter that will wait for any input:

```
Python 2.7.3 (default, Mar 14 2014, 17:55:54)
[GCC 4.6.3] on linux2
Type "help", "copyright", "credits" or "license" for more information.
>>>
```

We will provide the `"Hello world!"` input and watch the output:

```
>>> print "Hello world!"
Hello world!
>>>
```

We can leave the interpreter by pushing *Ctrl* + *D*. As an alternative, `quit()` at the prompt will also exit the Python interpreter.

The second option is editing a file (for example, `hello.py`) with the following content:

```
print "Hello world!"
```

Now we can invoke Python with this file as a parameter:

```
python hello.py
```

This will invoke the interpreter and deliver the same output as seen earlier.

A simple web server

Let's perform a more complex example: a simple web server. First, let's install a Python extension called `cherrypy` using the following command:

```
sudo apt-get install python-cherrypy3
```

After this, edit a file called `webserver.py` using the following command:

```
nano webserver.py
```

Fill this file with the following content:

```
import cherrypy
class HelloWorld(object):
    def index(self):
        return "Hello World!"
    index.exposed = True


cherrypy.quickstart(HelloWorld())
```

Contrary to other programming languages, Python uses indents for blocks that belong together. In the first line, the `cherrypy` Python extension is imported. The next four lines define a simple web server class called `HelloWorld`, just returning `"Hello world!"` on the main web page (index), which is visible (`index.exposed = True`). Finally, `cherrypy` is started with the `HelloWorld` object. The web server itself must be started as a root in order to get the rights to open required server ports:

```
sudo python ./webserver.py
```

This will start the web server and generate the following output:

```
[10/Feb/2015:10:22:18] ENGINE Listening for SIGHUP.
[10/Feb/2015:10:22:18] ENGINE Listening for SIGTERM.
[10/Feb/2015:10:22:18] ENGINE Listening for SIGUSR1.
[10/Feb/2015:10:22:18] ENGINE Bus STARTING
CherryPy Checker:
The Application mounted at '' has an empty config.

[10/Feb/2015:10:22:18] ENGINE Started monitor thread '_TimeoutMonitor'.
[10/Feb/2015:10:22:18] ENGINE Started monitor thread 'Autoreloader'.
[10/Feb/2015:10:22:18] ENGINE Serving on 127.0.0.1:8080
[10/Feb/2015:10:22:18] ENGINE Bus STARTED
```

As can be seen, `cherrypy` defaults the web port to port `8080`. Start a local web browser on Banana Pro providing the address `127.0.0.1:8080`. On my Banana Pro, I use `iceweasel` (`sudo apt-get install iceweasel`) get the following output:

Figure 11: Iceweasel showing the cherrypy minimal web server

Chromium, an open source version of Google Chrome, is also an excellent browser for Banana Pro. To install it, run this command:

```
sudo apt-get install chromium
```

The `cherrypy` module even shows a favicon (cherry). The web server can be stopped by pushing *Ctrl + C*. In *Chapter 3, Wireless Projects*, a complete measurement server example will be provided, combining C and the Python language.

Using Python for GPIO

There is also a python package available for the GPIO programming on Banana Pro. It must be installed from GitHub as follows:

```
git clone https://github.com/LeMaker/RPi.GPIO_BP -b bananapro
cd RPi.GPIO_BP
python setup.py install
sudo python setup.py install
```

According to the LeMaker Wiki page, `python setup.py install` needs to be executed twice: the first time without `sudo`, and the second time including `sudo`.

After the installation of the `Rpi.GPIO` library for Banana Pro, let's open the `gpio-test.py` file using the following command:

nano gpio-test.py

Then, we will write a small test program in the `gpio-test.py` file with the following content:

```
import RPi.GPIO as GPIO
GPIO.setmode(GPIO.BCM)
GPIO.setup(26, GPIO.OUT)
GPIO.output(26, GPIO.HIGH)
```

In the preceding code, the `RPi.GPIO` compiled library is imported with the name GPIO. All functions within this library can be called with `GPIO.function_name`. The GPIO mode is set to **BroadCom declaration Mode (BCM)**. The BCM pin 26 (identical to `GPIO.25`) is set as an output pin. Afterwards, this output pin is set to high. Run the preceding test program as a user root and check GPIO pins using `gpio readall`: the BCM pin 26 will be set to high. We can also ask Python to confirm the voltage level at the BCM pin 26. Add these lines to the preceding source code that's been provided, and restart Python with this file:

```
if GPIO.input(26):
    print("Pin 26 is HIGH")
else:
    print("Pin 26 is LOW")
```

The output will be as follows:

BAPI: revision(2)

Pin 26 is HIGH

 `GPIO.setmode(GPIO.BOARD)` sets the GPIO numbering to the board mode. This mode refers to the pin numbering on Banana Pro board itself, that is, the numbers printed on the board (for example, P1).

GPIO.setup() has a third optional parameter, which you can use to set pull-up or pull-down resistors. To use a pull-up resistor on a pin, add pull_up_down=GPIO. PUD_UP as a third parameter in GPIO.setup(). Or, if you need a pull-down resistor, use pull_up_down=GPIO.PUD_DOWN instead.

For example, to use a pull-up resistor on BCM pin 26, write this into your setup:

```
GPIO.setup(26, GPIO.IN, pull_up_down=GPIO.PUD_UP)
```

If nothing is declared in the third value, both the pull resistors will be disabled.

Banana Pro also features one **Pulse Width Modulation** (**PWM**) capable pin (the board pin 12 and BCM pin 18). PWM can be used in order to control motors or battery charging.

To initialize PWM, the GPIO.PWM(pin, frequency) function is used, and the *frequency* is provided in Hz. The pwm.start(duty cycle) function is used to set the initial value. Take a look at this example:

```
pwm = GPIO.PWM(18, 5000)
pwm.start(10)
```

We will set up the Banana Pro PWM pin with a frequency of 5 KHz and a duty cycle of 10%. The duty cycle indicates the percentage of time power that is applied over a given period. To adjust the value of the PWM output, use the pwm. ChangeDutyCycle(duty cycle) function. The duty cycle value can be any value between 0 and 100. The pwm.stop() function is used in order to turn PWM off.

 The PWM pin must be set as an output pin before using PWM.

Setting LEDs in Python

Python can also access /sys/class/led in order to switch the Banana Pro onboard LEDs on or off. Edit a file called led.py using the nano command and add the following content to it:

```
#!/usr/bin/env python
# coding=utf8

def led_on():
    value = open("/sys/class/leds/green:ph24:led1/trigger","w")
    value.write("default-on")
```

```
def led_off():
    value = open("/sys/class/leds/green:ph24:led1/trigger","w")
    value.write("none")

if __name__ == '__main__':
    from time import sleep
    while(1):
  led_on()
  sleep(1)
  led_off()
  sleep(1)
```

Save the preceding file as `led.py` and mark it as executable:

chmod +x led.py

Execute the program as follows:

sudo ./led.py

In the first line of code, we define python to be used with this file. Therefore, it can be started, as shown previously, without python included in the line. The second line defines utf8 as a coding scheme for the file (https://en.wikipedia.org/wiki/UTF-8). Furthermore, two functions without parameters are defined: `led_on()` and `led_off()`. These functions write to `/sys/class/led` in order to switch the green LED of Banana Pro on or off. The main entry point for the Python file provided earlier is `if __name__ == '__main__'`. Here, sleep is first imported from the time library. This function is used in order to switch the LED off for one second later on (`sleep(1)`). In an endless loop (`while(1)`), the green LED is switched on and off in a 1 second rhythm.

The last LED example fires the green Banana Pro LED on the LIRC input. As soon as an arbitrary button of any remote control pointing toward Banana Pro is pressed, the green LED will light up:

```
#!/usr/bin/env python
# coding=utf8

def led_on():
    value = open("/sys/class/leds/green:ph24:led1/trigger","w")
    value.write("default-on")

def led_off():
    value = open("/sys/class/leds/green:ph24:led1/trigger","w")
    value.write("none")
```

```
if __name__ == '__main__':
    from time import sleep
    import subprocess
    p = subprocess.Popen('irw', shell=True, stdout=subprocess.PIPE,
stderr=subprocess.STDOUT)
    while(1):
  led_off()
  output = p.stdout.readline()
  if output:
      led_on()
      output = ""
  else:
      led_off()
```

This example requires a working LIRC configuration (refer to *Chapter 5*, *A Multimedia Center*) and `irw` running. It is similar to the first Python LED example. The major difference is the main program: Here, the `irw` process is started and the `stdout` is piped to the `irw` process in an endless loop. Only if an output is available (the remote control key has been pressed), will the LED be switched on.

A Python window example

One very well-known extension for Python is `matplotlib`. The `matplotlib` library is a Python 2D plotting library, which produces publication quality figures and diagrams. It is available for many different platforms and will also run on Banana Pro. This section cannot provide a detailed look at `matplotlib` but it will, hopefully, capture your interest by providing a simple example. `matplotlib` can be installed using this command:

```
sudo apt-get install python-matplotlib
```

The following example draws the `sin` function for the x value range from `0` to `10` with a step width of `0.2`:

```
import matplotlib.pyplot as plt
import numpy as np
```

```
x = np.arange(0, 10, 0.2)
y = np.sin(x)

fig = plt.figure()

ax = fig.add_subplot(111)
ax.plot(x, y)

plt.grid()
plt.show()
```

The output is shown in this screenshot:

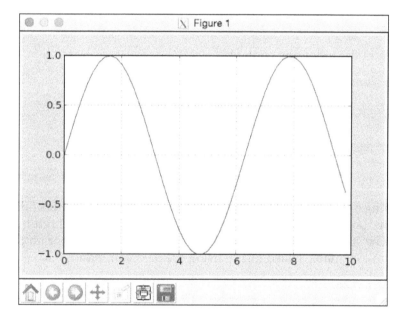

Figure 12: The Matplotlib output for the preceding example

 Do not call the matplotlib.py example. This will cause strange effects when executing this file with Python.

C/C++

Most Banana Pro programs found on the Internet are C/C++ programs. The main reasons for this are speed critical applications: interpreters, such as Python, are much slower compared to compiled programs such as C/C++ ones. In this section, we will have a closer look at the Linux C/C++ compiler called **GNU Compiler Collection (GCC)**. GCC includes frontends for both the C and C++ compiler as well as libraries for these languages. We install the C and C++ compiler with the following command:

```
sudo apt-get install gcc g++ make
```

Additionally, we install make, a utility that helps the compiling and linking of C/C++ files. We again start with a very simply "Hello world!" example, which we call hello.c:

```
nano hello.c
```

We can then add the following content:

```
#include <stdio.h>

int main(void)
{
    puts("Hello world!");
    return 0;
}
```

In the preceding example, we include standard input/output headers (stdio.h). The main entry point of the program has no arguments (void) and returns an integer value (int). The standard return value is 0 (for no errors). The program can be compiled to an executable called hello using the next command:

```
gcc -o hello hello.c
```

Invoking the compiled and linked program delivers this intended output:

```
./hello
Hello world!
```

When compiling and linking many different files, it would be a lot of work to include all the filenames in a single compile and linker line. In order to simplify this procedure, `Makefile` was invented. Edit a file called `Makefile` in the directory where `hello.c` is located, and place the following content in it:

```
VERSION    = 1.0
CPP = /usr/bin/g++
CFLAGS = -Wall -DVERSION=\"$(VERSION)\"
LDFLAGS =

OBJ = hello.o

BIN = hello

all: $(OBJ)
  $(CPP) $(CFLAGS) -o $(BIN) $(OBJ) $(LDFLAGS)

%.o: %.c
  $(CC) $(CFLAGS) -c $<

clean:
  rm -rf $(BIN) $(OBJ) *~
```

First, we'll invoke the `Makefile` and clean up the old build:

`make clean`

The `make` command itself invokes the file called `Makefile` and jumps to the `clean:` section. Everything belonging to this section is executed: `hello` (executable), `hello.o` (object file), and possible editor backup files (beginning with ~) are deleted. Calling the `make` command again rebuilds the `hello` executable. In the preceding example, `Makefile` also shows how `defines` can be passed to the source code (`-DVERSION` example).

> If a source file changes, `Makefile` will recompile the source. Incorrect date or time settings will confuse `Makefile`. Banana Pro does not feature a **Real Time Clock (RTC)**. Thus, be sure that `ntpdate` is running and providing the correct date and time. `ntpdate` can be installed as follows:
>
> **`sudo apt-get install ntpdate`**
>
> Then, to update the clock on the current computer, run the following command:
>
> **`sudo ntpdate -u time.nist.gov`**

The WiringBP C code example

In this section, we have already installed the WiringBP software. This software also includes a header file for C/C++ programs and a library in order to link these programs. In this section, first, a simple C code will be provided, which will define the GPIO pin 25 as an output pin and set its voltage to a logical high. In my example I've called the following `gpib_c.c` file:

```
#include <wiringPi.h>

int main (void)
{
  wiringPiSetup();
  pinMode (25, OUTPUT);
  digitalWrite (25, HIGH);
  return 0 ;
}
```

The program can be compiled as follows:

gcc -Wall -o gpio_c gpib_c.c -lwiringPi

The `-Wall` compiler switch switches on all warnings, which may arise during compile time. The output file is called `gpib_c`. In addition to this, the `wiringPi` library is used during the linking process (`-lwiringPi`). The output file itself can be started (as a root) by calling this command:

sudo ./gpio_c

> Do you remember, how GPIO settings can be read? A quick `gpio readall` shows whether our little example was executed successfully.

The preceding source example can be enhanced and used with an external LED:

```
#include <wiringPi.h>
int main (void)
{
  wiringPiSetup () ;
  pinMode (25, OUTPUT) ;
  for (;;)
  {
    digitalWrite (25, HIGH);
    delay(1000) ;
```

```
    digitalWrite (25,  LOW);
    delay(1000) ;
  }
  return 0 ;
}
```

The compilation should be clear: `for(;;)` generates an endless loop in C. The parameter of the `delay()` function is provided in ms. A value of 1,000 ms is equal to 1 s. We can now connect an external LED to Banana Pro. A red LED usually draws a current of 18 mA with a supply voltage of 1.6V. Thus, we need a voltage drop of *3.3 V – 1.6 V = 1.7 V* across the resistor. According to Ohm's law, the resistor size should be *1.7 V/0.018 A = 95 Ohm*.

C access to onboard LEDs

The C/C++ code can also be used in order to access the onboard LEDs of Banana Pro. Again, an example for blinking the green onboard LED is provided as follows. This time, it is C++. I've called this example file `led_cpp.cpp`:

```
#include<unistd.h>
#include<iostream>
#include<fstream>
#include<string>
using namespace std;

#define GREEN_LED_PATH "/sys/class/leds/green:ph24:led1/trigger"

int main(){
std::fstream fs;

    fs.open(GREEN_LED_PATH, std::fstream::out);

    while (1){
        fs << "default-on" << std::flush;
        usleep(1000000);
        fs << "none" << std::flush;
        usleep(1000000);
    }

    fs.close();
    return 0;
}
```

Compile the `led_cpp.cpp` file and start it:

```
g++ -o led_cpp led_cpp.cpp
sudo ./led_cpp
```

The `unistd.h` header provides the `usleep` function. This function expects time to sleep in microseconds as an argument. Thus, 10,00,000 μs is equal to 1 s.

In the next example, we switch off the LEDs of the Ethernet socket. The C source code has been provided to the Banana Pi forum by Roman Reichel. I changed it in order to only switch off the yellow and green Banana Pro Ethernet socket LEDs:

```c
#include <unistd.h>
#include <stdlib.h>
#include <stdio.h>
#include <ctype.h>
#include <string.h>
#include <errno.h>
#include <fcntl.h>
#include <getopt.h>
#include <time.h>
#include <syslog.h>
#include <sys/types.h>
#include <sys/socket.h>
#include <sys/ioctl.h>
#include <net/if.h>
#include <linux/sockios.h>
#include <linux/mii.h>


static int verbose = 1;
static int skfd = -1;
static struct ifreq ifr;

static int mdio_read(int skfd, int location) {

  struct mii_ioctl_data *mii = (struct mii_ioctl_data
    *)&ifr.ifr_data;
  mii->reg_num = location;
  if (ioctl(skfd, SIOCGMIIREG, &ifr) < 0) {
    fprintf(stderr, "SIOCGMIIREG on %s failed: %s\n",
      ifr.ifr_name, strerror(errno));
    return -1;
  }
```

```
    return mii->val_out;
}

static void mdio_write(int skfd, int location, int value) {

  struct mii_ioctl_data *mii = (struct mii_ioctl_data
*)&ifr.ifr_data;
  mii->reg_num = location;
  mii->val_in = value;
  if (ioctl(skfd, SIOCSMIIREG, &ifr) < 0) {
    fprintf(stderr, "SIOCGMIIREG on %s failed: %s\n",
      ifr.ifr_name, strerror(errno));
  }
}

enum {
  FUNC_10MBPS,
  FUNC_100MBPS,
  FUNC_1000MBPS,
  FUNC_ACTIVITY,
  FUNC_COUNT
};

#define CFG_10MBPS        (1 << FUNC_10MBPS)
#define CFG_100MBPS       (1 << FUNC_100MBPS)
#define CFG_1000MBPS      (1 << FUNC_1000MBPS)
#define CFG_ACTIVITY      (1 << FUNC_ACTIVITY)

enum {
  LED_YELLOW,
  LED_GREEN,
  LED_COUNT
};

typedef struct {
  int reg26_clear;
  int reg26_set;
  int reg28_clear;
  int reg28_set;
} led_config_t;

typedef struct {
  int func_mask;
  int func_value;
```

```
  } func_config_t;

static const char *led_name[] = {
  [LED_YELLOW] = "yellow",
  [LED_GREEN] = "green",
};

static const char *func_name[] = {
  [FUNC_10MBPS]   = "10Mbps",
  [FUNC_100MBPS]  = "100Mbps",
  [FUNC_1000MBPS] = "1000Mbps",
  [FUNC_ACTIVITY] = "Active (Tx/Rx)",
};

static const led_config_t led_config[LED_COUNT][FUNC_COUNT] = {
  [LED_YELLOW] = {
    [FUNC_10MBPS]   = {.reg28_set = 1 << 4},
    [FUNC_100MBPS]  = {.reg28_set = 1 << 5},
    [FUNC_1000MBPS] = {.reg28_set = 1 << 6},
    [FUNC_ACTIVITY] = {.reg26_set = 1 << 5},
  },
  [LED_GREEN] = {
    [FUNC_10MBPS]   = {.reg28_set = 1 << 0},
    [FUNC_100MBPS]  = {.reg28_set = 1 << 1},
    [FUNC_1000MBPS] = {.reg28_set = 1 << 2},
    [FUNC_ACTIVITY] = {.reg26_set = 1 << 4},
  },
};


static void led_config_apply(led_config_t *lcp, int set, const
led_config_t *lf) {
  if (set) {
    lcp->reg26_clear |= lf->reg26_clear;
    lcp->reg26_set   |= lf->reg26_set;
    lcp->reg28_clear |= lf->reg28_clear;
    lcp->reg28_set   |= lf->reg28_set;
  } else {
    lcp->reg26_clear |= lf->reg26_set;
    lcp->reg26_set   |= lf->reg26_clear;
    lcp->reg28_clear |= lf->reg28_set;
    lcp->reg28_set   |= lf->reg28_clear;
  }
```

```
}

static void led_mask_val(led_config_t *lcp, int led, const
  func_config_t *cfg) {
  if (cfg->func_mask & CFG_10MBPS) led_config_apply(lcp,
    !!(cfg->func_value & CFG_10MBPS),
    &led_config[led][FUNC_10MBPS]);
  if (cfg->func_mask & CFG_100MBPS) led_config_apply(lcp,
    !!(cfg->func_value & CFG_100MBPS),
    &led_config[led][FUNC_100MBPS]);
  if (cfg->func_mask & CFG_1000MBPS) led_config_apply(lcp,
    !!(cfg->func_value & CFG_1000MBPS),
    &led_config[led][FUNC_1000MBPS]);
  if (cfg->func_mask & CFG_ACTIVITY) led_config_apply(lcp,
    !!(cfg->func_value & CFG_ACTIVITY),
    &led_config[led][FUNC_ACTIVITY]);
}

static void led_set(const func_config_t *yellow,
  const func_config_t *green) {
  led_config_t lc;
  int reg26_old, reg28_old;
  int reg26_new, reg28_new;

  /* Parse configuration request */
  lc.reg26_clear = 0;
  lc.reg26_set = 0;
  lc.reg28_clear = 0;
  lc.reg28_set = 0;
  led_mask_val(&lc, LED_YELLOW, yellow);
  led_mask_val(&lc, LED_GREEN, green);

  /* Configure the phy */
  mdio_write(skfd, 0x1f, 0x0007);
  mdio_write(skfd, 0x1e, 0x002c);

  reg26_old = mdio_read(skfd, 26);
  reg26_new = (reg26_old & ~lc.reg26_clear) | lc.reg26_set;
  if (reg26_new != reg26_old)
    mdio_write(skfd, 26, reg26_new);

  reg28_old = mdio_read(skfd, 28);
  reg28_new = (reg28_old & ~lc.reg28_clear) | lc.reg28_set;
  if (reg28_new != reg28_old)
```

```
      mdio_write(skfd, 28, reg28_new);

   mdio_write(skfd, 0x1f, 0x0000);

}

int main(int argc, char** argv) {
  func_config_t yellow, green;



  (&yellow)->func_mask = ~0;  (&yellow)->func_value = 0;
  (&green)->func_mask = ~0;  (&green)->func_value = 0;

  if ((skfd = socket(AF_INET, SOCK_DGRAM, 0)) < 0) {
    perror("socket");
    exit(1);
  }

  strncpy(ifr.ifr_name, "eth0", IFNAMSIZ);

  if (ioctl(skfd, SIOCGMIIPHY, &ifr) < 0) {
    fprintf(stderr, "SIOCGMIIPHY on eth0 failed: %s\n",
    strerror(errno));
    close(skfd);
    return 1;
  }

  mdio_write(skfd, 0x1f, 0x0000);
  led_set(&yellow, &green);

  close(skfd);
  return 0;
}
```

The program can be compiled by typing the following command in a terminal, whereas I've called the eth_led_off.c source file:

```
gcc -o eth_led_off eth_led_off.c
```

Invoking the compiled and linked file as root will switch off the Ethernet socket LEDs.

Debugger

This final C/C++ section describes how programs can be debugged using the GNU debugger gdb. In the first step, gdb is installed using the following command:

```
sudo apt-get install gdb
```

Then, a very simple example called debug.c is generated:

```c
#include <stdio.h>
double div(double a, double b)
{
    return(a/b);
}

int main(void)
{
int a;

    for (a=4; a>0; a--)
     printf("10:%d = %lf\n", a, div(10,a));
    return 0;
}
```

The example includes a function called div, which takes two arguments, a and b, and delivers a divided by b as a return value. The main loop decrements an i variable from four to one and calculates 10 divided by i using the div function.

While compiling and linking the file, we include the debug information using the-ggdb compiler directivity:

```
gcc -ggdb -o debug debug.c
```

We start debugging the debug program by invoking the following command:

```
gdb debug
```

The list command shows the C-code within the gdb debugger:

```
(gdb) list
3       double div(double a, double b)
4       {
5           return(a/b);
6       }
7
```

```
8        int main(void)
9        {
10       int i;
11
12           for (i=4; i>=0; i--)
(gdb)
```

An additional `list` command will list the next lines of the source code.

The following table shows the most important `gdb` debugger commands:

Command	Action
run	This executes a loaded program
list	This shows a program's source code
break <source code line>	This set a breakpoint at <source code line>
cont	This continues the execution of a program after a break has been reached
watch <var>	This watches the <var> variable by permanently printing its value
next	This executes the next source code line
step	This steps into next source code line's function
set <var> = <value>	This sets the <var> variable to value <value>
up	This goes up one instance
down	This goes down one instance
quit	This exits a debugger
Help <command>	This provides additional help for the gdb command

Let's set a breakpoint in line 13:

```
(gdb) break 13
Breakpoint 1 at 0x83ee: file debug.c, line 13.
```

Next, let's start the program:

```
(gdb) run
Starting program: /home/pi/software/debug
```

```
Breakpoint 1, main () at debug.c:13
13              printf("10:%d = %lf\n", i, div(10.0,(double)i));
```

The debugger stops the execution of the program in line 12. The next command shows the first calculation result:

```
(gdb) next
10:4 = 2.500000
12          for (i=4; i>=0; i--)
```

Afterwards, the debugger stops in the source code line 12 again. Let's take a look at the i variable:

```
(gdb) watch i
Hardware watchpoint 2: i
```

A new next command shows the changed value of i:

```
(gdb) next
Hardware watchpoint 2: i

Old value = 4
New value = 3
0x00008420 in main () at debug.c:12
12          for (i=4; i>=0; i--)
```

An additional next command will reach the breakpoint in line 13:

```
(gdb) next

Breakpoint 1, main () at debug.c:13
13              printf("10:%d = %lf\n", i, div(10.0,(double)i));
```

We will now step into the div function:

```
(gdb) step
div (a=10, b=3) at debug.c:5
5           return(a/b);
```

Let's have a look at the value of a:

```
(gdb) print a
$1 = 10
```

As expected, a equals 10. Try other gdb commands, such as "up" and "down", which will go up and down one instance.

Exit the debugger using the quit command.

Scratch

Scratch is a programming language for children and teenagers. Graphical boxes have replaced all programming elements within this language. The language itself was invented and developed at MIT. The name is related to a scratching technique from turntables (mixing sounds). Scratch programs are event-driven with objects called sprites. Sprites can be either drawn or imported from external sources such as webcams.

Scratch can be used from a web interface. In addition to this, there is an **Integrated Development Environment** (**IDE**) available, which can be installed on Banana Pro using this command:

```
sudo apt-get install scratch
```

On many distributions, Scratch is already preinstalled.

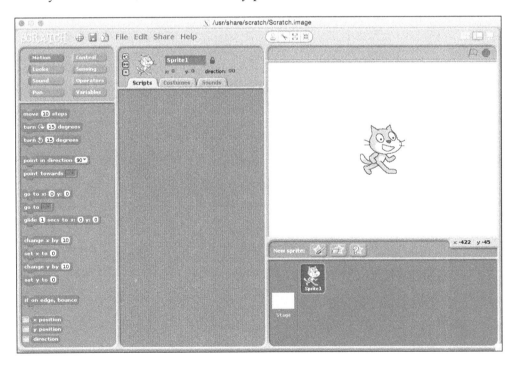

Figure 13

Typing the `scratch` command will start **Scratch**, as shown in the preceding screenshot. The IDE is split into three different parts: the left-hand side column contains all programming elements, the middle area can be used to place the programming elements in order to program functionality, and the right-hand side column shows the program output.

Hello world – example for Scratch

A very simple Scratch program is shown in the following screenshot. Hitting the green flag can start the Scratch program.

Figure 14

The output is shown in the speech balloon next to the cat:

Figure 15: In Scratch, texts are shown as speech balloon

Using LN Digital with Scratch

The Lenovaters LN Digital board has been already been introduced in *Chapter 1, Introduction to Banana Pro*. This section describes the usage of this add-on in combination with Scratch. In order to use LN Digital together with Scratch, the Mesh mode must be enabled. Mesh is a method allowing Scratch to interact with additional boards or even different computers by sharing, for example, variables or broadcasts. Moreover, different Scratch programs on different computers can interact once Mesh is enabled.

Mesh is not enabled by default in Scratch. Thus, as a first step, we will enable Mesh in order to allow interaction with the LN Digital board. This only needs to be done once the following the steps are described as `root`. Enabling Mesh requires the editing of Scratch's system browser, which can be done as follows:

1. Start Scratch in the X11 desktop:

   ```
   sudo scratch
   ```

2. Press and hold the *Shift* key and right-click the letter **R** within the Scratch logo.

3. Select **turn fill screen off**.

4. A white area at the bottom and right-hand side of Scratch will appear. Click on this white are and select **open**.

5. Select **browser**.

6. The system browser will appear. Go to **Scratch-UI-Panes | ScratchFrameMorph | menu/button actions | addServerCommandTo**.

7. Change the `t2 ← true` text in the code to `t2 ← false`.

8. Hold the *Ctrl* key, click on the system browser, and select **accept**.

9. Enter your initials and click on **accept**.

10. Close the system browser again.

11. Hold the *Shift* key down again, click the letter **R** of the **SCRATCH** logo again, and select **turn fill screen on**.

12. If you wish to save the edits to the system browser, shift-click **R** and select **save image for end-user**.

 If the Mesh mode has been saved but is not needed anymore, all the preceding steps can be reverted in order to remove the Mesh mode again. To get the ← symbol, press *Shift* + -.

LN Digital Installer is a set of Python programs that allow Banana Pro to control the LN Digital board. It is available in GitHub. In order to install the packages, switch to your home directory:

```
cd ~
```

Download these packages:

```
git clone https://github.com/LeMaker/LN_Digital_Installer.git
git clone https://github.com/LeMaker/LN_Digital_Scratch_Handler.git
git clone https://github.com/LeMaker/LN_Digital_Emulator.git
git clone https://github.com/LeMaker/LNdigitalIO.git
git clone https://github.com/LeMaker/LNcommon.git
```

Switch to the download directory and install the packages as follows:

```
cd ~/LN_Digital_Scratch_Handler
sudo python setup.py install
cd ~/LN_Digital_Emulator
sudo python setup.py install
cd ~/LNdigitalIO
sudo python setup.py install
cd ~/LNcommon
$ sudo python setup.py install
```

If you are using Python 3.x.x instead of Python 2.x.x, you will need to replace `python` in the preceding call with `python3`. Replace `Installer.py` with `unInstaller.py` in order to uninstall all the packages again.

In order to communicate with the LN Digital board, Banana Pro uses the SPI kernel module. Start the SPI driver manually with the following command:

```
sudo modprobe spi-sun7i
```

You can also add this module and the `spidev` module permanently in `/etc/modules`:

```
sudo nano /etc/modules
```

Both modules, `spi-sun7i` as well as `spidev`, need to be on separate lines within `/etc/modules` file. A reboot is required in order to make these changes effective.

If the module is blacklisted, be sure to comment the blacklisting out in the `/etc/modprobe.d/bpi-blacklist.conf` file.

The `/dev/spidev*` devices should appear in the device tree. This can be verified with the following command:

```
ls /etc/spidev*
```

SPI devices require special privileges for the `bananapi` user to access them. You can set these up by adding the following *udev rule* to the `/etc/udev/rules.d/50-spi.rules` file:

```
KERNEL=="spidev*", GROUP="spi", MODE="0660"
```

Create the `spi` group and add the `bananapi` user to this group:

```
sudo groupadd spi
sudo gpasswd -a bananapi spi
```

Replace the `bananapi` username with your username in case you are using a different username. The following command can be used in order to detect the current username:

```
whoami
```

LN Digital interrupts work by monitoring GPIO pins. Grant the `bananapi` user access to GPIO pins by adding the following udev rule to the `/etc/udev/rules.d/51-gpio.rules` file (all text to be in one line):

```
SUBSYSTEM=="gpio*", PROGRAM="/bin/sh -c 'chown -R root:gpio
/sys/class/gpio && chmod -R 770 /sys/class/gpio; chown -R root:gpio
/sys/devices/platform/gpio-sunxi/gpio && chmod -R 770
/sys/devices/platform/gpio-sunxi/gpio'"
```

Afterwards, create the `gpio` group and add the `bananapi` user:

```
sudo groupadd gpio
sudo gpasswd -a bananapi gpio
```

After setting the SPI and GPIO permissions, Banana Pro must be rebooted:

```
sudo reboot
```

In order to use the LN Digital board with Scratch, start Scratch as user `root`:

```
sudo scratch
```

The LN Digital handler can be started with this command

```
cd /usr/local/bin
sudo LN-Digital-Scratch-Handler
```

The handler itself provides inputs numbered from one to eight via sensor values. If you want to control LN Digital's output, you will need to create a variable for each pin named `LN-output1` to `LN-output8`.

The Banana Pro forum provides several Scratch example programs (take a look at `http://forum.lemaker.org/thread-12362-1-1-_demo1_control_the_ln_digital_board_with_scratch_on_banana_pro.html`).

New kernels

All Banana Pro operating systems have a kernel installed. Depending on OS functionality, such as multimedia or GPIO usage, different kernels may be used. Usually, kernel sources are not installed. However, in some cases, kernel sources need to be modified in order to add certain functionality to the OS. Even if others provide additional functionality to kernels on GitHub, users need to compile these changes and install a new kernel version. This section provides all the required principals: kernel sources are downloaded from GitHub and then configured and compiled. Finally, the new kernel will be installed. In *Chapter 4*, *An Arcade Cabinet*, we will add some additional functionality to the LeMaker's LeMedia kernel, which is required in order to run **Video Disk Recorder** (**VDR**) smoothly.

All Allwinner A20 kernels (such as the ones used for Banana Pro) are based on kernel version 3.4.x. The subversion x is 106 at the time of writing this book. Initial kernel versions, such as 3.17 and 3.19, are also available. However, these kernels can up till now only be used for the server mode as they do not provide a multimedia graphics driver. Moreover, the new versions are currently also missing support for some of the A20 hardware features.

Principally, there are two possibilities available in order to compile and install a new kernel. Kernel sources can either be compiled natively on Banana Pro or cross-compilers can be used. In the second case, compiled kernels and modules need to be transferred from a host system to Banana Pro. However, compilation time depends on the host system and requires a minimum of only 10 to 15 minutes. Compiling the source directly on Banana Pro will take much longer time (up to several hours). However, changes can be made quickly, and there is no need to transfer kernel and kernel modules from the host system to Banana Pro. In this section, the compilation of kernel sources on Banana Pro and kernel installation are described in detail. Additionally, some hints are provided for cross-compilation on a Linux host system.

Compiling on Banana Pro

For operating systems, such as Microsoft Windows or Mac, no kernel compilation is required. Patches will be provided by vendors themselves, and new hardware drivers are delivered as closed source add-ons. The situation in Linux is different. While kernel version 4 is currently under development, the only kernel version recognizing all Banana Pro hardware is 3.4. This is especially true for a graphics driver. In the following example, we will install the LeMedia kernel from GitHub. This kernel features accelerated video drivers, which we will need later on. In *Chapter 4*, *An Arcade Cabinet*, we will add additional functionality to this kernel. Kernel sources can be checked out using this command:

```
sudo su
cd /usr/local/src
git clone -b lemaker-3.4-dev-lemedia https://github.com/LeMaker/linux-sunxi.git
```

Downloading the sources will take a long time. In order to compile the kernel sources later on, the following packages are required:

```
sudo apt-get install libncurses5-dev build-essential
```

By default, the kernel configuration is saved within the kernel directory in a file called .config. This file contains configurations with respect to installable modules and supported hardware. Changes to this file can be easily done invoking the following command:

```
Cd /usr/local/src/linux-sunxi
sudo make menuconfig
```

A working config file is available in the linux/arch/arm/defconfig directory. This file contains default hardware configuration for Sunxi-7 Allwinner devices such as Banana Pro. Simply copy this file to the kernel main directory before invoking make menuconfig:

```
cd /usr/local/src/linux
cp arch/arm/defconfig/sun7i_defconfig .config
```

Kernel and modules can be compiled, linked, and installed using this command chain:

```
make uImage
make modules
sudo cp arch/arm/boot/uImage /boot/uImage
sudo make modules_install
```

The installation of kernel modules can be checked with this command:

```
ls /lib/modules/$(uname -r)
```

> Remember to copy the kernel and modules to an SD card in case `rootfs` is booted from the SATA disk. Provide individual names for kernels This will avoid the old (`/lib/modules/$(uname -r)`) module directory to be overwritten by `make modules_install`. Also, remember to back up the old kernel image (`cp /boot/uImage /boot/uImage.old`) before replacing it with new ones. If the new kernel does not boot, remove the SD card and replace the new kernel with the backup version. The boot kernel image can be set in the `uEnv.txt` file (*Chapter 1, Introduction to Banana Pro*).

Cross-compilation

In order to save some time in software development for embedded boards, software can be developed and compiled on a much more powerful host system compared to Banana Pro. This is especially true for kernel compilation, which easily consumes hours when executed on a Banana Pro, but only 10 to 15 minutes when executed on a very fast X86 computer.

This section briefly describes the required steps. As a cross-compilation platform, I use the Debian X86 system. Debian now has cross-tool chains present in an archive, superseding those at `emdebian.org`. Backported cross-compilers for testing are available at `people.debian.org/~wookey/tools/debian`. Cross compilation of kernels work as follows:

- In the first step, we install a cross-compiler and `build utils` on the host system as follows:

  ```
  sudo dpkg --add-architecture armhf
  sudo apt-get update
  sudo apt-get install g++-arm-linux-gnueabihf
  ```

- Moreover, some additional tools are required to build a sunxi kernel, which is not related to the cross-compiler:

  ```
  sudo apt-get install build-essential git debootstrap u-boot-tools
  ```

- After the kernel download (previous section), the default configuration for Allwinner A20 kernels can be set as follows:

  ```
  make ARCH=arm CROSS_COMPILE=arm-linux-gnueabihf- sun7i_defconfig
  ```

- After the default configuration has been set, the kernel configuration can be fine-tuned. For this, you will need the `ncurses` development code installed. So, run the following command:

```
sudo apt-get install libncurses5-dev
```

- Now you can run `menuconfig` and edit your configuration:

```
Sudo make ARCH=arm CROSS_COMPILE=arm-linux-gnueabihf- menuconfig
```

- Note that the sunxi kernel is based on an obsolete kernel version with vendor hacks thrown in to support the sunxi hardware. As a result, some configurations that are possible to select will not build or work.

- In particular, some sunxi-specific drivers were not fixed to work as built-on code or as modules. Moreover, IPv6 only works as a kernel built-in function. Built-in code is part of the main kernel and is always available, regardless of whether it's needed or not. Kernel modules can be inserted into a kernel if they're needed, removed, or no longer needed. In doing so, kernel modules save memory.

- In order to build the new kernel on the host, make sure you have the `u-boot-tools` package installed. Then, call the following command:

```
make -j4 ARCH=arm CROSS_COMPILE=arm-linux-gnueabihf- uImage
modules
```

- The `-j4` option runs four `make` instances in parallel to a speed-up compilation. Adjust this with regard to the number of CPU cores/thread execution units that are available. You can determine this easily with Python.

- Run `python`, after the `>>>` notation appears, and type these two commands:

```
import multiprocessing
print(multiprocessing.cpu_count())
```

- When you hit enter, the number it shows is the number of virtual processors that are available on the current computer.

- Finally, create the full module tree:

```
make ARCH=arm CROSS_COMPILE=arm-linux-gnueabihf INSTALL_MOD_
PATH=output modules_install
```

- The `INSTALL_MOD_PATH` option specifies the directory where the full module tree will be made available; in this example, it will be the output directory under the kernel build directory itself.

- After compilation, the kernel tree is available in the form of the following directory structure:

```
arch/arm/boot/uImage
output/lib/modules/3.4.XXX/
```

The `uImage` file (the kernel minus the modules) needs to be started by u-boot, so it is usually copied to a boot partition where u-boot will find it, load it to the RAM, and then transfer control to it (u-boot can also pass parameters to the kernel). The module directory needs to be copied to `/lib/modules` on the target root filesystem.

In order to perform these operations, mount the Banana Pro SD card on the host system and copy both the `uImage` kernel and modules to the SD card. Afterwards, unmount the SD card and boot Banana Pro with it:

```
sudo mount /dev/mmcblk0p1 /mnt
sudo cp arch/arm/boot/uImage /mnt/boot
cp -R output/lib/modules/* /mnt/lib/modules
sudo umount /mnt
```

Summary

In this chapter, we learned how to remote connect to Banana Pro in order to program an embedded board. Different kinds of IDEs have been introduced to you. In most cases, a terminal and `vi` editor will do the job. You have now learned the basics of shell programming, C/C++, Python, and Scratch.

Examples have been provided dealing with Banana Pro onboard LEDs and GPIOs. Last but not least, you have also learned how to compile, install, and booted your own kernel.

The next chapter deals with wire projects. You will learn how Banana Pro can be used as a hotspot, or provide an AirPlay server for wireless audio transmission. Moreover, we will take a look at databases that host web pages.

3
Wireless Projects

In this chapter, several wireless projects that use Banana Pro are presented. The OpenVPN server allows connecting from the Internet to Banana Pro at home using a secure channel. In doing so, Banana Pro can act as a gateway that allows the control of home equipment while travelling.

The next section deals with wireless connections. You will learn how to use Banana Pro in order to connect to a wireless LAN. Moreover, Banana Pro can even serve as a wireless hotspot. You will also learn how this hotspot can be enabled, and how hotspot traffic can be routed through the Internet.

Did you ever want to use your printer in order to print pages from a mobile phone? The *On air* section explains how any available printer can be used as an AirPrint device by simply connecting it to a Banana Pro or a Banana Pro accessible network. The same applies to AirPlay: Banana Pro can be connected to audio equipment, allowing wireless transmission of audio files from a mobile phone.

A Banana Pro that runs all year long will only consume electricity worth 5 € a year and is, therefore, well suited as a web server. *Serving web pages* explains how web pages can be served using a content management system and database.

Finally, a practical example will show you how a hotspot and web server can be combined in order to control application boards, which are connected to Banana Pro via a USB.

This chapter contains the following topics in detail:

- OpenVPN
- WLAN
- On air
- Serving web pages
- Creating a measurement server

OpenVPN

In this section, we will install the **Virtual Private Network** (**VPN**) server, OpenVPN (`https://openvpn.net`). Every computer connecting from the outside to the Banana Pro VPN server is virtually connected to a home network: It can access every other home computer, which Banana Pro can also access. This procedure will provide a secure connection to a home **Network Attached Storage** (**NAS**) or allow the remote programming of VDR timers (refer to *Chapter 4*, *An Arcade Cabinet*). Additionally, clients are not only available for PCs or laptops, but also for mobile phones running iOS or Android. Before we take a look at possible clients, we will install the server first:

```
sudo apt-get install openvpn openssl easy-rsa
```

The preceding command install the OpenVPN server in addition to the SSL encryption, which is required to generate keys for both servers and clients. After installation, we can copy the `easy-rsa` directory into the OpenVPN configuration directory. We need to do this as a user `root` due to write right restriction:

```
su
cd /etc/openvpn
cp -r /usr/share/doc/openvpn/examples/easy-rsa/2.0 ./easy-rsa
```

Now, switch to the `easy-rsa` directory, and edit the `vars` file:

```
cd easy-rsa
nano ./vars
```

Replace the `export EASY_RSA="`pwd`"` line with `export EASY_RSA="/etc/openvpn/easy-rsa"`.

Save your changes and exit the editor. In the following step, we complete the installation by calling the following commands within the `easy-rsa` directory:

```
source ./vars
./clean-all
./pkitool --initca
ln -s openssl-1.0.0.cnf openssl.cnf
```

The source command adds the recently changed EASY-RSA variable to the shell environment. The clean-all command erases all data from the `/etc/openvpn/2.0/keys`. The `pkitool` call initializes the key generation. ln sets a link from `openssl-1.0.0.cnf` to `openssl.cnf`.

Now it is time to generate the keys required for the OpenVPN connection. For this purpose, call the following commands:

```
./build-ca OpenVPN
./build-key-server server
./build-key client1
```

These commands generate a private key for the server (called `server`) and a public key for the client (called `client1`). While generating the keys, a user is prompted with several questions. I've provided the following answers:

```
Country Name (2 letter code) [GB]:DE
State or Province Name (full name) [Berkshire ]:NRW
Locality Name (eg, city) [Newbury ]: Mettmann
Organization Name (eg , company ) [My Company Ltd ]: IMST GmbH
Organizational Unit Name (eg , section ) []: Webservice
Common Name (eg , your name or your server 's hostname ) []: R. Follmann
Email Address []: rudi@follmann.name
Please enter the following 'extra ' attributes to be sent with your
certificate request
A challenge password []:
An optional company name []:
```

The complete installation of keys follows after the next commands:

```
./build-dh
exit
```

Also, the output indicated that it was going to take a long time, but it only took about a minute. The final `exit` command disconnects the `root` user from terminal.

In the next step, we will provide a configuration file for OpenVPN. For this, switch to the `/etc/openvpn` directory:

```
cd /etc/openvpn
```

Also, create a file called `openvpn.conf` as the user `root`:

```
sudo nano ./openvpn.conf
```

Fill the following content in this file:

```
dev tun
proto udp
port 1194
ca /etc/openvpn/easy-rsa/keys/ca.crt
cert /etc/openvpn/easy-rsa/keys/server.crt
key /etc/openvpn/easy-rsa/keys/server.key
dh /etc/openvpn/easy-rsa/keys/dh1024.pem
user nobody
group nogroup
server 10.8.0.0 255.255.255.0
persist-key
persist-tun
status /var/log/openvpn-status.log
verb 3
client-to-client
push "redirect-gateway def1"
# DNS Server setzen
push "dhcp-option DNS 8.8.8.8"
push "dhcp-option DNS 8.8.4.4"
log-append /var/log/openvpn
comp-lzo
duplicate-cn
keepalive 10 120
push "explicit-exit-notify 3"
```

What is going on here? In the preceding file, we tell OpenVPN where our keys are located, and which IP address range we will use for the OpenVPN connection. For the OpwnVPN server, we define the IP address range as 10.*. Later on, we can supply this IP address range to the AirPrint server also. This will allow printer access from outside networks using the VPN connection. Moreover, we define the log file and use Google's public name servers (8.8.8.8 and 8.8.4.4). Principally, the connection from the outside to Banana Pro will work already—with the exception that IP traffic is not yet routed through the eth0 cable Internet connection. For this purpose, we use iptables, which is the default firewall for Linux:

```
sudo sh -c 'echo 1 > /proc/sys/net/ipv4/ip_forward'
sudo iptables -t nat -A POSTROUTING -s 10.0.0.0/8 ! -d 10.0.0.0/8 -o eth0
-j MASQUERADE
```

The preceding commands enable IP-forwarding. This is a precondition to route IP packages from one address room to another. Finally, we route all packets from the 10.*-address room (our OpenVPN server) to the Ethernet (eth0) interface, which is the wired Internet connection. In order to enable IP forwarding permanently, the following entry must be activated within the /etc/sysctl.conf (sudo nano / etc/sysctl.conf) file:

```
net.ipv4.ip_forward=1
```

We do not want to type the preceding commands again after a reboot. Thus, we will use crontab in order to make the commands reboot-resistant. cron is a Linux service, which can start scripts and programs at a given time. The -e option opens the crontab table for editing. Type the following command:

```
sudo crontab -e
```

Now, supply the following information:

```
@reboot sudo /etc/openvpn/iptables.sh
```

The /etc/openvpn/iptables.sh script must include the preceding provided iptables command. This command will be executed once after each reboot:

```
sudo iptables -t nat -A POSTROUTING -s 10.0.0.0/8 ! -d 10.0.0.0/8 -o eth0
-j MASQUERADE
```

After this preliminary work, OpenVPN can almost be used. We only need to generate a client key package before the first connection can be initiated. Switch over to the user root for this purpose, and then to the /etc/openvpn/easy-rsa/keys directory. Edit a file called bananapro.ovpn:

```
su
cd /etc/openvpn/easy-rsa/keys
nano bananapro.ovpn
```

Copy the following content into this file:

```
dev tun
client
proto udp
remote ip-address 1194
resolv-retry infinite
nobind
persist-key
persist-tun
ca ca.crt
cert client1.crt
key client1.key
comp-lzo
verb 3
```

Replace the word `ip-address` with the IP address of your Banana Pro. This IP address must be accessible from an outside network. An `ifconfig` command may be helpful to detect this IP address. As a final step, we will generate a zipped key package, which we can copy to the client:

```
tar czf openvpn-keys.tgz ca.crt client1.crt client1.csr client1.key
bananapro.ovpnmv openvpn-keys.tgz /home/pi
```

```
chown pi:pi /home/pi/openvpn-keys.tgz
```

```
exit
```

The preceding commands assume the user `pi`, which is located in `group pi` (`pi:pi`). Change both according to your user and group. The `id` command will show the current user and group. Restart the OpenVPN server now in order to make all preceding changes available:

```
sudo /etc/init.d/openvpn restart
```

Keys for an additional client can be generated in a way similar to the key for a client:

```
cd /etc/openvpn/easy-rsa/
```

```
sudo su
```

```
source ./vars
```

```
./build-key client2
```

Remember the client number (for example, `client2`) also for the `bananapro.ovpn` file. The also applies to the generation of a client key:

```
cd /etc/openvpn/easy-rsa/keys
tar czf openvpn-keys-client2.tgz ca.crt client2.crt client2.csr client2.
key bananapro.ovpn
mv openvpn-keys-client2.tgz /home/pi
chown pi:pi /home/pi/openvpn-keys-client2.tgz
exit
```

Copy the preceding generated key to the client. This will allow the client to connect with the OpenVPN server. An example of this is provided in the next section.

Connecting from Android

In this section, the connection from an Android mobile phone to the OpenVPN server is described. Install the OpenVPN client from the Google Play Store first:

OpenVPN in the Google Play Store

After installation, connect your Android device to a PC, unzip and untar the key files, and copy the files to Android (for example, on an external SD card). Start OpenVPN on Android and import the key files. The OpenVPN client will now show the IP address of the Banana Pro device, and connection to Banana Pro is possible:

Figure 1: The OpenVPN connection to Banana Pro

 Replace the IP address of Banana Pro with a dynamic DNS address if you want to access Banana Pro OpenVPN outside your home network. Additionally, forward the port 1194 UDP and TCP to Banana Pro's internal IP. These settings are provided in the menu of your DSL router.

DSL routers usually provide an internal DHCP network. Clients, such as Banana Pro, can connect via Ethernet or WLAN and will automatically receive an IP address. If the IP address range of the DSL router is 192.168.178.x, Banana Pro may have the 192.168.178.20 IP address. It can be addressed by this IP address only from the internal network. The DSL router itself is connected to the Internet using an IP address assigned by the DSL provider (for example, 87.163.198.17). Very often, this IP address changes on a daily basis. Using a DynDNS service, such as www.noip. com, a fixed name (such as mydslbox.noip.com) will be provided for the IP address of the DSL router. Even if this IP address changes on a daily basis, the router itself will remain accessible using the DynDNS name (that is, mydslbox.noip.com). In order to access Banana Pro, which is located in the home network (192.168.178.20), from the outside using VPN, port 1194 (UDP and TCP) must be forwarded from the DSL router to the internal IP address of Banana Pro. This can be done in the menu of most DSL routers. Be aware of the fact that Banana Pro will always get the same internal IP address; otherwise, port forwarding may not work.

WLAN

Banana Pro features a WLAN chip called AP6210 (http://linux-sunxi.org/ Cubietruck/AP6210), providing a wireless LAN. Additionally, this chip can be set to the access point mode. In this mode, Banana Pro can act as a wireless hotspot. This section describes the principal usage of the WLAN chip connecting to a hotspot. Moreover, the setup of a Banana Pro access point is described. In this mode, Banana Pro will be connected to the internal net by Ethernet and will offer this connection over the Pro's Wi-Fi adapter.

Setting up WLAN

The kernel module communicating with the AP6210 WLAN chip is called ap6210. Make sure that /etc/modules (sudo nano /etc/modules) contains a contains a line loading the ap6210 kernel module:

```
ap6210
```

Without a network manager, WLAN connection can be set in the /etc/network/ interfaces file. My interfaces file is provided as follows:

```
# Wired adapter #1
auto eth0
  iface eth0 inet dhcp
#  iface eth0 inet static
#  address 192.168.178.86
#  netmask 255.255.0.0
```

```
#   gateway 192.168.178.1
  hwaddress ether 01:02:03:04:05:10
#   pre-up /sbin/ifconfig eth0 mtu 3838 # setting MTU for
    DHCP, static just:
 mtu 3838

# Wireless adapter
auto wlan0
  allow-hotplug wlan0
  iface wlan0 inet dhcp
  wpa-ssid access_point
  wpa-psk password

#
# Local loopback
auto lo
iface lo inet loopback
```

The Ethernet adapter gets its Ethernet address from the DHCP server. Static IP address settings are commented out. The Ethernet hardware address is set in the `hwaddress ether` line. Replace `01:02:03:04:05:10` with the MAC address that you want to associate with the `eth0` interface.

> If no MAC address is set for the Ethernet, Banana Pro will provide a random address. With a random address, the DHCP server will provide another IP after reboot. Therefore, it definitely makes sense to set the hardware Ethernet address.

A wireless adapter is configured afterwards. Replace `access_point` with the name or the IP address of the access point (SSID) you want to connect to and `password` with the password required for the connection.

After the reboot, Banana Pro will connect to WLAN automatically if the Ethernet interface is commented out.

Setting up an access point mode

An access point in Linux is provided by a software called `hostapd` (`https://w1.fi/hostapd/`). Unfortunately, `hostapd` is provided by apt-get from Debian resources and does not work with the AP6210 chip. Therefore, `hostapd` needs to be compiled from sources. I had to install `libnl-3-dev` in order to get the compilation process through:

```
git clone git://w1.fi/srv/git/hostap.git
sudo apt-get install hostapd libnl-3-dev libnl-genl-3-dev
```

In the next step, copy `defconfig` to `.config`:

```
cd hostap/hostapd
cp defconfig .config
```

Also, uncomment the `#CONFIG_LIBNL32=y` line:

```
CONFIG_LIBNL32=y
```

Finally, compile `hostapd`, and back up the original file and replace it:

```
sudo mv /usr/sbin/hostapd /usr/sbin/hostapd.backup
make
sudo cp hostapd /usr/sbin
```

Contrary to the WLAN mode, the access point mode of AP6210 requires the additional `op_mode=2` parameter. Add/change the following line in `/etc/modules`:

```
ap6210 op_mode=2
```

Reboot Banana Pro in order to make the loading of this module effective.

Afterwards, create and edit the `hostapd.conf` file in `/etc/hostapd/`:

```
sudo mkdir -p /etc/hostapd
vi /etc/hostapd/hostapd.conf
```

My `hostapd.conf` looks like this (`https://wiki.gentoo.org/wiki/Hostapd`):

```
interface=wlan0
driver=nl80211
ssid=bananapro
channel=6
hw_mode=g
macaddr_acl=0
auth_algs=1
ignore_broadcast_ssid=0
wpa=2
wpa_passphrase=password
wpa_key_mgmt=WPA-PSK
wpa_pairwise=TKIP
rsn_pairwise=CCMP
```

Replace bananapro with the hotspot name you want to provide. Additionally, replace the password with one that's required for connection later on. In the next configuration step, /etc/network/interfaces must be changed:

```
# Hotspot
allow-hotplug wlan0
iface wlan0 inet static
address 192.168.100.1
netmask 255.255.255.0
```

As for the router address, I've chosen 192.168.100.1. Comment all other wlan0 settings (for example, WLAN connection settings). Now, we will install the DHCP server, providing IP addresses for clients connecting to the Banana Pro hotspot:

```
sudo apt-get install udhcpd
```

I've edited the /etc/udhcp.conf file as follows (http://manpages.ubuntu.com/manpages/hardy/man5/udhcpd.conf.5.html):

```
# The start and end of the IP lease block
start    192.168.100.101   #default: 192.168.0.20
end      192.168.100.254   #default: 192.168.0.254
#The interface that udhcpd will use
interface   wlan0      #default: eth0
#Examles
option  subnet  255.255.255.0
opt     router  192.168.100.1
opt     wins    192.168.100.1
option  dns     8.8.8.8
option  domain  local
option  lease   864000
```

According to the IP address of the router (access point), clients from 192.168.100.101 to 254 are allowed. In addition to this, Google's 8.8.8.8 nameserver is used as a **Domain Name Service (DNS)**. Before this, however, the DHCP server, hostapd can be started, and the wlan0 interface must be bridged to eth0.

Open /etc/sysctl.conf and add the following line at end of the file (if you've not already done this in the previous section):

```
net.ipv4.ip_forward=1
```

IP forwarding can be directly activated by typing this:

```
sudo sh -c "echo 1 > /proc/sys/net/ipv4/ip_forward"
```

Now, we route all network traffic from wlan0 through the eth0 interface:

```
sudo iptables -t nat -A POSTROUTING -o eth0 -j MASQUERADE
sudo iptables -A FORWARD -i eth0 -o wlan0 -m state --state
RELATED,ESTABLISHED -
j ACCEPT
sudo iptables -A FORWARD -i wlan0 -o eth0 -j ACCEPT
```

In the next step, we make that persistent by typing the following command:

```
sudo sh -c "iptables-save > /etc/iptables.ipv4.nat"
```

Also, we add the following line at the end of /etc/network/interfaces:

```
up iptables-restore < /etc/iptables.ipv4.nat
```

Finally, we start the DHCP server and hostpad:

```
sudo /etc/init.d/udhcp start
/usr/sbin/hostapd /etc/hostapd/hostapd.conf
```

In order to make udhcp start rebooting persistently, edit /etc/default/udhcp and add the comment character (#) in front of the following line:

```
#DHCPD_ENABLED="no"
```

Finally, start hostpad using the following command:

```
sudo hostapd /etc/hostapd/hostapd.conf -B
```

Afterwards, the Banana Pro hotspot will be available. On my iPhone connection to Banana Pro, the hotspot looks similar to what is shown in the following screenshot. When asked for a password, type in the password provided in the `hostapd.conf` file.

Figure 2: The iPhone connection to the WLAN hotspot.

The installation of OpenVPN clients for different operating systems is similar to what we have just seen: Simply download the client and provide the key files for the installation to take place.

On air

This section describes the usage of Banana Pro as an AirPlay and an AirPrint server.

An AirPlay receives music that's streamed from an iPhone or iPad. Moreover, an Android software that provides this feature is also available.

AirPrint allows iDevices and Android devices to print documents using a WLAN connection.

The AirPlay protocol

The AirPlay protocol is implemented in all recent iOS versions. While AirPlay sound systems are rather expensive, Banana Pro and an old audio system can do the job. This section describes the installation of an AirPlay server on Banana Pro, and the usage of this server when connecting to an Apple or Android device. Moreover, the installation of a USB soundcard, in addition to Banana Pro, is described, which provides the **Sony/Philips Digital Interface Format** (**SPDIF**) audio output. There are different AirPlay servers available on the Internet. I've had some good experience using one from `https://github.com/abrasive/shairport`. The installation of this can be done quickly. Switch to a directory of your choice and download the AirPlay server as follows:

```
git clone https://github.com/abrasive/shairport.git
```

Additionally, we need to install a few software packages, which are required in order to compile the AirPlay server correctly:

```
apt-get install libssl-dev libavahi-client-dev libasound2-dev
```

The AirPlay server itself is compiled, linked, and installed using these commands:

```
cd shairport
./configure
make
sudo make install
```

If the last step is skipped, the executable will be available within the `shairport` directory.

Make sure that the `/etc/asound.conf` file contains the following settings:

```
pcm.dmixer {
  type dmix
  ipc_key 1024
  slave {
  pcm "hw:3,0"
  period_size 3000
  buffer_size 24000
  rate 48000
  format S16_LE
  }
}

pcm.sunxihdmi {
  type plug
  slave.pcm dmixer
}
```

The "hw:3,0" value represents the audio output device. The available devices are listed using the aplay -l command, which comes with alsa-utils.

Start the AirPlay server using the following command:

```
sudo /home/pi/shairport/shairport -d -a AirBanana -o ao -- -n sunxihdmi
```

The preceding command assumes that shairport is installed in the home directory of the user pi. As an audio device, we provide sunxihdmi, which has been defined in /etc/asound.conf, and links to the audio device we want to use (hw:3,0 in our example). The -d parameter starts shairport as a daemon. The server itself is called AirBanana. Devices connecting to the Banana Pro server will show this name. It can be changed arbitrarily.

While Apple devices can directly access the Banana Pro AirPlay servers, Android devices require compatible software. The only one without rooting requirements that I've found in the Google Play Store is called **AOA Player Trial**.

Figure 3: Android connecting to the Banana Pro AirPlay server

Banana Pro does provide the electrical SPDIF output on the 40-pin GPIO header (*Chapter 4, An Arcade Cabinet*). However, it does not provide the optical SPDIF output.

Using an external USB SPDIF soundcard

For those of you who own a stereo amplifier with the optical SPDIF input, I recommend that you use the Delock 61961 USB soundcard (*Figure 4*):

Figure 4: The Delock USB soundcard with the optical SPDIF output (source: Delock)

This soundcard requires an adapter similar to what is shown here:

Figure 5: The 3.5 mm TOSLINK adapter (source: Amazon.com)

The soundcard itself identifies as (lsusb):

```
Bus 003 Device 002: ID 040d:3400 VIA Technologies, Inc.
```

My `aplay -l` Banana Pro provides the following output for this soundcard:

```
card 4: Dongle [VIA USB Dongle], device 0: USB Audio [USB Audio]
  Subdevices: 1/1
  Subdevice #0: subdevice #0
card 4: Dongle [VIA USB Dongle], device 1: USB Audio [USB Audio #1]
  Subdevices: 1/1
  Subdevice #0: subdevice #0
```

The first card 4 subdevice is the SPDIF device. Thus, use `"hw:4,0"` in `/etc/asound.conf` for the optical SPDIF output. The `snd-usb-audio` kernel driver recognizes this Delock USB soundcard automatically (`dmesg`):

```
input: VIA Technologies Inc. VIA USB Dongle as /devices/platform/sw-
ohci.1/usb3/3-1/3-1:1.3/input/input3

generic-usb 0003:040D:3400.0001: input,hidraw0: USB HID v1.00 Device [VIA
Technologies Inc. VIA USB Dongle] on usb-sw-ohci-1/input3

usbcore: registered new interface driver snd-usb-audio
```

AirPrint

AirPrint is an interface, which was developed by Apple. It allows wireless printing using operating systems, such as iOS and the MAC OS. There is also software for Android available. AirPrint is designed to only work with certain printers. However, when using a Banana Pro, every printer can be tuned to be an AirPrint printer. This section explains the required setup and configuration. The heart of the installation is the Common Unix Printing System (CUPS). CUPS can be installed using the following commands:

```
sudo apt-get install avahi-daemon cups cups-pdf python-cups
```

The so-called `gutenprint`-package contains many drivers for many printers. The probability is quite high that the required printer driver for your printer is included in this package. Therefore, we will install this package in the next step:

```
sudo apt-get install printer-driver-gutenprint
```

A list of all available printers in the gutenprint package is available at `http://gimp-print.sourceforge.net/p_Supported_Printers.php`. There are additional printer drivers available. The required printer driver should not be available within the `gutenprint` package:

```
sudo apt-get install printer-driver-c2050 #printer driver for Lexmark
2050 Color Jetprinter
```

```
sudo apt-get install printer-driver-c2esp #printer driver for Kodak ESP
AiO color inkjet Series

sudo apt-get install printer-driver-cjet #printer driver for Canon LBP
laser printers

sudo apt-get install printer-driver-escpr #printer driver for Epson
Inkjet that use ESC P-R

sudo apt-get install printer-driver-foo2zjs #printer driver for ZjStream-
based printers

sudo apt-get install printer-driver-hpcups #HP Linux Printing and Imaging
- CUPS Raster driver (hpcups)

sudo apt-get install printer-driver-hpijs #HP Linux Printing and Imaging
- gs IJS driver (hpijs)

sudo apt-get install printer-driver-m2300w #printer driver for Minolta
magicolor 2300W 2400W color laser printers

sudo apt-get install printer-driver-min12xxw #printer driver for
KonicaMinolta PagePro 1[234]xxW

sudo apt-get install printer-driver-pnm2ppa #printer driver for HP-GDI
printers

sudo apt-get install printer-driver-postscript-hp #HP Printers PostScript
Descriptions

sudo apt-get install printer-driver-ptouch #printer driver Brother
P-touch label printers

sudo apt-get install printer-driver-pxljr #printer driver for HP Color
LaserJet 35xx 36xx

sudo apt-get install printer-driver-sag-gdi #printer driver for Ricoh
Aficio SP 1000s SP 1100s

sudo apt-get install printer-driver-splix #Driver for Samsung and Xerox
SPL2 and SPLc laser printers
```

Select the requisite printer driver for your printer and install it according to the previously mentioned installation command. For those of you who've connected their printer via a **Network Attached Storage** (**NAS**), I recommend that you install the smbclient package:

```
sudo apt-get install smbclient
```

Some vendors provide their printer data via the so-called **PPD** (**Postscript Printer Description**) files. The foomatic-filters package converts Postscript into a printer language using these PPD files. Non-postscript printers are supported by the hpijs package. The aforementioned packages can be installed as follows:

```
sudo apt-get install foomatic-filters hpijs
```

After the installation of all the required printer drivers, we will now configure CUPS.

Configuring CUPS

The global CUPS configuration file is located in the `/etc/cups` directory and is called `cupsd.conf`. We need to apply a few changes to this file because we want to access the CUPS server from the **Local Area Network (LAN)**:

```
# Only listen for connections from the local machine.
Listen localhost:631
```

Replace the preceding lines with the following lines:

```
# Only listen for connections from the local machine.
Port 631
```

Additionally, add the `Allow @Local` phrase to the following locations within the CUPS configuration file:

```
# Restrict access to the server...
<Location />
  Order allow,deny
  Allow @Local
</Location>

# Restrict access to the admin pages...
<Location /admin>
  Order allow,deny
  Allow @Local
</Location>

# Restrict access to configuration files...
<Location /admin/conf>
  AuthType Default
  Require user @SYSTEM
  Order allow,deny
  Allow @Local
</Location>
```

In order to make these changes effective, we need to restart CUPS:

```
sudo /etc/init.d/cups restart
```

Before we start the CUPS web interface for further configurations, we will add the user `pi` to the `lpadmin` group:

```
sudo adduser pi lpadmin
```

Replace the `pi` username in accordance with your default username. For final configurations, we can now open a web browser with Banana Pro's IP and port number `631`. If you set up everything correctly, the main CUPS screen will appear in your web browser as shown in the following screenshot:

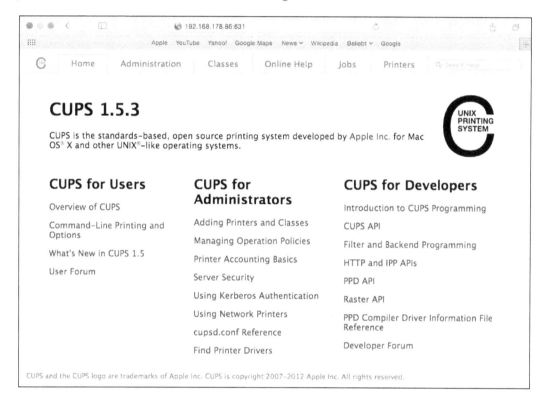

Figure 6: Configuring a script from a web browser

After the CUPS menu has appeared, click on `Administration` and check `Share printers connected to this system` (*Figure 7*). After this, click on `Change Settings` in order to save the preceding change.

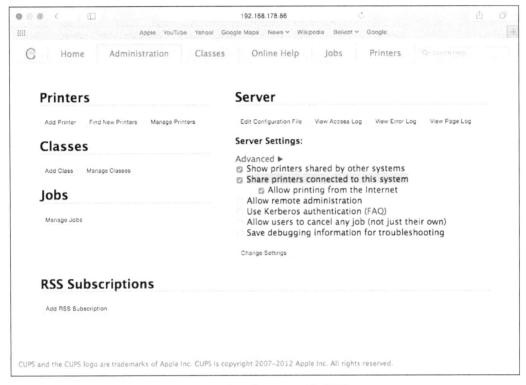

Figure 7: Shared printers with CUPS

A login box will appear when clicking on `Change Settings`. Provide the `pi` username and the associated password. After this prework, we can now install the printer itself.

Be sure that the printer is connected to either Banana Pro via a USB or to any other computer that's located in your network. Also, make sure that the printer and the connected computer are switched on. Select `Add Printer` in the `Administration` main menu. This will open a menu similar to what is shown in here:

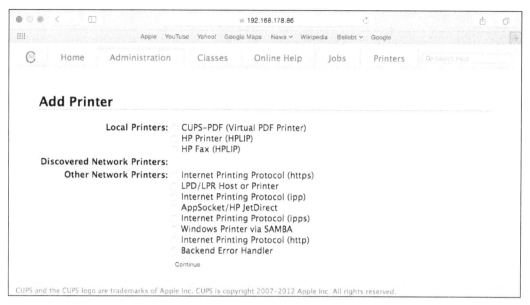

Figure 8: Add a new printer with CUPS

In most cases, CUPS will automatically detect your printer and list it. My printer is connected via a **Network Attached Storage** (**NAS**) and can be accessed by using samba. In a similar case, select Windows Printer via SAMBA and provide the connection line as follows:

```
smb://192.168.178.200/Brother_lp0
```

The smb keyword tells CUPS to use a samba connected printer. Change the IP address according to yours. Finally, you will see that Brother_lp0 is the name of the printer queue.

 The usage of samba printers requires smbclient to be installed. If smbclient is not installed, CUPS will not show the samba entry.

After clicking on `Continue`, a new window will open (*Figure 9*). Add your printer description in it and click on `Continue` again.

Figure 9: Adding a printer description

This will open a new window (*Figure 10*) where the printer driver can be selected. In my case (**Brother HL2140**), I had to download and provide the PPD from the manufacturer's web page.

Figure 10: Adding a printer driver

A final click on **Add Printer** will add the printer to CUPS. In order to check the installation, a test page can be printed. For this purpose, select the `Administration` main menu again. In this menu, select `Manage Printers` and click on the recently installed printer. The `Maintenance` drop-down menu contains the entry `Print Test Page`.

The new version of CUPS (that is 1.5.3) already contains an AirPrint server. Thus, no special AirPrint software must be installed on Banana Pro.

Printing from Android and iOS

While Apple devices can use iOS routines in order to print on AirPrint printers, Android needs special software. For Android, I recommend that you use **Let's Print Droid**. It can easily be installed from the Google Play Store and is free of charge (*Figure 11* and *Figure 12*).

Figure 11: The Let's Print Droid software from Google Play allows printing to CUPS devices

Once the installation is complete, every document can be sent to **Let's Print Droid** for printing.

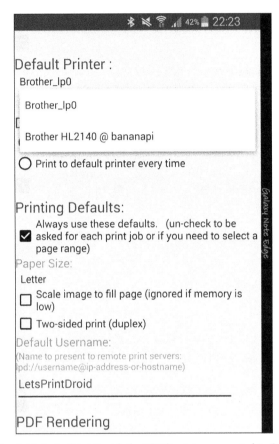

Figure 12: As a default print in Let's Print Droid, the CUPS printer connected to Banana Pro can be chosen

Serving web pages

In this section, we will install the content management system, Contao. Contao can display web pages. The content can be easily edited and is stored in a database. Though it's independent of user rights or devices (for example, a mobile browser or browser on a full HD screen), content is generated in a short amount of time before it is displayed. Contao requires a running web server. One of the most popular web servers under Linux is Apache. It can be installed using the following command:

```
sudo apt-get install apache2
```

After installation, Apache is already running and shows a simple web page when invoked (*Figure 13*). For this test, provide the IP address of Banana Pro in a web browser once Apache has been installed.

Figure 13: Apache shows a simple test page after installation

The content of this test web page is located in the /var/www directory, which is within the index.html file.

When you encounter the **apache2: Could not determine the server's fully qualified domain name, using 127.0.0.1 for ServerName** error message, edit the /etc/apache2/conf.d/fqdn file, add the line following line of code to it, and then save the file:

```
ServerName localhost
```

This all can be done using a single command:

```
echo "ServerName localhost" | sudo tee /etc/apache2/
conf.d/fqdn
```

Installing PHP and MySQL

Contao requires the installation of php:

```
sudo apt-get install php5 libapache2-mod-php5
```

After the php installation, Apache requires a restart in order to recognize the php installation:

```
sudo /etc/init.d/apache2 restart
```

The php installation itself can be tested by the following source code lines, which we place as the `test.php` file in the `/var/www` directory:

```php
<?php
phpinfo();
?>
```

On Banana Pro, the test can be executed using the `http://localhost/test.php` address. Using any other computer, the IP address of Banana Pro must be provided (*Figure 14*).

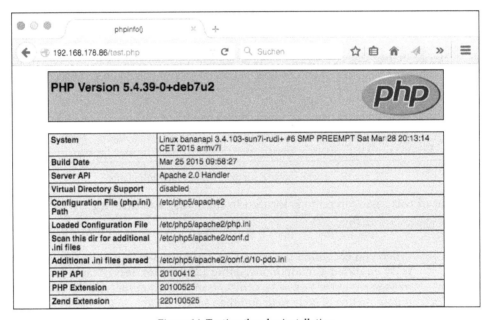

Figure 14: Testing the php installation

Contao makes use of the `mysql` database to serve web pages. The following commands will install the `mysql` database and all the add-ons that are required:

```
sudo apt-get install mysql-server php5-mysql mysql-client
```

During installation, a password for `mysql` is required. Note this password. It will be required again later on. The `mysql` database can be administrated from a web server using `phpmyadmin`. Install it as follows:

```
sudo apt-get install libapache2-mod-auth-mysql phpmyadmin
```

During the installation of the preceding packages, users need to answer two questions:

- The webserver to be configured is `apacha2` and not `lighttpd`

- Please answer all upcoming questions with `yes`.

Additionally, the password for mysql is required (I hope you've noted it) and a new password for `phpmyadmin`. We will now test the `phpmyadmin` installation by calling the associated configuration web page. Type the IPaddress of your Banana Pro in your web browser followed by the `phpmyadmin` directory. In my case, the browser line looks like this:

`http://192.168.178.86/phpmyadmin`

Log in as the user `root` with the password provided during the `phpmyadmin` installation. The browser will open the `phpmyadmin` login page, which also allows switching of the language (*Figure 15*).

If the `phpadmin` page is not shown properly, an additional link must be placed in the `/var/www` directory. Provide this link by typing the following commands within a terminal:

```
su
cd /var/www
ln -s /usr/share/phpmyadmin/
```

Figure 15: The phpmyadmin login page

After the correct login, the `phpmyadmin` configuration page is shown as follows:

Figure 16: The phpmyadmin configuration page

 The maximum file size for mysql files is rather low by default. However, it can be changed within the `/etc/php5/apache2/php.ini` file.

Installing contao

Finally, we install the `contao` content management system (CMS). The most recent `contao` version can be downloaded from `https://contao.org/de/download.html`. Download the zipped tar version (`*.tgz`) and copy it to your Banana Pro. Alternatively, download the version using any browser available on Banana Pro such as `iceweasel`. After the download, the `contao` installation needs to be copied to the `/var/www` directory and unzipped as follows:

```
su

cp contao-3.4.5.tgz /var/www
```

```
cd /var/www
tar xvfz contao-3.4.5.tgz
mv contao-3.4.5 demo
chown -R www-data:www-data contao
```

In parallel, we have renamed the `contao` installation to `demo` because we are going to install a demo web page soon. Moreover, we've changed the owner and group of the demo directory to `www-data`. This will allow `contao` to access the new directory.

After principal installation of `contao`, we will now add a new database to `mysql` using `phpmyadmin`. Using the **Databases** tab, we define a new database called `db_demo`.

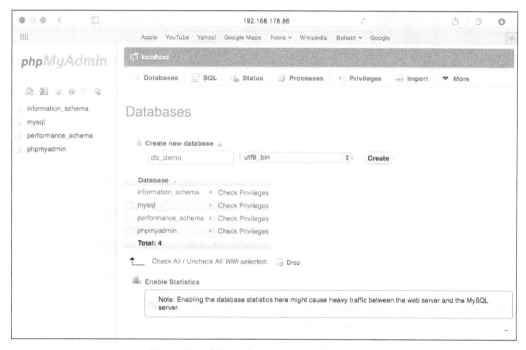

Figure 17: Adding a database using phpmyadmin

Using the **Privileges** tab, we select **Add a new user** and define a new user called
`demo`. Choose a password that you like. It will be required later on.

Figure 18: Adding a new user for a database in phpmyadmin

Additionally, grant all the rights to the database `db_demo`.

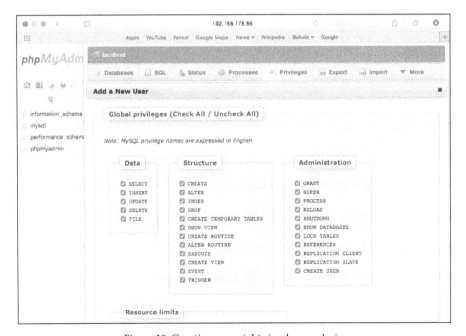

Figure 19: Granting user rights in phpmyadmin

Finally, add the user by clicking on the **Create User** button. The connection between `contao` and the database comes next. Call the `ip-address/demo/contao/install.php` URL in a web browser, and replace `ip-address` with the IP address of your Banana Pro. The browser will ask you to accept the license agreement and also ask for an installation password. After this, the browser will show a window (*Figure 17*), which allows the connecting of `contao` to the database.

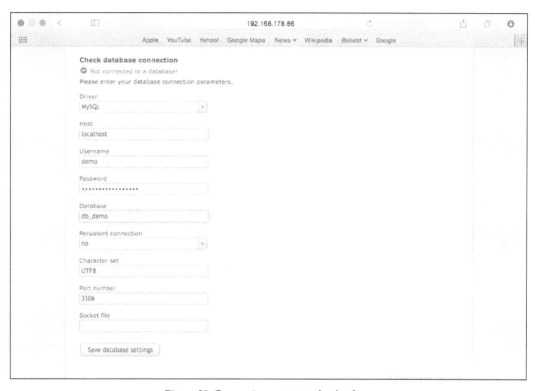

Figure 20: Connecting contao to the database

Provide all the settings that are shown in the preceding screenshot. As for the password, use the password that was provided when granting the user demo all the rights to the db_demo database within phpmyadmin. Then, update the database settings. When asked to update the database, do so.

Figure 21: Updating the contao database

Save the database settings. Finally, create an admin user account as shown in the following screenshot:

Figure 22: Adding a contao backend user

After connection to the database has been established, we log in to the contao backend and install a demo web page. In doing so, call the `ip-address/demo/contao` address in your web browser. As always, `ip-address` is the IP address of your Banana Pro (*Figure 18*). Enter the username and password that were provided earlier.

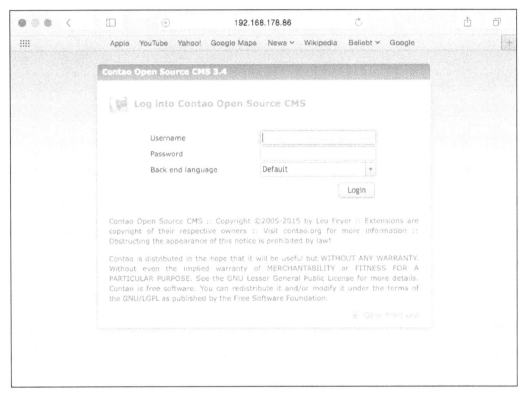

Figure 23: The Contao backend login

Select **Extension catalog** from left-hand side menu, search for **official_demo**, and install this extension.

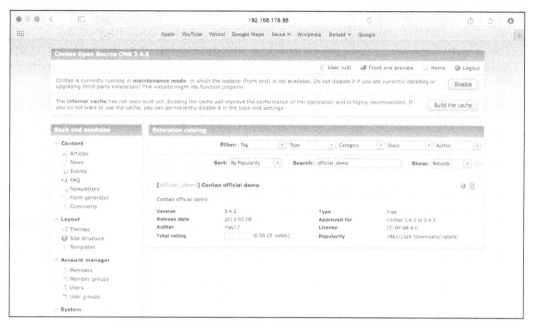

Figure 24: Installing the contao official demo

In order to activate the demo, call the `contao` installation script (`ip-address/demo/contao/install.php`) again and select the official demo template.

Figure 25: Importing the Contao official demo template

Then, import the template. This will delete all existing data, including the Contao backend account. However, the template provides a new backend user called k.jones with the kevinjones password. Use this data to log in to the backend again by calling ip-address/demo/contao. In the very last step, disable the maintenance mode, and then click on the **Build the cache** button to build the contao cache.

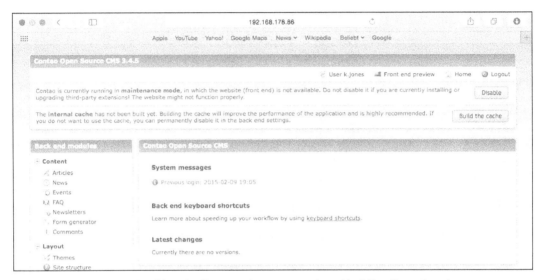

Figure 26: Disabling the Contao maintenance mode and building Contao's cache

The demo web page will now be available using the ip-address/demo IP address (remember to replace ip-address with the IP address of your Bananan Pro, for example, 192.168.178.86/demo).

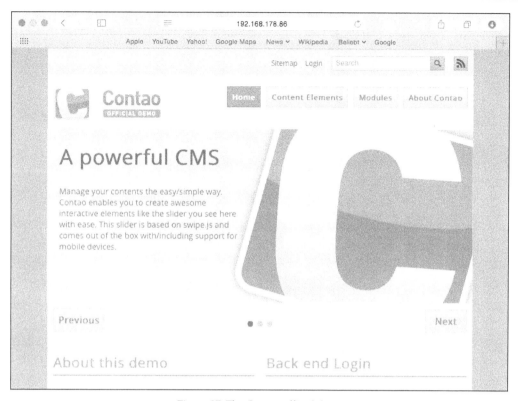

Figure 27: The Contao official demo

A measurement server

In the last section of this chapter, we will merge the things you've learned in the previous chapter into one project: We will build a measurement server providing a web-based interface through a hotspot. This interface can be used in order to program circuits using their dedicated interface, such as Serial Peripheral Interface (SPI). With regard to the example of a fractional-N frequency synthesizer, you will learn how to connect Banana Pro's USB port to a test circuit, convert USB signals into serial signals, and finally, program the test circuit. The measurement server itself is realized in Python using CherryPy (*Chapter 2*, *Programming Languages*). As a USB interface, the **Future Technology Device International** (**FTDI**) chip is used, which is available at www.ftdichip.com. Though in this section, the example of a fractional-N synthesizer is used, the software can be easily transferred to any other application board providing a USB interface via FTDI.

The following picture shows a fractional-N synthesizer board, which can be programmed via the FTDI chip.

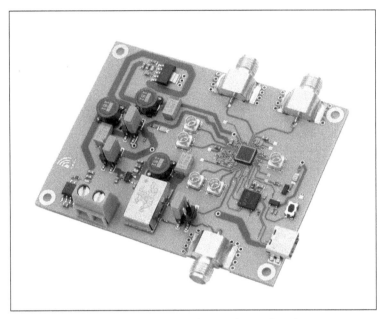

Figure 28: The fractional-N synthesizer board

Our measurement server requires the installation of the following packages:

```
sudo apt-get install libftdi-dev python-dev python-cherrypy3
```

The FTDI/SPI control of devices

As mentioned in the preveious section, the FTDI chip can translate USB signals into serial signals using the ftdi library called `libftdi`. The synthesizer itself provides a serial interface featuring the following three or four interface lines, which is similar to many other application boards:

- **Clock line**: This line provides the clock required for programming the application board. The maximum clock frequency usually depends on the application board itself and is usually less than 100 MHz.

- **Enable line**: For low-enabled application boards, this line needs to be *low* in order to read or write data. For high-enabled application boards, this line needs to be *high* in order to transfer data to input or to output lines.

- **Write line**: This line provides the data to be set within the clock. Data will be read after the enable line has been set.

- **Read line**: This line reads data out of the application boards using the clock line once enable has been set. Not all application boards feature a read line. Moreover, some boards feature a write line, which can be switched to a read line (a bidirectional read).

As Banana Pro features an SPI over GPIO, there is typically no need to make use of the FTDI chip if the application board provides direct access to the SPI lines. The following timing diagram shows the interaction between all four SPI lines:

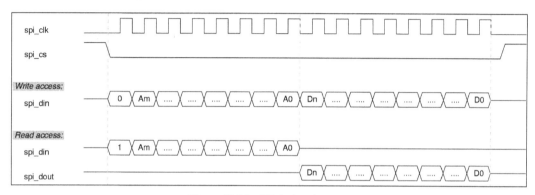

Figure 29: The SPI timing diagram

The timing diagram is low-enabled: As soon as the enable line is low, data can be written into the synthesizer or settings can be read out of the synthesizer. The first bit sent distinguishes the read and write modes from each other: low (0) enables write access and high (1) enables read access. Read and write lines are also often marked as data-out and data-in lines. In the prceding timing diagram,**D** stands for data and **A** for address. The function of data and address registers are explained in the application board data sheet. For our fractional-N synthesizer, the registers are as follows:

Control registers (addresses that range from 0000 to 1011 registers are read-write).

Address	Bit	Name	Function	Default
"0000" Divisor_reg_0	15...0	divisor(35:20)	Divisor bits 7...0, -1...-8	0x2D00
"0001" Divisor_reg_1	15...0	divisor(19:4)	Divisor bits -9...-24	0x0000
"0010" Divisor_reg_2	15...12	divisor(3:0)	Divisor bits -25...-28	"0000"
	11...0	unused		

Address	Bit	Name	Function	Default
"0011" Config_reg	15...8	unused		
	7	reset_sd	Low-active reset for SD	'0'
	6...5	sd_mux	Number of accu stages: "00", "01", "10", "11" = 1,2,3,4	"00"
	4	clk_tune_en	0: unshifted ref clk/1: shifted ref clk	'0'
	3...0	ctrl_ref_div	Divisor for reference clock divider. Setting "0000" will activate the divider bypass.	"0000"
"0100" Preload_reg	15...0	Preload	Preloads first accu bits -1...-16	0x0000
"0101" CP_reg	15...10	Unused		
	9...5	cp_fine	This sets the charge pump fine current	"01000"
	4...0	cp_coarse	This sets the charge pump coarse current	"01000"
"0110" Offset_reg	15...10	Unused		
	9...5	offset_fine	This sets the fine offset current	"00001"
	4...0	offset_coarse	This sets the coarse offset current	"00001"
"0111" VCO_reg	15...7	Unused		
	6...3	vco_band_ctrl	This is the band selection for internal VCO array	"0011"
	2...0	vco_ctrl	This is enabled for all VCOs, internal or external	"000"
"1000" GPO_reg	15...8	gpo_default_1	This general purpose function outputs with the as '1'	0xFF
	7...0	gpo_default_0	This general purpose function outputs with the default as 0	0x00

Status registers (address range `1100` to `1111` registers are read-only).

Address	Bit	Name	Function	Default
"1100" Status_reg	15...8	gpi	These are general purpose inputs	
	7...4	version	This version number increases on full mask run	"1001"
	3...0	subversion	This subversion number increases on metal change run	"0000"
"1101" Error_reg	15...11	unused		
	10	lock_detect	This is the PLL lock detect	
	9...0	error_cnt	This is the triple mode error count	

In order to read the synthesizer version number, for example, bits 0...3 (subversion) and bits 4...7 (version) of the `1100` address must be read.

A web server

The complete source code of the measurement server is located in the `novelo` directory:

```
pi@bananapi:~/novelo$ ls -l
total 196
-rw-r--r-- 1 pi pi  1147 Mai  9 17:43 convert.cpp
-rw-r--r-- 1 pi pi   326 Mai  9 17:43 convert.h
drwxr-xr-x 2 pi pi  4096 Mai  9 17:43 data
-rw-r--r-- 1 pi pi  3254 Mai  9 17:43 FTDI_Basic_IO.cpp
-rw-r--r-- 1 pi pi   306 Mai  9 17:43 FTDI_Basic_IO.h
-rw-r--r-- 1 pi pi  9615 Mai  9 17:43 FTDI.cpp
-rw-r--r-- 1 pi pi  1075 Mai  9 17:43 FTDI.h
-rw-r--r-- 1 pi pi 11655 Mai  9 17:43 lo9.cc
-rw-r--r-- 1 pi pi  2213 Mai  9 17:43 L09_FTDI.h
-rw-r--r-- 1 pi pi   923 Mai  9 17:43 L09.h
-rw-r--r-- 1 pi pi  3265 Mai  9 17:43 lo.py
-rw-r--r-- 1 pi pi   465 Mai  9 17:43 Makefile
-rw-r--r-- 1 pi pi 10612 Mai  9 17:43 novelo.cc
-rw-r--r-- 1 pi pi   827 Mai  9 17:43 novelo.h
-rw-r--r-- 1 pi pi 12822 Mai  9 17:43 novelo_main.cpp
-rw-r--r-- 1 pi pi 20542 Mai  9 17:43 novelo_sub.cpp
-rw-r--r-- 1 pi pi   616 Mai  9 17:43 novelo_sub.h
-rw-r--r-- 1 pi pi   159 Mai  9 17:43 server.ini
-rw-r--r-- 1 pi pi 21574 Mai  9 17:43 server.py
-rw-r--r-- 1 pi pi   902 Mai  9 17:43 setup.py
-rw-r--r-- 1 pi pi  1009 Mai  9 17:43 simple.c
drwxr-xr-x 2 pi pi  4096 Mai  9 17:43 styles
-rw-r--r-- 1 pi pi  6323 Mai  9 17:43 test.cpp
-rw-r--r-- 1 pi pi 22635 Mai  9 17:43 Write_Read_L09_Regs.cpp
pi@bananapi:~/novelo$
```

Figure 30: The measurement server source code located in the novelo directory

The source code can be compiled using the following commands:

```
cd novelo
```

```
make
```

```
make python
```

The first `make` command compiles and links a C program (refer to *chapter 2, Programming Languages*) called `novelo`, which allows programming the synthesizer within a shell. The second `make python` command generates a shared library for Python, which can be accessed by the Python web server. The web server can by started within the `novelo` directory by issuing this command:

```
sudo python server.py
```

The server must be started as superuser `root` due to USB write rights. Make sure that the `server.ini` file contains the IP address of your Banana Pro before using this command. In my case, this file contains the following:

```
#*******************************
# Banana Pro server ini file
#*******************************

IP_ADDRESS = "192.168.178.86"
PORT = 1000
```

The measurement web server will be started at port `1000`. Once the server has been started on Banana Pro, it can be accessed by any web browser in the same net using the `http://192.168.178.86:1000` URL. Change the IP address and port number according to your needs. The server itself is password protected. The default username and password is `bananapro`.

Figure 31: Password protection for the measurement web server

If no application board is attached to Banana Pro, the results should look similar to what is shown in the following screenshot:

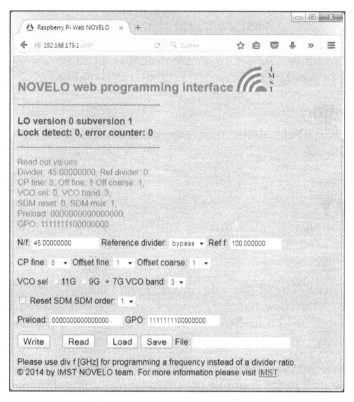

Figure 32: The measurement server within a web browser

Explanations

This section provides some explanation for the source code included in the `novelo` directory.

The Python web server

The Python web server itself is located in the `server.py` file. It is based on CherryPy and provides all the settings for the application board. It can be easily adapted to other application boards. The Python code makes use of a shared C-module library called `novelo.so`. This library contains all the C-code modules required for communication with the FTDI chip and application boards via SPI. Web server images are located in the `images` directory, and settings can be saved or restored within the `data` directory. The `style` directory contains a **Customized Style Sheets (CSS)** file, describing the look of the web page itself.

The Python/C interface

The Python/C interface is located in the `novelo.cc` source code file. Within this file, all the functions that can be called within the `server.py` file are defined, for example, `novelo_read`, which will read all the settings from the synthesizer application board. The `novelo.cc` source code file itself makes use of low-level and high-level FTDI routines. The `setup.py` file describes all additional files, which will be used in order to generate the `novelo.so` shared Python library.

C programming

The remaining (`*.cpp`) files define the communication with the FTDI chip and SPI of the application board.

Summary

In this chapter, different wireless projects were presented. You learned how OpenVPN can be used, for example, to allow wireless connections to a home network while traveling.

Additionally, Banana Pro can not only connect to an Ethernet connection, but also to a WLAN hotspot. Moreover, Banana Pro itself can serve as a secure wireless hotspot. Another section described how Banana Pro could be used as a printer server or an audio server.

Due to its low power consumption, Banana Pro is predestined to serve web pages. You learned how web pages could be provided using a content management system and database.

Last but not least, the section on the measurement server combined wireless hotspot functionality and web server functionality in order to control applications boards via USB and/or SPI.

4
An Arcade Cabinet

Everyone born between the 1980s and 1990s has had the experience of playing arcade kiosk games. They may have often thought that they could buy one and play it all day and night at home. But, one thing is for sure: these games were too expensive. These days, a PC is powerful enough to play many cool games, but there are still many people who install an emulator on their PC and play arcade games, such as 1942, KOF, Metal Slug, and so on. However, when we play on PCs, they're not convenient to carry. Now, though, a small SBC Banana Pro can take on the role of a PC, and we can play the games on it.

In this chapter, I will introduce you to how we can build a portable arcade cabinet with Banana Pro that can run different emulator games, such as iMAME4ALL, SENS, and PCSX. We can play these games with a joystick using an LCD or HDMI monitor as our display. In addition to this, it also can just act as a portable computer that's powered by Banana Pro.

We will firstly open the hardware acceleration function on Banana Pro as it is closed by default. We'll then install the iMAME4ALL and SENS emulators as the libretro core to play the two different emulator games. Also, we will build the PCSX emulator standalone without the libretro support. After all the different software is installed, we will design and make the arcade cabinet structure for Banana Pro. The arcade cabinet described in this chapter is just one design; you can also find many other appearance arcade cabinets from the Internet. The following topics are explained in detail:

- Implementing hardware acceleration
- Implementing libretro emulators
- Building PCSX
- Making cabinets for Banana Pro

Implementing hardware accelerations

For the good performance of games and smooth animation, we need first to open the hardware acceleration support of the Mali GPU on Banana Pro. For a framebuffer version `mali` binary driver, we just need to build the libdri2, libump, and sunxi-mali drivers from scratch, but for the X11 version, we also need to build the xf86-video-fbturbo driver to enable the GLES capable X11. So, in upcoming sections, there are two version build processes, framebuffers, and the X11 version. Choose only one version, and follow all the processes for the one you choose. The X11 version will let you play a game in a window, while the framebuffer version will let you play the game in full screen. However, the framebuffer version doesn't refresh a display when you exit games; you need to plug out of the display monitor or forcefully refresh the display through other script. This is not a good experience.

Installing dependencies

First, download and install the `Raspbian_For_BananaPro` image from `http://www.lemaker.org/product-bananapro-download-16.html`.

At the time of writing this chapter, I'm using the `Raspbian_For_BananaPro_v1412` version as the base kernel image.

Installing modules

By default, the OS image has `mali` and `ump` drivers built in, so we should first make sure that the `mali`, `mali_drm`, and `ump` drivers have been loaded as follows:

```
sudo modprobe mali
sudo modprobe mali_drm
sudo modropbe ump
lsmod
```

The output should be like this:

```
mali_drm            2608   1
drm               209226   2 mali_drm
mali              111427   0
ump                52415   4 mali,disp_ump
```

We'd better add the three driver modules, mentioned earlier, to the `/etc/modules` to load the driver automatically as shown in the following figure:

```
# /etc/modules: kernel modules to load at boot time.
#
# This file contains the names of kernel modules that should be loaded
# at boot time, one per line. Lines beginning with "#" are ignored.

ump
mali
mali_drm
```

Installing packages

To make the build process successfully, we need to install all these necessary packages:

```
sudo apt-get update

sudo apt-get install git build-essential make gcc autoconf libtool debhelper \

dh-autoreconf pkg-config automake xutils-dev libx11-dev libxext-dev libdrm-dev \

x11proto-dri2-dev libxfixes-dev xorg-dev libltdl-dev mesa-utils
```

Installing a directory

Create a directory that acts as the workspace to save and compile the downloaded source code:

```
cd ~

mkdir acrade_cabinet
```

So, `~/acrade_cabinet` will be the directory for all the upcoming source code.

Installing libdri2

The `libdri2` library is necessary to build the `sunxi-mali` driver, so we'll build `libdri2` first:

```
cd ~/acrade_cabinet

git clone https://github.com/robclark/libdri2.git

cd libdri2

./autogen.sh

./configure --prefix=/usr

make

sudo make install

sudo ldconfig
```

Installing libump

The `libump` is a **unified memory provider** (**UMP**) user-space library. We can build it according to the following process:

```
cd ~/acrade_cabinet
git clone https://github.com/linux-sunxi/libump.git
cd libump
dpkg-buildpackage -b
sudo dpkg -i ../libump_3.0-0sunxi1_armhf.deb
sudo dpkg -i ../libump-dev_3.0-0sunxi1_armhf.deb
```

You can check if the `libump` library has successfully installed into the system by running this command:

```
sudo find /usr/include/ -name ump*
```

You will see this output now:

```
bananapi@lemaker ~ $ sudo find /usr/include/ -name ump*
/usr/include/ump
/usr/include/ump/ump_platform.h
/usr/include/ump/ump_ref_drv.h
/usr/include/ump/ump.h
```

Now, run this command:

```
sudo find / -name *UMP*
```

You will see this output:

```
bananapi@lemaker ~ $ sudo find / -name *UMP*
/usr/lib/arm-linux-gnueabihf/libUMP.a
/usr/lib/arm-linux-gnueabihf/libUMP.so.3
/usr/lib/arm-linux-gnueabihf/libUMP.so.3.0.0
/usr/lib/arm-linux-gnueabihf/libUMP.so
```

Installing the sunxi-mali driver

After `libdri2` and `libump` are installed, we can then build the `sunxi-mali` driver. However, you'll first need to download this source code:

```
cd ~/acrade_cabinet
git clone https://github.com/linux-sunxi/sunxi-mali.git
cd sunxi-mali
git submodule init
git submodule update
```

In order to avoid possible RetroArch build errors later, it's better to replace the `gl2.h` and `gl2ext.h` files, since, these two original header files provided by the `sunxi-mali` repository lack the GLchar definitions required when building RetroArch. In order to build successfully, we can replace the two original head files with the following two downloads:

```
wget https://raw.githubusercontent.com/Tony-HIT/game_emulations/master/
patch/sunxi-mali/gl2.h -O ./include/GLES2/gl2.h
```

```
wget https://raw.githubusercontent.com/Tony-HIT/game_emulations/master/
patch/sunxi-mali/gl2ext.h -O ./include/GLES2/gl2ext.h
```

To build the `sunxi-mali` driver, we need to have different X11 and framebuffer versions.

The X11 version of the sunxi-mali driver

We will install the X11 version of the `sunxi-mali` drive using the following set of commands:

```
cd ~/acrade_cabinet/sunxi-mali

make config

sudo make install
```

The framebuffer version of the sunxi-mali driver

If we choose to use `framebuffer` to play the game, we need to install the `framebuffer` version of `sunxi-mali`:

```
cd ~/acrade_cabinet/sunxi-mali

make config ABI=armhf VERSION=r3p0 EGL_TYPE=framebuffer

sudo make install
```

Installing xf86-video-fbturbo

If you want to use OplenGLES that's capable X11, then you will need to install the `xf86-video-fbturbo` driver like this:

```
cd acrade_cabinet

git clone https://github.com/ssvb/xf86-video-fbturbo.git

cd xf86-video-fbturbo

autoreconf -v -i

./configure --prefix=/usr

make
```

After building `xf86-video-fbturbo`, configure your system to tell X11 to use the preceding driver. You will, therefore, need to create the `/etc/X11/xorg.conf.d/99-fbturbo.conf` file like this:

```
mkdir -p /etc/ X11/xorg.conf.d
touch /etc/X11/xorg.conf.d/99-fbturbo.conf
```

Then, fill the `99-fbturbo.conf` file with this content:

```
Section "Screen"
        Identifier      "My Screen"
        Device          "Allwinner A10/A13 FBDEV"
        Monitor         "My Monitor"
EndSection


Section "Device"
        Identifier      "Allwinner A10/A13 FBDEV"
        Driver           "fbturbo"
        Option          "fbdev" "/dev/fb0"
        Option          "SwapbuffersWait" "true"
        Option          "AccelMethod" "G2D"
EndSection


Section "Monitor"
        Identifier      "My Monitor"
        Option          "DPMS" "false"
EndSection
```

Getting device permission

The default permissions of `/dev/ump`, `/dev/mali`, `/dev/disp`, `/dev/g2d`, `/dev/fb*`, and `/dev/cerdar_dev` make these drivers unusable for normal users. Add a file to `/etc/udev/rules.d`, perhaps called `50-mali.rules`, with the following content:

```
KERNEL=="mali", MODE="0660", GROUP="video"
KERNEL=="ump", MODE="0660", GROUP="video"
KERNEL=="disp", MODE="0660", GROUP="video"
KERNEL=="g2d", MODE="0660", GROUP="video"
KERNEL=="fb*", MODE="0660", GROUP="video"
KERNEL=="cedar_dev", MODE="0660", GROUP="video"
```

Make sure that your user is in the `video` group. If a command group does not show any videos, you will have to assign a group to the user using this command:

```
sudo usermod -aG video &USER
```

Testing hardware acceleration

After all the hardware acceleration dependencies have been built, we need to restart the system to see the result using this command:

```
sudo reboot
```

Firstly, we could check if the `xf86-video-fbturbo` driver has been loaded; we can take a look at this information in the `/var/log/Xorg.0.log`:

```
grep -i fbturbo /var/log/Xorg.0.log
```

Then, you should see this output:

```
[    17.540] (II) LoadModule: "fbturbo"
[    17.541] (II) Loading /usr/lib/xorg/modules/drivers/fbturbo_drv.so
[    17.555] (II) Module fbturbo: vendor="X.Org Foundation"
[    17.556] (II) FBTURBO: driver for framebuffer: fbturbo
[    17.557] (WW) Falling back to old probe method for fbturbo
[    17.567] (II) FBTURBO(0): using /dev/fb0
[    17.567] (II) FBTURBO(0): Creating default Display subsection in
Screen section
[    17.567] (==) FBTURBO(0): Depth 24, (==) framebuffer bpp 32
[    17.567] (==) FBTURBO(0): RGB weight 888
[    17.567] (==) FBTURBO(0): Default visual is TrueColor
[    17.567] (==) FBTURBO(0): Using gamma correction (1.0, 1.0, 1.0)
[    17.567] (II) FBTURBO(0): hardware:   (video memory: 16200kB)
[    17.567] (**) FBTURBO(0): Option "fbdev" "/dev/fb0"
[    17.568] (**) FBTURBO(0): Option "SwapbuffersWait" "true"
[    17.568] (II) FBTURBO(0): processor: ARM Cortex-A7
[    17.568] (II) FBTURBO(0): checking modes against framebuffer
device...
[    17.568] (II) FBTURBO(0): checking modes against monitor...
[    17.570] (--) FBTURBO(0): Virtual size is 1920x1080 (pitch 1920)
[    17.570] (**) FBTURBO(0):  Built-in mode "current": 148.5 MHz, 67.5
kHz, 60.0 Hz
```

```
[    17.570] (II) FBTURBO(0): Modeline "current"x0.0   148.50   1920 2008
2052 2200   1080 1084 1089 1125 +hsync +vsync -csync (67.5 kHz b)

[    17.570] (==) FBTURBO(0): DPI set to (96, 96)

[    17.603] (II) FBTURBO(0): using backing store heuristics

[    17.633] (II) FBTURBO(0): enabled G2D acceleration

[    17.633] (==) FBTURBO(0): Backing store disabled

[    17.635] (II) FBTURBO(0): using sunxi disp layers for X video
extension

[    17.635] (II) FBTURBO(0): using hardware cursor

[    17.699] (II) FBTURBO(0): tear-free zero-copy double buffering needs
more video memory

[    17.699] (II) FBTURBO(0): please set fb0_framebuffer_num >= 3 in the
fex file

[    17.700] (II) FBTURBO(0): and sunxi_fb_mem_reserve >= 24 in the
kernel cmdline

[    17.700] (II) FBTURBO(0): enabled display controller hardware
overlays for DRI2

[    17.700] (II) FBTURBO(0): Wait on SwapBuffers? enabled

[    17.700] (II) FBTURBO(0): [DRI2] Setup complete

[    17.700] (II) FBTURBO(0): [DRI2]    DRI driver: lima

[    17.700] (II) FBTURBO(0): [DRI2]    VDPAU driver: sunxi

[    17.700] (II) FBTURBO(0): using DRI2 integration for Mali GPU (UMP
buffers)

[    17.700] (II) FBTURBO(0): Mali binary drivers can only accelerate
EGL/GLES

[    17.700] (II) FBTURBO(0): so AIGLX/GLX is expected to fail or
fallback to software
```

Secondly, we can test the `sunxi-mali` driver. We also have two test methods that are different for the X11 and framebuffer versions, respectively.

To test the X11 `sunxi-mali` version, use this command:

```
cd ~/acrade_cabinet/sunxi-mali

cd test

cc -Wall -o test test.c -lEGL -lGLESv2 -lX11

./test
```

To test the sunxi-mali framebuffer version, use this command:

```
cd ~/acrade_cabinet/sunxi-mali
cd test
make test
./test/test
```

You should be able to see a smoothed triangle, either written out in the top-left corner of the framebuffer or in an X window.

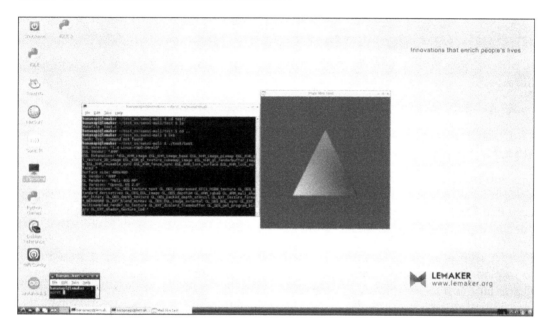

The console will tell you which renderer is being used by passing this command:

```
...
GL Vendor: "ARM"
GL Renderer: "Mali-400 MP"
GL Version: "OpenGL ES 2.0"
...
```

We can see from this output that the `mali` drivers use OpenGL ES, so, in the leftover building process, we will choose the OpenGL ES as the graphic support.

Implementing libretro emulators

Libretro is a simple but powerful development interface that allows you to easily create emulators, games, and multimedia applications that can plug straight into any libretro-compatible frontend. This development interface is open to others so that they can run these pluggable emulators and game cores in their own programs or devices also. Here, we will focus on the emulators of games that work with libretro. Libretro frontends and libretro cores are two different parts of implementing libretro emulators; we will build them separately in the upcoming sections.

Installing dependent packages

In order to get audio when we play games, we can install `sdl` relevant developing libraries like this:

```
sudo apt-get install libsdl1.2-dev libsdl-image1.2-dev
```

Installing libretro frontend - RetroArch

Libretro frontends are programs that have implemented the libretro API specification. When properly implemented, this allows a program to run any libretro core that has been developed. There are many different kinds of libretro frontends, such as RetroArch, minir, Arcan, Phoenix, RetroPlayer, and so on.

RetroArch is the official reference frontend for the libretro API. It is usually the first to implement new features added to the libretro API. It is written almost entirely in C and targets a large number of platforms. It tries to be as portable as possible, while providing impeccable audio/video performance. It does not feature a WIMP UI of any kind as of now.

To let building of `RetroArch` be successful, we need to change to a special commit after we download this source code:

```
cd ~/acrade_cabinet/
git clone https://github.com/libretro/RetroArch.git
cd RetroArch
git checkout 9e132a0
sudo mkdir -p /opt/retroarch
```

To build RetroArch, there is also an X11 version or another framebuffer version with different build commands.

The X11 version of RetroArch

With the RetroArch X11 version, we can only play a game in a window using this command:

```
./configure --enable-gles --disable-oss --disable-sdl --disable-netplay
--prefix=/opt/retroarch
make
sudo make install
```

The framebuffer version of RetroArch

With the RetroArch framebuffer version, we can play a game in full screen, but we will encounter a problem where the screen cannot be refreshed after exiting the game.

Before building the RetroArch framebuffer version, we need to first patch the `mali_fbdev_ctx.c` file:

```
wget https://raw.githubusercontent.com/Tony-HIT/game_emulations/master/patch/RetroArch/mali_fbdev_ctx.c -O ./gfx/context/mali_fbdev_ctx.c
```

After patching the file, we can build the RetroArch framebuffer version like this:

```
./configure --disable-vg --disable-ffmpeg --disable-sdl --disable-x11
--disable-xvideo --enable-gles --disable-kms --enable-neon --enable-
fbo --enable-mali_fbdev --enable-lakka --enable-freetype --enable-glui
--prefix=/opt/retroarch
make
sudo make install
```

Then, you can check whether the RetroArch has been installed:

```
ls /opt/retroarch/bin/retroarch
```

It should output like this:

```
bananapi@lemaker ~/RetroArch $ ls /opt/retroarch/bin/retroarch
/opt/retroarch/bin/retroarch
```

Installing libretro cores

After installing RetroArch as a `libretro` frontend, we still need a `libretro` core to run special game ROMs.

Libretro cores are individual standalone programs that implement the libretro API specification as glue code. If a core is correctly implemented, this program can then be executed on any `libretro` frontend. Here, we will choose iMAM4ALL and SENS as the libretro cores so that we can play games supported by these two different emulators.

Installing iMAM4ALL libretro core

To install the iMAM4ALL libretro core, we need to download the `imame4all-libretro` source code and use ARM configuration:

```
cd ~/acrade_cabinet/
git clone https://github.com/libretro/imame4all-libretro.git
cd imame4all-libretro/
make -f makefile.libretro ARM=1
```

After the build process has finished, we will get a dynamic library called libretro. So, we can copy and rename it into a separate place using this command:

```
sudo mkdir -p /usr/lib/libretro
sudo cp libretro.so /usr/lib/libretro/libretro-imame4all.so
```

Installing the SNES libretro core

To install the SNES libretro core, we can download and build the `pocketsnes-libretro` source code:

```
cd ~/acrade_cabinet/
git clone https://github.com/ToadKing/pocketsnes-libretro.git
cd pocketsnes-libretro/
make
```

After the build process has finished, we will also get a dynamic library called libretro. So, we will still copy and rename it in the `/usr/lib/libretro` directory using this command:

```
sudo cp libretro.so /usr/lib/libretro/libretro-pocketsnes.so
```

Configuration

We should also first set some values in the RetroArch configuration file that's located at /etc/retroarch.cfg so that we can use the RetroArch more conveniently.

Set the libretro_directory using this command. This command tells RetroArch about the directory that can be searched for libretro core implementations:

```
libretro_directory = "/usr/lib/libretro/"
```

This tells RetroArch about the directory that can be searched for libretro core implementations.

Set rgui_browser using this command:

```
rgui_browser_directory = /opt/retroarch/roms/
```

This tells RetroArch the start directory for a menu content browser so that we can quickly find the game ROMs.

If you want to set the default libretro core to run, you can set libretro_path using this command:

```
libretro_path = "/usr/lib/libretro/libretro-imame4all.so"
```

Here, we'll set it as the iMAME4ALL core.

Set the video_driver using this command:

```
video_driver = "gl"
```

This tells the video_driver which OpenGL context implementation to use. If you're using the RetroArch framebuffer version, the following values also need to be set:

```
video_gl_context = "mali-fbdev"
```

For framebuffer, we use "mali-fbdev". In X11, you don't need to specify it. All the games in the *Testing games* section have been tested under the X11 window.

Playing games

First, we need to download some game ROMs from the Internet. To download the ROMs, the reference link is `http://www.theoldcomputer.com/roms/index.php?folder=MAME/Mame-0.37b5`.

For iMAM4ALL game ROMs, we should choose version 0.37b5 or we will not be able to play the iMAM4ALL game normally.

To play a game, we can just enter a special command to boot a special game, or, we can firstly enter into the RetroArch menu interface, and then select the core and game content.

Playing a game directly with a command line

Using this method, we can just play a special game with the special libretro core. By default, the control mode is `keyboard`; we will configure it in later content. As we have built two different libretro cores, we will have separate commands to run different libretro cores.

iMAM4ALL games

To play the iMAM4ALL games, we need use libretro-imame4all.so as the core:

```
/opt/retroarch/bin/retroarch -c /etc/retroarch.cfg -L /usr/lib/libretro/
libretro-imame4all.so [PATH_TO_YOUR_ROM]
```

For example, the Metal Slug game ROM is located at `/opt/retroarch/roms/mame037b5/mslug.zip`:

```
/opt/retroarch/bin/retroarch -c /etc/retroarch.cfg -L /usr/lib/libretro/
libretro-imame4all.so /opt/retroarch/roms/mame037b5/mslug.zip
```

For SNES

To play the SNES games, we need use libretro- pocketsnes.so as the core:

```
/opt/retroarch/bin/retroarch -c /etc/retroarch.cfg -L /usr/lib/libretro/
libretro-pocketsnes.so [PATH_TO_YOUR_ROM]
```

For example, the Mario Kart game ROM is located at `/opt/retroarch/roms/snes/Super\ Mario\ Kart.zip`:

```
/opt/retroarch/bin/retroarch -c /etc/retroarch.cfg -L /usr/lib/libretro/
libretro-imame4all.so /opt/retroarch/roms/ snes/Super\ Mario\ Kart.zip
```

Playing a game from the RetroArch menu interface

Contrary to playing a special game with a special command, we can also first boot into the RetroArch menu interface, and then select the corresponding core to run the right game ROMs.

Now, let's boot into the RetroArch menu interface:

```
/opt/retroarch/bin/retroarch -c /etc/retroarch.cfg --menu
```

When you've booted into the system for the first time, you may see the following control instructions:

We can press the X key to select items:

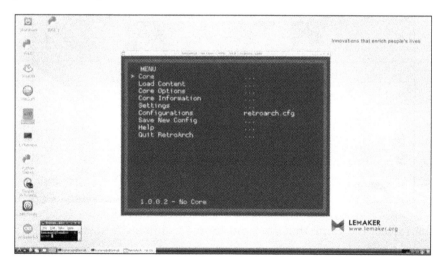

Firstly, we need to select a core to run corresponding game ROM. Navigate to the top of the **MENU** interface and select the **CORE** item, and then navigate to the right location of the libretro cores. As described in the following screenshot, the location of the libretro cores in this chapter is /usr/lib/libretro/.

We can select **libretro-imame4all.so** to run the iMAME4ALL ROM, or we can select **libretro-pocketsnes.so** to run the SNES ROMs as shown in the following figure:

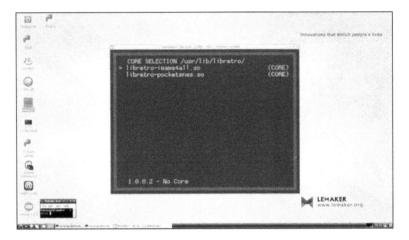

After selecting the core, we need enter the Load Content menu item, and navigate to the location of the game ROM to select the suitable game. For example, we have chosen **libretro-imame4all.so** as the core, so navigate to the ROM's location at /opt/retroarch/roms/mame037b5:

We can then select the game that we want to run and press *X* to start it.

Testing games

Here are some games that have been tested on Banana Pro:

1. The iMAME4ALL games:
   ° Metal Slug
   ° Metal Slug2
   ° Bubble Bobble
   ° 1942
   ° 1943
   ° Golden Axe

2. SNES games:
   ° Mario World
   ° Mario Kart

Building PCSX

PCSX is a free console emulator that allows software that's designed to be used with PlayStation to be used with personal computers and a signal board computer such as Banana Pro.

We can build a PCSX standalone or the libretro version that acts as a RetroArch core. Still, I recommend that you use the standalone version as it performs better than the libretro version.

Installing dependent packages

Just like building RetroArch, we also need to install the `sdl` relevant developing libraries in order to get audio to work:

```
sudo apt-get install libsdl1.2-dev libsdl-image1.2-dev
```

Installing PCSX

PCSX ReARMed is yet another PCSX fork that's based on the PCSX-Reloaded project that itself contains code from PCSX, PCSX-df, and PCSX-Revolution. This version is ARM architecture-oriented and features the MIPS->ARM recompiler by Ari64, NEON GTE code, and more performance improvements. So, we will use the PCSX ReARMed version as the PCSX emulator.

Downloading PCSX ReARMed

Download the source code and compile it using the following command:

```
cd ~/acrade_cabinet/
git clone https://github.com/notaz/pcsx_rearmed.git
cd pcsx_rearmed
git submodule init
git submodule update
./configure
make
```

Patching

The default directory for the PSX BIOS is ~/bios. If you want to configure it later in your ~/.pcsx/pcsx.cfg, you need to edit the frontend/menu.c file, find the CE_CONFIG_STR(Bios) line, and add the CE_CONFIG_STR(BiosDir) line below it:

```
static const struct {
        const char *name;
        size_t len;
        void *val;
} config_data[] = {
        CE_CONFIG_STR(Bios),
        CE_CONFIG_STR(BiosDir),
        CE_CONFIG_STR_V(Gpu, 3),
        CE_CONFIG_STR(Spu),
```

Compiling and installing

We'll use the following configure command to generate configuration files:

```
./configure
```

We then need to edit the resulting config.mak file to remove all the parameters behind SOUND_DRIVERS except sdl so that the file looks like this:

```
# Automatically generated by configure
# Configured with: './configure'
CC = gcc
CXX = g++
AS = as
CFLAGS += -mfpu=vfp -I/usr/include/SDL -D_GNU_SOURCE=1 -D_REENTRANT
-Wno-unused-result
ASFLAGS += -mfpu=vfp
```

```
LDFLAGS +=
MAIN_LDFLAGS +=
MAIN_LDLIBS += -L/usr/lib/arm-linux-gnueabihf -lSDL -lpulse -lasound
-lpng  -ldl -lm -lpthread -lz
PLUGIN_CFLAGS +=   -fPIC

ARCH = arm
PLATFORM = generic
BUILTIN_GPU = unai
SOUND_DRIVERS =  sdl
PLUGINS = plugins/spunull/spunull.so plugins/dfxvideo/gpu_peops.so
plugins/gpu_unai/gpu_unai.so plugins/gpu-gles/gpu_gles.so
HAVE_TSLIB = 1
HAVE_GLES = 1
CFLAGS_GLES =
LDLIBS_GLES = -lEGL -lGLESv1_CM
USE_DYNAREC = 1
```

After the modification has been made, we can run the `make` command:

`make`

It will take some time to finish the build process; after this, we can add the resulting pcsx binary file to the `/usr/local/bin` path so that we can use `pcsx` directly:

`sudo cp pcsx /usr/local/bin/`

Playing PCSX games

We can download some PCSX game ROMs from the Internet, place them in an SD card, and then use the following command to play games:

`pcsx -cdfile [PSX_IMAGE_FILE]`

Configuration

When we first play games, the `pcsx` emulator would mention that we do not have a bios file, so we can download this bios file, which is sometimes called `scph1001.bin`, from the Internet and move it to the `~/bios` directory:

`cp scph1001.bin ~/bios`

Since we have patched `frontend/menu.c` before we compiled it, we can edit the `~/.pcsx/pcsx.cfg` file to configure the bios path like this:

`Bios = scph1001.bin`

`BiosDir = /home/bananapi/.pcsx/bios`

So, if we have a special the `bios` path, we can place the `bios` file in a patch that sets in `~/.pcsx/pcsx.cfg`:

```
mkdir -p /home/bananapi/.pcsx/bios
cp scph1001.bin /home/bananapi/.pcsx/bios
```

Testing PCSX games

Most PCSX games can be played very smoothly. However, there are two games that have been tested:

- Final Fantasy
- Crash Bandicoot

Making an arcade cabinet for Banana Pro

All the preceding games are set up in the arcade cabinet software environment, and now, we will build a portable arcade cabinet using Banana Pro. There are many different arcade cabinet shapes on the Internet; you can also build one like those shown on the Internet.

Preparing the materials

In order to build a nice and cool arcade cabinet, we first need to prepare some necessary materials.

A suitcase

In order to take the Banana Pro arcade emulator walkaround, we need to first prepare a suitcase to put Banana Pro, joysticks, LCD, and so on inside it. We can either buy one or find something that looks like this:

A joystick

The default controller method uses a keyboard. As we would make an arcade cabinet, we should also play a game with a joystick. We can find many different USB joysticks in online shops.

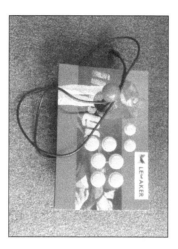

We can then break a joystick, and take out its button, stick, and circuit aboard. We will put all of these into a suitcase.

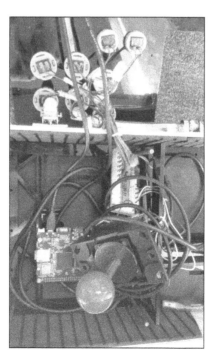

A micro USB extended line

In order to power Banana Pro (inside the suitcase) outside the suitcase, we need a micro USB extended line to connect to the Banana Pro power USB connector and leave the other side of the micro USB extended line out of the suitcase.

A USB hub

We also need to lead the USB port of Banana Pro outside the suitcase, so we'll need a USB hub device to achieve this.

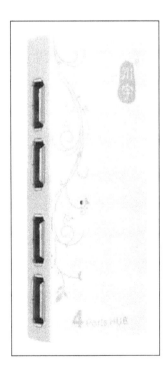

An LCD display

By default, we use HDMI as the display output, but if we take the arcade cabinet outside of the house, we will not have the HDMI monitor all the time. So, we can use an LCD as the display output. We can find an official 7 inch LCD for Banana Pro on the Internet; it is easier to install and use. Here, I've used a 10.1 inch LCD, but I do not suggest any of you to use it because you need to make modifications to it on your own.

An audio extended line

In order to listen to audio when playing games, we also need to connect earphones to the Banana Pro audio jack. So, we will use an audio extend line to achieve this.

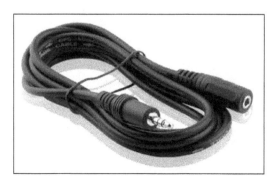

A mini keyboard

We also need to prepare a mini keyboard that we can use when configuring systems.

Designing a frame

After preparing all the parts, we need to design a frame to mount all these parts together. In order to make the arcade cabinet look cool, we'll leave all the parts, except the stick and buttons, above the frame.

You can find the CAD file of the frame at `https://github.com/Tony-HIT/game_emulations/tree/master/cases`.

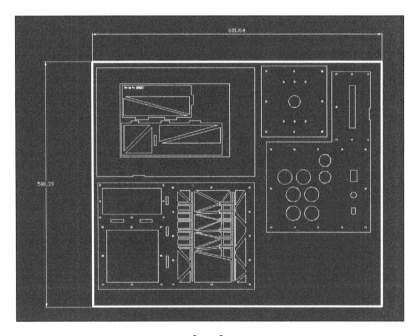

The frame consist of three layers: the bottom layer is used to fix the box and the components in the box; the middle layer is used to place parts, such as Banana Pro, a joystick circuit and so on; and the top layer is used to fix a stick, buttons, and some interfaces, such as USB, audio and so on.

The LCD is fixed inside the cover of the suitcase.

The frame would look like the following screenshot after we mount it well:

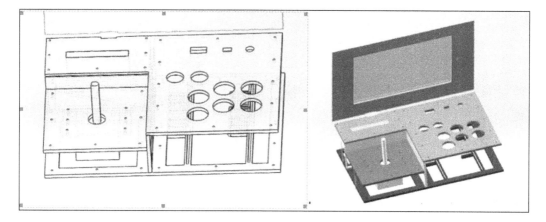

We can then adjust the size according to the suitcase and LCD panel.

Assembling

After we design the frame, we can find an online shop to help us produce it out. Then, we need to assemble the frame and other parts together into the suitcase.

Assembling a base frame

The base frame has many position holes on it. The left-hand side of the base frame is used to fix the joystick and adapter board for the LCD. The right-hand side of the base frame is used to fix Banana Pro.

Assembling Banana Pro and a joystick

We should first fix the joystick on the joystick board and put these on the left-handside of the base frame. Then, we'll fix Banana Pro on the right-hand side of the base frame and connect the joystick circuit board to Banana Pro via a USB. Also, we need to connect the extended audio line and micro USB line to Banana Pro.

The joystick is shown as follows:

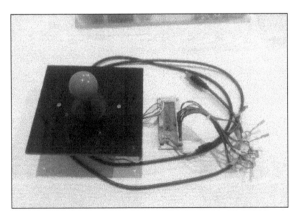

The assembled joystick and Banana Pro in the suitcase are shown as follows:

Mounting an LCD

To use a 10.1 inch LCD, we need an adapter board and an FPC cable.

We then need to mount the LCD inside the top cover of the suitcase using the frames for the LCD. We'll then connect the LCD to the adapter board with the FPC cable, and then connect the adapter board to the Banana Pro display connector with the FPC cable.

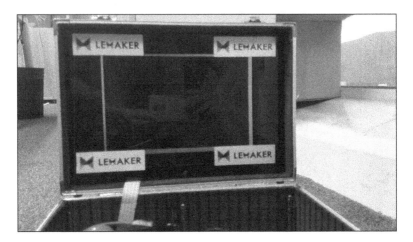

Assembling a top frame

The top frame is used to mount the buttons, USB hub, audio jack, and the USB power and connector as shown here:

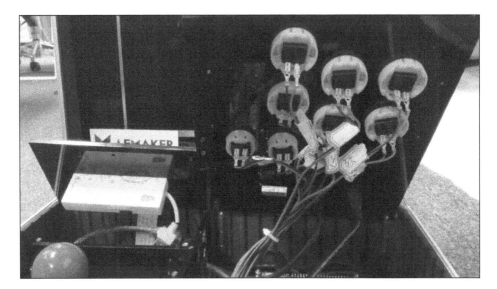

Playing the Banana Pro arcade cabinet

After we have finished setting up the arcade cabinet, we need to perform some configurations so that we can play games using a joystick and LCD display.

Configuring output to an LCD

In the preceding software configurations, the display output mode is HDMI, so we need to first change the display output to an LCD. We used a 10.1 inch LCD here, so we need to adjust the parameters to accommodate it.

Power on Banana Pro again, and try to connect it through SSH or just use HDMI. In order to use the LCD as the display output, we need to change the parameters in the `script.bin` file. To do so, we need will install the `sunxi-tools` to edit the `script.bin` file:

```
cd ~
git clone https://github.com/linux-sunxi/sunxi-tools.git
sudo apt-get install libusb-1.0-0-dev
cd sunxi-tools/
make
```

We then need to compile `script.bin` file to a `.fex` format file:

```
sudo mount  /dev/mm cblk0p1 /mnt
cd /mnt
sudo cp script.bin script.bin.bak
sudo ~/sunxi-tools/bin2fex scritp.bin script.fex
```

Next, edit the `script.fex` file and modify the following parameters to make it fit into the LCD panel:

```
screen0_output_type = 1
screen0_output_mode = 5

[lcd0_para]
lcd_used = 1
lcd_x = 1280
lcd_y = 800
lcd_dclk_freq = 67
lcd_pwm_not_used = 0
lcd_pwm_ch = 0
lcd_pwm_freq = 22000
```

```
lcd_pwm_pol = 0
lcd_max_bright = 240
lcd_min_bright = 64
lcd_if = 3
lcd_hbp = 80
lcd_ht = 1370
lcd_vbp = 20
lcd_vt = 1650
lcd_vspw = 10
lcd_hspw = 50
lcd_hv_if = 0
lcd_hv_smode = 0
lcd_hv_s888_if = 0
lcd_hv_syuv_if = 0
lcd_lvds_ch = 0
lcd_lvds_mode = 0
lcd_lvds_bitwidth = 0
lcd_lvds_io_cross = 0
lcd_cpu_if = 0
lcd_frm = 0
lcd_io_cfg0 = 268435456
lcd_gamma_correction_en = 0
lcd_gamma_tbl_0 = 0x0
lcd_gamma_tbl_1 = 0x10101
lcd_gamma_tbl_255 = 0xffffff
lcd_bl_en_used = 1
lcd_bl_en = port:PH07<1><0><default><1>
lcd_power_used = 1
lcd_power = port:PH08<1><0><default><1>
lcd_pwm_used = 1
lcd_pwm = port:PB02<2><0><default><default>
```

```
lcdd0 = port:PD00<3><0><default><default>
lcdd1 = port:PD01<3><0><default><default>
lcdd2 = port:PD02<3><0><default><default>
lcdd3 = port:PD03<3><0><default><default>
lcdd4 = port:PD04<3><0><default><default>
lcdd5 = port:PD05<3><0><default><default>
lcdd6 = port:PD06<3><0><default><default>
lcdd7 = port:PD07<3><0><default><default>
lcdd8 = port:PD08<3><0><default><default>
lcdd9 = port:PD09<3><0><default><default>
lcdd10 = port:PD10<2><0><default><default>
lcdd11 = port:PD11<2><0><default><default>
lcdd12 = port:PD12<2><0><default><default>
lcdd13 = port:PD13<2><0><default><default>
lcdd14 = port:PD14<2><0><default><default>
lcdd15 = port:PD15<2><0><default><default>
lcdd16 = port:PD16<2><0><default><default>
lcdd17 = port:PD17<2><0><default><default>
lcdd18 = port:PD18<2><0><default><default>
lcdd19 = port:PD19<2><0><default><default>
lcdd20 = port:PD20<2><0><default><default>
lcdd21 = port:PD21<2><0><default><default>
lcdd22 = port:PD22<2><0><default><default>
lcdd23 = port:PD23<2><0><default><default>
lcdclk = port:PD24<2><0><default><default>
lcdde = port:PD25<2><0><3><default>
lcdhsync = port:PD26<2><0><3><default>
lcdvsync = port:PD27<2><0><3><default>
```

After modifications have been made, we need to transform the FEX file into the script
.bin file:

```
sudo ~/sunxi-tools/fex2bin scritp.fex script.bin
```

Then, reboot the system. The system will be visible on the LCD display when it's booted again:

Configuring a joystick controller

By default, the controller method is just for keyboards, so if we want to use the joystick, we need configure some parameters.

For RetroArch, it is easy to achieve this; we can use a menu interface to configure and save the new `.cfg` file to `retroarch.cfg`:

```
sudo /opt/retrparch/bin/retroarch -c /etc/retroarch.cfg -menu
```

Then, select **Settings | Input** to be used for our keyboard, and configure all the joysticks and buttons according to your preference. When you've finished, exit to the top **MENU** interface and save the new configuration using the **Save New Config item**. The system will tell you which filename it is saved by such as `Retroarch-201505051111.cfg`. Now, we need to use a new configuration file:

```
sudo cp /etc/retroarch.cfg /etc/retroarch.cfg.bak
sudo mv /etc/Retroarch-201505051111.cfg /etc/retroarch.cfg
```

Here are some parameters that we need to pay attention to because we may edit the parameters according to our own configuration:

1. Path parameters:

```
libretro_path = "/usr/lib/libretro/libretro-imame4all.so"
libretro_directory = "/usr/lib/libretro/"
system_directory = "/opt/retroarch/roms/mame037b5/"
rgui_browser_directory = "/opt/retroarch/roms/"
```

2. Joystick and keyboard control parameters:

```
input_player1_b = "z"
input_player1_b_btn = "3"
input_player1_b_axis = "nul"
input_player1_y = "a"
input_player1_y_btn = "1"
input_player1_y_axis = "nul"
input_player1_select = "rshift"
input_player1_select_btn = "7"
input_player1_select_axis = "nul"
input_player1_start = "enter"
input_player1_start_btn = "4"
input_player1_start_axis = "nul"
input_player1_up = "up"
input_player1_up_btn = "nul"
input_player1_up_axis = "-1"
input_player1_down = "down"
input_player1_down_btn = "nul"
input_player1_down_axis = "+1"
input_player1_left = "left"
input_player1_left_btn = "nul"
input_player1_left_axis = "-0"
input_player1_right = "right"
input_player1_right_btn = "nul"
input_player1_right_axis = "+0"
input_player1_a = "x"
input_player1_a_btn = "0"
input_player1_a_axis = "nul"
```

```
input_player1_x = "s"
input_player1_x_btn = "2"
input_player1_x_axis = "nul"
input_player1_l_x_plus = "nul"
input_player1_l_x_plus_btn = "nul"
input_player1_l_x_plus_axis = "+0"
input_player1_l_x_minus = "nul"
input_player1_l_x_minus_btn = "nul"
input_player1_l_x_minus_axis = "-0"
input_player1_l_y_plus = "nul"
input_player1_l_y_plus_btn = "nul"
input_player1_l_y_plus_axis = "+1"
input_player1_l_y_minus = "nul"
input_player1_l_y_minus_btn = "nul"
input_player1_l_y_minus_axis = "-1"
input_menu_toggle = "f1"
input_menu_toggle_btn = "6"
input_menu_toggle_axis = "nul"
```

Playing the game on the arcade cabinet

After configuring the LCD and joystick, we can play games using a joystick and LCD. The method to play the game is the same as the instructions we covered in the *Playing games* section. If you do not want to enter a command in the terminal every time, you can write an execute shell script to run the command. However, we will not go into a detailed description of this here. Following is a picture of playing game 1942:

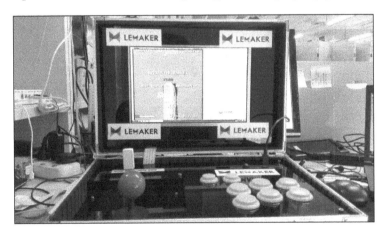

Summary

In this chapter, we built different software that need to support playing games smoothly, such hardware acceleration support and different game emulators. This was done so that we can play kinds of emulators in it, such as iMAME4ALL, SNES, and PCSX.

Then, we used a suitcase to place all the parts in it so that we can take an arcade anywhere. We designed frames, mounted all the parts, and configured controllers and a display. We also added a power bank in the suitcase so that we can play games on the go.

Finally, our initial purpose was to not only make an arcade cabinet to play games, but also build it in such a way that the arcade cabinet can act as a small portable computer that we can program and watch videos on.

5
A Multimedia Center

Embedded boards have become increasingly popular when using a multimedia center. Although Banana Pro is not yet perfectly suited for Kido (formerly known as XBMC and Xbox Media Center), it is highly recommended when watching TV, especially HDTV. Several years ago, watching HDTV required a huge CPU consumption or special graphics cards running **Video Decode and Presentation API for Unix** (**VDPAU**). Today, Banana Pro can do this job while consuming only a few watts of power.

In this chapter, we will build a multimedia center, which can receive **Digital Video Broadcast** (**DVB**) television signals. In addition to this, it can be remote controlled, provides hard disk recording, and allows you to watch, for example, DVDs, or listen to audio CDs. Moreover, timers can be programmed in order to record movies.

We will install VDR and customize it using TV station logos and different plugins. This chapter provides all required preparations, starting with the kernel and required graphics libraries. Although Kodi does not yet work perfectly on Banana Pro, an outlook is provided on how it can be installed and used.

This chapter contains the following in detail:

- Kernel preparation
- Video Disk Recorder (VDR)
- A remote control
- VDR plugins
- Xbox Media Center (XBMC)

Kernel preparation

In *Chapter 2, Programming Languages*, the LeMedia kernel was installed from sources. This kernel is now used as a base for the multimedia center with the following additions/changes:

- The I2S audio device is added and enabled

- In addition to this, graphics memory for TV decoding is set to a maximum of 190 MB.

- Additionally, some kernel debug messages are deactivated. This prevents the log daemon from flooding `/var/log/syslog` in case of a VDR crash.

- Moreover, the *key repetition* in the IR driver is activated: when a remote control button is pressed and not released, the remote button is recognized several times.

- Banana Pro features a `mali` **Graphics Processing Unit (GPU)**. Although there are patches available for the `mali` driver version r3p2 and higher, Kodi only shows videos in the accelerated mode using `mali` r3p0. Therefore, the `mali` driver version will not be updated.

- Before compiling the kernel, DVB USB devices are activated.

Finally, a bug in the display driver, which is responsible for slightly dark pictures, will be corrected.

In the meantime, Daniel Andersen has implemented most of the changes described in the following section in his kernel, which is located at `https://github.com/dan-and/linux-sunxi`.

Adding the I2S audio device

1. Using the I2S audio, the reader can connect an audio DAC to the Banana Pro GPIO header. I checked out the LeMedia kernel in the `/usr/local/src/linux-sunxi-lemaker` directory using this command:

   ```
   sudo su

   git clone -b lemaker-3.4-dev-lemedia https://github.com/LeMaker/
   linux-sunxi.git /usr/local/src/linux-sunxi-lemaker
   ```

2. The I2S audio device is located in the `sound/soc/sunxi/i2s` subdirectory. In the first step, I copied the existing nonworking I2S driver into a backup directory:

   ```
   cd /usr/local/src/linux-sunxi-lemaker/sound/soc/sunxi/i2s

   mkdir backup

   mv * backup
   ```

3. Afterwards, I checked out the dan-and kernel and copied the associated files into the LeMaker kernel branch:

```
cd /usr/local/src

git clone https://github.com/dan-and/linux-sunxi.git linux-sunxi-
danand

cp -R danand/sound/soc/sunxi/i2s linux-sunxi-lemaker/sound/soc/
sunxi/i2s
```

4. Make sure that the I2S audio is activated in the kernel menu. This can be done using the sudo make menuconfig command (refer to *Chapter 2, Programming Languages*) in the kernel directory, as shown here:

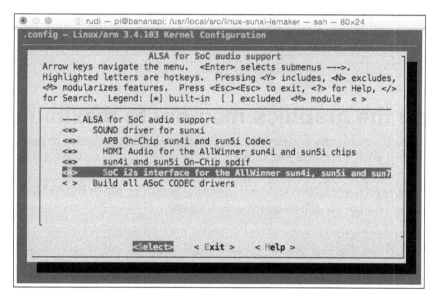

Figure 1: Activating the Banana Pro I2S audio in the Linux kernel

 In order to detect all the available audio devices, the following command can be used:

```
aplay -l
```

5. For the LeMedia kernel that's been patched as described previously, the output should look similar to what is shown in this screenshot:

```
rudi — pi@bananapi: /usr/local/src/linux-sunxi-lemaker — ssh — 80×15
pi@bananapi:/usr/local/src/linux-sunxi-lemaker$ aplay -l
**** List of PLAYBACK Hardware Devices ****
card 0: sunxicodec [sunxi-CODEC], device 0: M1 PCM [sunxi PCM]
  Subdevices: 1/1
  Subdevice #0: subdevice #0
card 1: sunxisndspdif [sunxi-sndspdif], device 0: SUNXI-SPDIF sndspdif-0 []
  Subdevices: 1/1
  Subdevice #0: subdevice #0
card 2: sunxisndi2s [sunxi-sndi2s], device 0: SUNXI-I2S sndi2s-0 []
  Subdevices: 1/1
  Subdevice #0: subdevice #0
card 3: sunxisndhdmi [sunxi-sndhdmi], device 0: SUNXI-HDMIAUDIO sndhdmi-0 []
  Subdevices: 1/1
  Subdevice #0: subdevice #0
pi@bananapi:/usr/local/src/linux-sunxi-lemaker$
```

Figure 2

Setting the graphics memory to maximum

The graphics driver memory is limited to 80 MB by default. In order to use libvdpau in combination with VDR and the softhddevice plugin (video output), we need to enlarge this memory to 190 MB. Therefore, edit the /usr/local/src/linux-sunxi-lemaker/drivers/media/video/sunxi/sunxi_cedar.c file in the LeMedia kernel directory, and change the file in line 934 as follows:

```
#ifdef CONFIG_CMA
        /* If having CMA enabled, just rely on CMA for memory
allocation */
        resource_size_t pa;
        ve_size = 190 * SZ_1M;
```

This will set the maximum allowed graphics driver memory to 190 MB instead of the default of 80 MB.

Deactivating display driver kernel logging

If, in a later stage, VDR is killed or crashes, the kernel will flood the system log file with messages. In order to avoid this, a few lines in the display driver must be commented out. Comment out the print messages in the `s32 img_sw_para_to_reg(u8 type, u8 mode, u8 value)` function in the `disp_layer.c` file, which can be found in the `/usr/local/src/linux/linux-sunxi-lemaker/drivers/video/sunxi/disp` directory (line 95 to 99):

```
/*      else {
            DE_WRN("not supported yuv channel format:%d in "
                    "img_sw_para_to_reg\n", value);
            return 0;
        }*/
```

The same applies to lines 125 to 129:

```
/*      else {
          DE_WRN("not supported yuv channel pixel sequence:%d "
                    "in img_sw_para_to_reg\n", value);
            return 0;
        }*/
```

You can also apply this to lines 168 to 172:

```
/*      else {
          DE_WRN("not supported image0 pixel sequence:%d in "
                    "img_sw_para_to_reg\n", value);
            return 0;
        }*/
```

Finally, comment out the following line as well (near line 175):

```
//   DE_WRN("not supported type:%d in img_sw_para_to_reg\n", type);
```

Activating IR driver key repetition

By default, the infrared driver recognizes a remote button key press only once, no matter how long it is kept pressed. When changing, for example, the volume of a television program, it would be nice if we could simply hold the remote button pressed until the intended volume has been reached, rather than pressing the same button several times. For the activation of this feature, we add one additional line into the `sunxi-ir` driver, which is called `/usr/local/src/linux-sunxi-lemaker/drivers/input/keyboard/sunxi-ir.c`:

```
static u32 ir_gpio_hdle;

#define REPORT_REPEAT_KEY_VALUE

#de0fine SYS_CLK_CFG_EN
```

> If the Banana Pro IR receiver also listens to the remote control of another device, the `sunxi-ir` driver can be set to the fixed address of the Banana Pro remote control. In this case, add an additional definition to the `sunxi-ir` driver (it should be same as listed above—`sunxi-ir.c`):
>
> ```
> #define IR_ADDR_CODE 0xff00 /* Add the remote control
> address here */
> ```

Activating the sunxi lirc driver

The previously mentioned `sunxi-ir` driver can only be used for NEC remote protocols (`https://en.wikipedia.org/wiki/Consumer_IR`). This limits the range of usable remote controls. There is another **Linux Infrared Remote Control** (**LIRC**) driver available, which does not filter any specific protocol. Again, the driver can be copied from the `linux-sunxi-danand` kernel branch to the staging directory of the LeMaker kernel, as follows:

```
cd /usr/local/src
git clone https://github.com/dan-and/linux-sunxi.git linux-sunxi-danand
cp /usr/local/src/linux-sunxi/drivers/staging/media/lirc/* /usr/local/src/linux-sunxi-lemaker/drivers/staging/media/lirc
```

The sunxi LIRC driver must be enabled as the staging driver after invoking `sudo make menuconfig`. This is shown in the following screenshot:

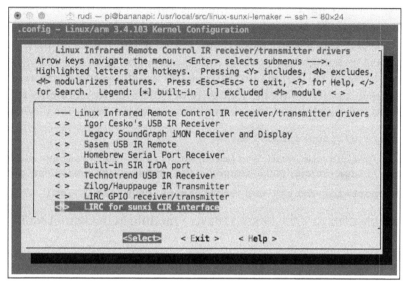

Figure 3

Correcting display driver brightness

The original display driver contains the following illogical line of code or something similar to it in the `drivers/video/sunxi/disp/de_fe.c` file around line 1385:

```
bright = (bright*64)/100;
bright = (saturation*64/100);
bright = (contrast*64/100);
bright = (hue*64)/100;
```

The `bright` variable is set four times to different values and only the very last setting is valid. Change these lines as follows:

```
bright = DIV_ROUND_CLOSEST((clamp(bright, 0, 100) * 63), 100);
saturation = DIV_ROUND_CLOSEST((clamp(saturation, 0, 100) * 63), 100);
contrast = DIV_ROUND_CLOSEST((clamp(contrast, 0, 100) * 63), 100);
hue = DIV_ROUND_CLOSEST((clamp(hue, 0, 100) * 63), 100);
```

Adding the DVB-SKY S960 USB box

A very good DVB-S2 USB box is currently being offered by DVB-SKY, China (`http://www.dvbsky.net`). The company was founded in 2010 and focuses on multimedia products, such as PC tuners and embedded digital video systems. Although DVB-SKY already provides many kernel drivers, none of their drivers for S960 on their web page has worked with Banana Pro. While S960 has had Linux support since kernel 3.19, Banana Pro images still use the kernel version of 3.4.x. However, there is a patch available that provides the S960 functionality on Banana Pro. Download this patch into Linux kernel directory and apply it as follows:

```
cd /usr/loca/src/linux-sunxi-lemaker
```

```
wget https://github.com/vonfritz/meta-sunxi/raw/test-master/recipes-kernel/linux/linux-sunxi/0001-support-for-dvbsky-usb-receiver.patch
```

```
cat 0001-support-for-dvbsky-usb-receiver.patch | patch –sp1
```

Be sure to enable `CONFIG_DVB_M88DS3103` as a module in the kernel config (`make menuconfig`).

After all the changes have been applied, compile the new kernel and install it as described in *Chapter 2*, *Programming Languages*.

Installing the accelerated mali driver

In this section, we will install the `mali` driver from sources. In addition to this, we will install the X11 framebuffer turbo driver. You can skip this step if the driver has already been installed as described in *Chapter 1*, *Introduction to Banana Pro*. The following packages need to be installed before executing the `mali` driver installation:

```
sudo apt-get install git build-essential autoconf libtool libx11-dev libxext-dev libdrm-dev x11proto-dri2-dev libxfixes-dev automake xorg-dev xutils-dev x11proto-dri2-dev libltdl-dev
```

1. In the first step, we will install the `ump` module from sources:

    ```
    sudo su
    cd /usr/local/src
    git clone https://github.com/linux-sunxi/libump.git
    cd libump
    autoreconf -i
    ./configure --prefix=/usr
    make
    make installldconfig
    ```

2. Before we can install the `mali` driver, we need to install `libdri2` first:

```
sudo su

git clone https://github.com/robclark/libdri2
cd libdri2
./autogen.sh
./configure --prefix=/usr
make
make install
ldconfig
```

3. In the next step, we will install the `mali` driver:

```
sudo su
cd /usr/local/src

git clone --recursive https://github.com/linux-sunxi/sunxi-mali.
git
cd sunxi-mali
make config
make install
```

4. If you didn't do this in *Chapter 1, Introduction to Banana Pro*, install the X11 framebuffer turbo driver now:

```
sudo su
cd /usr/local/src

git clone https://github.com/ssvb/xf86-video-fbturbo.git
cd xf86-video-fbturbo
autoreconf -vi
./configure --prefix=/usr
make
make install
cp xorg.conf /etc/X11/xorg.conf
```

Video Disk Recorder (VDR)

Klaus Schmidinger's VDR (http://www.tvdr.de) is a very popular software that's used to watch TV. Using a DVB stick or card, VDR provides a full-featured hard disk recorder for terrestrial (DVB-T), cable (DVB-C), or satellite (DVB-S) television. In this chapter, we will compile VDR from sources, including all its prerequisites.

Setting display settings

This chapter assumes a running X-desktop environment using the xf86-video-fbturbo driver (*Chapter 1, Introduction to Banana Pro*). In the first step, we set the television output to the full HD (1920x1080) progressive mode. Later on, we will add a deinterlacer to libvdpau. This deinterlaver will enhance picture quality for interlaced video content. Make sure that your /boot/uEnv.txt file contains the following entries:

```
console=tty1

root=/dev/mmcblk0p1 rootwait

#root=/dev/sda2 rootwait

extraargs=rootfstype=ext4 sunxi_ve_mem_reserve=190 sunxi_g2d_mem_
reserve=16 sunxi_fb_mem_reserve=32 hdmi.audio=EDID:1 disp.screen0_output_
mode=1920x1080p50 panic=10 consoleblank=0

script=bananapi.bin

kernel=uImage
```

The first line defines the tty1 terminal (boot terminal) as the console. All boot messages will be shown in this terminal. The root filesystem is booted from the first partition of memory block devices (the mmcblkp1 microSD card). The additional rootwait parameter will wait until the boot device is available. The third line is commented out. It can be commented in instead of the second line if the root filesystem is located on a hard disk drive. In the preceding example, the second partition (/dev/sda2) on the hard disk is used for the root filesystem. The extraargs line provides the following parameters:

- This rootfstype parameter describes the root filesystem type. In the preceding case, the .ext4 filesystem is used.

- Older Linux kernels allow the reservation of memory for the graphics driver, on-screen-display, and the framebuffer. We reserve the maximum possible amount of memory for our Multimedia Center. The graphics driver memory is ignored if the kernel **Contiguous Memory Allocator** (**CMA**) mode is switched off. In the preceding section, we set this memory to 190 MB (the maximum available value).

- `hdmi.audio=EDID:1` defaults the audio output to the HDMI audio. A value of `0` (instead of `1`) can be used in order to activate the analog audio output. The audio source can be changed within the VDR later if the connected device is not EDID-capable.

- The `disp-section` overwrites the setting of the FEX file (*Chapter 1, Introduction to Banana Pro*). We set the display output to full HD (1920x80) and progressive (50 frames per second). If later on the deinterlacer of the TV is used rather than the `deinterlacer` of `libvdpau`, the `p50` parameter can be replaced by `i50` for a 50 Hz output or `i60` for a 60 Hz output. If your TV does not support full HD, set the mode to another resolution (as seen in *Chapter 1*).

- `panic=10` defines 10 seconds of default time, which the kernel will wait after a kernel panic to reboot itself. The default value of `0` would wait forever.

- `consoleblank=0` disables the screensaver for the console. A value that's different from `0` will activate the console screensaver after the given amount time in seconds. The default value is 600 (10 minutes).

The `script` line will use the `bananapi.bin` file for the configuration of Banana Pro's parameters (*Chapter 1, Introduction to Banana Pro*). Name this file in accordance with your configuration that's located in the `/boot` directory. Finally, for the boot kernel, the `uImage` file is used (refer to *Chapter 2, Programming Languages*). After changing the `uEnv.txt` file, a reboot is required in order to make the changes effective.

Setting locales

Locales in Linux are used in order to define the system language as well as additional properties. This includes a formatted output for some things, for example, date/time, numbers and decimal places, and currency. Using the correct locales is important for the correct **Electronic Program Guide** (**EPG**) representation. In the first step, we will install the required tools to configure locales. Afterwards, we will configure locales and define **Coordinated Universal Time** (**UTC**) as the time zone. An appropriate time setting is required later on to set the correct wake-up time for the timer. Let's install the required tools and configure the locales and time now as the `root` user:

```
sudo su
apt-get install mc console-data console-tools console-common debconf
dpkg-reconfigure locales
echo UTC > /etc/timezone
dpkg-reconfigure tzdata
```

Choose the UTF-8 locales for your country (for example, `en_US.UTF-8`). If a menu shows up for the `keymap` selection, choose **Don't touch keymap**.

The `ntpdate` program can be used in order to set or synchronize both date and time.

Adding (non-free) Debian multimedia packages

In a later step, some Debian packages are required. Therefore, we add the associated repository to our `sources.list` file that's located in `/etc/apt` directory:

```
deb http://www.deb-multimedia.org wheezy main non-free
```

Make sure you call the following two lines after adding the preceding line:

```
sudo apt-get update
sudo apt-get upgrade
```

Loading required modules

Using Banana Pro requires quite a few modules to be loaded during the system boot. These modules can be found in the `/etc/modules` file:

```
# Unified Memory Provider module
ump
# Mali kernel driver modules
mali
mali_drm
# IR driver
sunxi-ir
# Video engine module
sunxi_cedar_mod
```

Make sure that all the modules listed here are loaded in your `module` file. The `module` file can be edited by executing this:

```
sudo nano /etc/modules
```

A network address

This chapter assumes a running network connection as described in *Chapter 3, Wireless Projects*. The network will be required for the `tvscraper` plugin. This plugin displays movie information within **Electronic Program Guide** (**EPG**) or audio-recordings.

Editing the FEX file

The principle of the FEX file has already been described in *Chapter 1, Introduction to Banana Pro*. Make sure that the FEX file in *Chapter 1* includes the following `disp-` section:

```
[disp_init]
disp_init_enable = 1
disp_mode = 0
screen0_output_type = 3
screen0_output_mode = 4
screen1_output_type = 2
screen1_output_mode = 11
fb0_framebuffer_num = 4
fb0_format = 10
fb0_pixel_sequence = 0
fb0_scaler_mode_enable = 0
fb1_framebuffer_num = 2
fb1_format = 10
fb1_pixel_sequence = 0
fb1_scaler_mode_enable = 0
lcd0_backlight = 197
lcd1_backlight = 197
lcd0_bright = 50
lcd0_contrast = 50
lcd0_saturation = 57
lcd0_hue = 50
lcd1_bright = 50
lcd1_contrast = 50
lcd1_saturation = 57
lcd1_hue = 50
```

Remember to translate the FEX file into a binary file (refer to *Chapter 1*) using this command:

```
fex2bin bananapi.fex bananapi.bin
```

After changing the FEX and `.bin` files, a reboot is required (`sudo reboot`) in order to activate the changes.

Installing required packages

In this section, we will install the packages required for the Multimedia Center. First, we will install `deb-multimedia-keyring`, a package containing unofficial applications that could not be added to the official Debian repositories because they are released under a proprietary license:

```
sudo apt-get update
sudo apt-get install deb-multimedia-keyring
sudo apt-get update
```

Answer the question arising during the installation with y for yes. Afterwards, we will install the remaining required packages:

```
sudo apt-get install git build-essential autoconf libtool gettext
automake xutils-dev pkg-config xserver-xorg-dev libdrm-dev x11proto-
xf86dri-dev xserver-xorg debhelper dh-autoreconf x11proto-xext-dev
libxext-dev libxfixes-dev libvdpau-dev libfreetype6-dev libfontconfig1-
dev libjpeg8-dev libcap-dev libxcb-screensaver0-dev libxcb-randr0-
dev libxcb-dpms0-dev libxcb-icccm4-dev libx11-xcb-dev libxcb-ewmh-dev
alsa-base alsa-utils libasound2-dev libudev-dev libglib2.0-dev libxcb-
xv0 libxcb-shm0 libxcb-dpms0 libxcb-util0 libxcb-screensaver0 libxcb-
keysyms1 libxcb-icccm4 libxcb-glx0 libxcb-randr0 psmisc libncurses5-dev
libncursesw5-dev
```

The `softhddevice` VDR output device requires the `ffmpeg` package, which we will install from sources as the `root` user. The compilation processes will take approximately 45 minutes:

```
su
cd /usr/local/src/
wget http://ffmpeg.org/releases/ffmpeg-2.4.4.tar.bz2
tar xfvj ffmpeg-2.4.4.tar.bz2
cd ffmpeg-2.4.4
./configure --enable-shared --prefix=/usr
make
make install
```

Installing and patching VDPAU

In this section, we will install the **Video Decode and Presentation API for Unix (VDPAU)** library. This library provides accelerated video decoding and is used by `softhddevice` for both SD and HD TV decoding. Jens Kuske has provided the original branch for the Allwinner Mali devices (SUNXI) in GitHub `https://github.com/linux-sunxi/libvdpau-sunxi`. For the Multimedia Center, I've used a modified version located at `https://github.com/zillevdr/libvdpau-sunxi`:

`su`

`cd /usr/local/src/`

`git clone -b deint https://github.com/zillevdr/libvdpau-sunxi/`

`cd libvdpau-sunxi`

`make`

`make install`

The preceding commands fetch the deinterlace branch of `libvdpau`, and then compile and install it. The initial tests that have been done with this VDPAU-library have delivered a picture, which is somewhat dark. A user with the name `Johns` provided the following patch for the VDPAU-library, which corrects this problem:

```
diff --git a/presentation_queue.c b/presentation_queue.c
index d71af3c..7377c00 100644
--- a/presentation_queue.c
+++ b/presentation_queue.c
@@ -26,6 +26,7 @@
 #include <unistd.h>
 #include <string.h>
 #include <sys/ioctl.h>
+#include <math.h>

 #include "queue.h"

@@ -83,7 +84,7 @@ VdpStatus vdp_presentation_queue_
display(VdpPresentationQueue presentation_queue
   if (!os)
      return VDP_STATUS_INVALID_HANDLE;

- task_t *task = (task_t *)calloc(1, sizeof(task_t));
+ task_t *task = (task_t *)malloc(sizeof(task_t));
   task->when = vdptime2timespec(earliest_presentation_time);
```

```
    task->clip_width = clip_width;
    task->clip_height = clip_height;
@@ -91,6 +92,7 @@ VdpStatus vdp_presentation_queue_
display(VdpPresentationQueue presentation_queue
    task->queue_id = presentation_queue;
    os->first_presentation_time = 0;
    os->status = VDP_PRESENTATION_QUEUE_STATUS_QUEUED;
+   os->first_presentation_time = 0;

    if(q_push_tail(queue, task))
    {
@@ -252,14 +254,24 @@ static VdpStatus do_presentation_queue_
display(task_t *task)
      // set doing this unconditionally is costly.
      if (os->csc_change) {
        ioctl(q->target->fd, DISP_CMD_LAYER_ENHANCE_OFF, args);
-       args[2] = 0xff * os->brightness + 0x20;
+
+       VDPAU_DBG(">bright %g contrast %g saturation %g hue %g",
+       (double)os->brightness, (double)os->contrast,
+         (double)os->saturation, (double)os->hue);
+
+       args[2] = (os->brightness + 1.00) * 50;
        ioctl(q->target->fd, DISP_CMD_LAYER_SET_BRIGHT, args);
-       args[2] = 0x20 * os->contrast;
+       if ( os->contrast <= 1.00 )
+         args[2] = os->contrast * 50;
+       else
+         args[2] = 50 + (os->contrast - 1) * 50 / 9;
        ioctl(q->target->fd, DISP_CMD_LAYER_SET_CONTRAST, args);
-       args[2] = 0x20 * os->saturation;
+       if ( os->saturation <= 1.00 )
+         args[2] = os->saturation * 50;
+       else
+         args[2] = 50 + (os->saturation - 1) * 50 / 9;
          ioctl(q->target->fd, DISP_CMD_LAYER_SET_SATURATION, args);
-         // hue scale is randomly chosen, no idea how it maps exactly
-       args[2] = (32 / 3.14) * os->hue + 0x20;
+       args[2] = 50 + (50 / M_PI) * os->hue;
        ioctl(q->target->fd, DISP_CMD_LAYER_SET_HUE, args);
        ioctl(q->target->fd, DISP_CMD_LAYER_ENHANCE_ON, args);
        os->csc_change = 0;
```

Without the preceding code patch, the picture provided to the TV is somewhat dark. By applying the changes above, this problem is solved and the picture has the correct level of brightness.

The preceding patch was written for an older version of `libvdpau`. Thus, the Linux command patch cannot be used in order to apply this patch. The patch needs to be applied manually. In order to do this, edit the `presentation_queue.c` file within the `libvdpau` directory (`/usr/local/src/libvdpau-sunxi`). Uncomment all the lines within this file, where the patch shows - as the first character, and add all the lines that have + as the first character. Take a look at this example:

```
-   task_t *task = (task_t *)calloc(1, sizeof(task_t));
+   task_t *task = (task_t *)malloc(sizeof(task_t));
```

The preceding lines will look like this:

```
// task_t *task = (task_t *)calloc(1, sizeof(task_t));
task_t *task = (task_t *)malloc(sizeof(task_t));
```

In the meantime, the deinterlace branch of `libvdpau` is available at `https://github.com/linux-sunxi/libvdpau-sunxi/tree/staging`, which can be checked out as follows:

```
git clone -b staging https://github.com/linux-sunxi/libvdpau-sunxi/
```

Compiling VDR

Now that all the required libraries have been installed, we can download and compile the VDR itself. Later on, we will add several plugins to VDR, for example, when watching DVDs or audio CDs. For now, we will only install the `softhddevice` video output device. Again, the compilation is done as the `root` user because we use the `/usr/local/src` directory:

```
su
cd /usr/local/src
wget ftp://ftp.tvdr.de/vdr/vdr-2.2.0.tar.bz2
git clone git://projects.vdr-developer.org/vdr-plugin-softhddevice.git
git clone git://projects.vdr-developer.org/vdr-plugin-streamdev.git
tar xfvj vdr-2.2.0.tar.bz2
ln -s vdr-2.2.0 VDR
cd VDR/PLUGINS/src/
ln -s ../../../vdr-plugin-softhddevice/ softhddevice
```

Before the compilation process is started, we need to apply the changes to `Makefile` of *softhddevice*. In doing so, edit `/usr/local/src/vdr-plugin-softhddevice/` `Makefile`. The first change removes the comment sign in the following line:

```
CONFIG += -DUSE_BITMAP # VDPAU, use bitmap surface for OSD
```

In the second change, we add the `-fsigned-char` compile option to the end of the following lines:

```
override CXXFLAGS += $(_CFLAGS) $(DEFINES) $(INCLUDES) \
  -g -W -Wall -Wextra -Winit-self -Werror=overloaded-virtual -fsigned-char
override CFLAGS  += $(_CFLAGS) $(DEFINES) $(INCLUDES) \
  -g -W -Wall -Wextra -Winit-self -Wdeclaration-after-statement -fsigned-char
```

Run the following commands after the preceding changes are made:

```
cd /usr/local/src/VDR
make clean
makemake plugins
make install
```

This will install VDR in `/usr/local/bin` and the plugins in `/usr/local/lib/vdr`. In the next step, we generate a directory in which recordings are saved. In addition to this, we change the rights for this directory:

```
sudo mkdir /video
sudo chmod 775 /video
```

All the configuration files for VDR are located in the `/var/lib/vdr` directory. The most important configuration file is `channels.conf` (`http://vdr-wiki.de/wiki/` `index.php/Channels.conf`). Herein, TV channels for DVB-SCT are stored as follows:

```
:-> DVB-S example
Das Erste;ARD:11837:HC34M2S0:S19.2E:27500:101=2:102=deu@3,103=mis@3;10
6=deu@106:104;105=deu:0:2810
6:1:1101:0
:-> DVB-T example
RTL Television,RTL;RTL World:538000000:B8C23D12G4I0M16T8Y0:T:27500:337
=2:338=deu@4:343:0:16405:846
8:8706:0
```

The `commands.conf` file contains commands, that can be executed once VDR has been started. This file does not exist by default. I filled it with the following commands:

```
Eject CD/DVD: /usr/bin/eject
Reboot: sudo /sbin/reboot
Halt: sudo /sbin/halt -p
```

Later on, Banana Pro will eject a DVD/CD with the help of the first command. The second and third command will reboot or halt Banana Pro. In order to software-eject a DVD or CD from a USB drive, the `eject` package must be installed if it's not already available:

```
sudo apt-get install eject
```

The remaining configuration files save the VDR settings (`setup.conf`), configure the **Digital Satellite Equipment Control (DISEQC)** settings (`diseqc.conf`), or configure remote controls (`remote.conf`). The `keymacros.conf` file defines actions that are related to certain remote control keys. Recording timers are stored in `timers.conf`. The INSTALL file, located in the `/usr/local/src/VDR` directory, contains a more detailed description of these configuration files.

In order to control VDR for the first experiments done on a keyboard, I generated the file `remote.conf` and added the following entries to it:

```
KBD.Up          00000000001B5B41
KBD.Down        00000000001B5B42
KBD.Menu        000000000000006D
KBD.Ok          000000000000000D
KBD.Back        000000000000007F
KBD.Left        00000000001B5B44
KBD.Right       00000000001B5B43
KBD.Red         0000000000000072
KBD.Green       0000000000000067
KBD.Yellow      0000000000000079
KBD.Blue        0000000000000062
KBD.0           0000000000000030
KBD.1           0000000000000031
KBD.2           0000000000000032
KBD.3           0000000000000033
KBD.4           0000000000000034
KBD.5           0000000000000035
KBD.6           0000000000000036
KBD.7           0000000000000037
KBD.8           0000000000000038
```

```
KBD.9           0000000000000039
KBD.Info        0000000000000069
KBD.Power       0000000000000070
KBD.Volume+     000000000000002B
KBD.Volume-     000000000000002D
KBD.Mute        000000000000006C
```

This file maps some keys of the keyboard to functions of VDR. Pressing *M* will show the menu later on. The arrow key will allow navigation in the VDR menu, and the red, green, yellow and blue buttons are represented by the *R*, *G*, *Y*, and *B* keys. *OK* is represented by the *Enter* keypress. Additionally, numbers (0…9) are provided by the associated keys. In a later section of this chapter, we will add remote control keys to this file.

Defining a sound device

In the first section of this chapter, we added an additional audio device to Banana Pro, namely the I2S audio. In this section, we will define the standard sound device for the Linux sound system **Advanced Linux Sound Architecture** (**ALSA**). Furthermore, I will show you a very simple circuit, which can be used in order to send the electrical SPDIF audio signal from the Banana Pro board. Many home theatre setups accept this audio signal.

Adding a default sound device

In order to define the default ALSA sound device, we add a file called `asound.conf` to the `/etc` directory with the following content:

```
pcm.dmixer {
  type dmix
  ipc_key 1024
  slave {
    pcm "hw:3,0"
    period_size 3000
    buffer_size 24000
    rate 48000
    format S16_LE
  }
}

pcm.sunxihdmi {
  type plug
  slave.pcm dmixer
}
```

This file defines an audio device called `sunxihdmi`. The default device is defined in the `pcm "hw:3,0"` line. Replace `3` with the card number that's provided by the `aplay -l` command. For my configuration (*Figure 2*), card 3 refers to the HDMI audio. Replace `3` with `0` for the analog audio or with 1 for the electrical SPDIF (refer to the next section).

Using an electrical SPDIF with Banana Pro

SPDIF must be activated in the kernel configuration (*Figure 1*). This section assumes an activated SPDIF device (first section of this chapter). Moreover, select the appropriate ALSA device for `asound.conf` (refer to the last section). The following figure shows the assignment of the CON6 connector of Banana Pro.

The SPDIF audio output signal is provided to pin 33 [IO-8 and SPDIF-DO (digital-out)]. In addition to this pin, a ground pin is required. This is provided by pin 34 (GND).

Both Banana Pro pins (CON6) must be connected to a circuit, as follows:

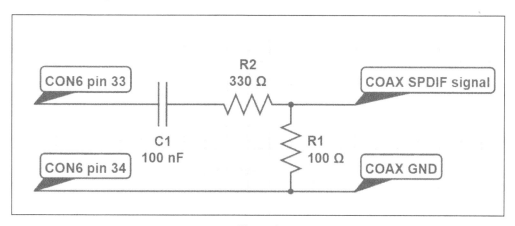

Figure 4

This circuit consists of two resistors (**330 Ω** and **100 Ω**) and one capacitor (**100 nF**). The resistors form a voltage divider, providing the correct voltage level to a coaxial electrical SPDIF cable. The capacitance decouples the SPDIF receiver from Banana Pro. **Pin 33** and **pin 34** of the Banana Pro **CON6** connector need to be connected to the left-hand side of this little circuit. One end of the coaxial cable needs to be connected to the right-hand side of the circuit.

Configuring a remote control

In this section, we will add a remote control to our Multimedia Center. For the VDR operation, we need a remote control, which features different colored buttons (red, green, yellow, and blue), arrow keys, menu key, the OK key, and the back key. One well-suited example of a remote control is shown in this image:

Figure 5: The Philips SRP2008B/86 remote control (source: Philips)

With the kernel changes shown in the first section of this chapter, there are two different IR drivers available: `sunxi_ir` and `sunxi_lirc`. As the first driver can only deal with NEC protocol remote controls, we will use the latter one. This driver works with many more remote controls. If this driver has been compiled as a module, it will be inserted using the following command:

```
sudo modprobe sunxi_lirc
```

The following step-by-step guide shows you how a remote control can be used with Banana Pro:

1. Add `sunxi_lirc` to `/etc/modules` in order to make this driver persistent. A successful insertion of the `lirc` driver will generate the `/dev/lirc0` device. If you have a remote at your fingertips, you may test the driver in a terminal, as follows:

```
sudo cat /dev/lirc0
```

2. The terminal will show a remote control button press by outputting characters.

 Only one IR driver can be loaded at a time. Therefore, be sure to not load `sunxi_ir` together with `sunxi_lirc`.

3. In the next step, we install the remote control `lirc` package. LIRC is a package that allows you to decode and send the infrared signals of many (but not all) commonly used remote controls. This package contains programs, such as `irw` or `irexec`, which will be required later on, for example, to start VDR by pushing the remote control power button. In addition to this, this package includes the `lirc` startup script:

```
sudo apt-get install lirc
```

4. Make sure that the `lirc` daemon is not running while we program a configuration file for our remote control:

```
sudo /etc/init.d/lirc stop
```

5. Before we start connecting our remote control to `lirc`, we look for valid `lirc` key names:

```
irrecord -l | grep KEY
```

6. This will list all the possible `lirc` key names, such as KEY_1 or KEY_POWER. The remote control learning process is started as follows:

```
sudo su
cd /etc/lirc
irrecord -d /dev/lirc0 lircd.conf
```

7. Follow the instructions provided by `irrecord`. If I provide the first key name for my remote control (for example, KEY_POWER) and push the remote power button afterwards, `irrecord` will provide an error message called Something went wrong. In this case, press the *Enter* key two times; `irrecord` will ask you to push one remote control button several times as fast as you can in order to recognize the key repetition rate. After this, the `/etc/lirc/lircd.conf` file will include the following content:

```
begin remote

  name   lircd.conf
  bits           33
  flags  SPACE_ENC
  eps            30
  aeps          100

  one           476   1707
  zero          476    595
  ptrail        483
  repeat       8764   2269
  gap         21693
  repeat_gap  16275
  toggle_bit_mask 0x0

    begin codes
    end codes

end remote
```

8. Now we will check if our remote control sends the key repetition code, while we keep pressing the remote control button:

    mode2 -d /dev/lirc0 -m

9. Push the remote control button and keep it pressed for a while after invoking the preceding command. For my remote control, the terminal output can be seen in the following screenshot (*Figure 4*). The mode2 command can be stopped by pressing *Ctrl* + *C*. As we can see from the output in shown in *Figure 4*, the number 16275 appears several times. It marks the end of the remote control command. The remote control repeat code can be seen in the same line as the end code. For my remote control, it is 8788 2261. Open the lircd.conf file with an editor and apply the following changes:

```
●  ◉  ●                    ⚔ rudi — pi@bananapi: ~ — ssh — 80×24
pi@bananapi:~$ mode2 -d /dev/lirc0 -m
     8724-pulse      4458-space       533-pulse       575-space      469-pulse
1706-space
         512     1663       491      575      491      575
         469      597       512      618      448     1685
         512     1727       448     1706      512     1663
         512     1706       469      575      491     1706
         469      618       469      554      533      597
         469     1685       491      554      533      575
         491      575       469      597      491      597
         491      575       469     1706      469      618
         469     1706       491     1706      491     1685
         491     1663       512     1685      491     1706
         512    21693      8767     2282      512    16275
        8788     2261       491    16275     8788     2218
         555    16275      8767     2239      533    16275
        8788     2218       533    16275     8767     2239
         512    16275      8831     2197      576    16275
        8788     2239       469    16275     8788     2282
         469    16275      8788     2303      469    16275
        8767     2261       491    16275     8810     2218
         491    16275      8746     2261      512    16275
        8788     2261       491    16275     8788     2261
         512    16275      8788     2218      491    16275
```

Figure 6: The Mode2 output when keeping a remote control button pressed

```
begin remote
  name   test
  bits   32 <- For my remote control I had to reduce this number by
1
  flags SPACE_ENC
  eps            30
  aeps          100

  one           476   1704
  zero          476    597
  ptrail        480
  repeat       8877   2261 <- Enter first 2 numbers of repeat code
here
  gap          21693
  repeat_gap   16275
  toggle_bit_mask 0x0

     begin codes
     end codes
```

As shown in the preceding example, I had to lower the number of bits by one in order to make `irrecord` work.

10. After applying these changes, we repeat the preceding `irrecord` command:

```
su

cd /etc/lirc

irrecord -d /dev/lirc0 lircd.conf
```

11. Now, connecting the remote control keys to the pressed buttons should work as expected. After all the remote control keys have been recognized, irrecord will generate a new file called /etc/lirc/lircd.conf.conf. Copy this file to /etc/lircd.conf as follows:

```
rm /etc/lirc/lircd.conf

mv /etc/lirc/lircd.conf.conf /etc/lirc/lircd.conf
```

12. My key definition is as follows:

```
KEY_POWER              0x58A7
KEY_EPG                0x39C6
KEY_MENU               0xC936
KEY_INFO               0xF10E
KEY_BACK               0x619E
KEY_OK                 0x08F7
KEY_UP                 0xD12E
KEY_DOWN               0x8976
KEY_LEFT               0x11EE
KEY_RIGHT              0xB946
KEY_RED                0xF807
KEY_GREEN              0x7887
KEY_YELLOW             0x20DF
KEY_BLUE               0x906F
KEY_CHANNELUP          0xE01F
KEY_CHANNELDOWN        0x61F4807F
KEY_0                  0x708F
KEY_1                  0x40BF
KEY_2                  0xC837
KEY_3                  0x30CF
KEY_4                  0x6897
KEY_5                  0x28D7
KEY_6                  0xE817
KEY_7                  0x18E7
KEY_8                  0xB04F
KEY_9                  0x9867
```

13. In the following step, we adapt the `/etc/lirc/hardware.conf` file to suit the requirements of Banana Pro:

```
# /etc/lirc/hardware.conf
#
# Arguments which will be used when launching lircd
LIRCD_ARGS=""

#Don't start lircmd even if there seems to be a good config file
#START_LIRCMD=false

#Don't start irexec, even if a good config file seems to exist.
#START_IREXEC=false

#Try to load appropriate kernel modules
LOAD_MODULES=true

# Run "lircd --driver=help" for a list of supported drivers.
DRIVER="default"
# usually /dev/lirc0 is the correct setting for systems using udev
DEVICE="/dev/$(ls /sys/devices/platform/sunxi_lirc.0/lirc/)"
MODULES=""

# Default configuration files for your hardware if any
LIRCD_CONF="/etc/lirc/lircd.conf"
LIRCMD_CONF=""
```

14. After we provide the preceding `hardware.conf` file, we start the `lirc` daemon again and test the working of the `lirc` configuration by calling it in a terminal:

```
sudo /etc/init.d/lirc start
irw
```

The `irw` will show the key code of the button we pushed on the remote control like this:

```
0000000061f440bf 00 KEY_1 lircd.conf
```

The `irw` command can be stopped by pressing *Ctrl* + *C*.

irexec

Later on, we want to start VDR by pushing the power button of our remote control. The `irexec` program can do this job for us. First, we start `irexec` in the `/etc/rc.local` file by adding it as follows:

```
sudo /usr/bin/irexec -d
```

Starting `irexec` from the `hardware.conf` file did not work for me. After doing this, we need to edit the `/etc/lirc/lirc/lircrc` file with the following content:

```
begin
  prog = irexec
  button = KEY_POWER
  config = /usr/local/bin/runvdr
end
```

This configuration will start the `/usr/local/bin/runvdr` script, which we will generate later. In this file, we will start VDR.

Adding a USB DVB stick

In order to watch TV, we need to add at least one DVB stick. In this section, I will explain the installation of a DVB-T stick using the kernel driver, two DVB-S2 sticks using the kernel driver, and a DVB-S2 stick using userspace drivers.

The DVB kernel driver

Figure 7

The installation of a DVB kernel driver follows certain steps: first, the driver must be activated in the kernel; second, the associated firmware file(s) must be copied into the `/lib/firmware` directory. We will now use the Elgato EyeTV DVB-T stick (*Figure 5*). This stick is one of the smallest that's available worldwide. In the LeMaker kernel (the LeMedia branch), the Elgato driver is called `dvb_as102` and is available in the kernel staging directory.

Activate this driver in the kernel configuration (*Chapter 2, Programming Languages*), as shown in the following screenshot:

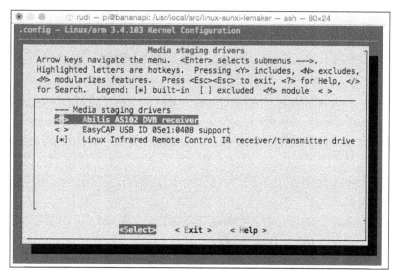

Figure 8

The firmware consists of two parts and is available at www.kernellabs.com. It must be downloaded and installed in the `/lib/firmware` directory. If `wget` is already installed, the installation of this package will not be required:

```
su
sudo apt-get install wget
cd /lib/firmware
wget http://kernellabs.com/firmware/as102/as102_data1_st.hex
wget http://kernellabs.com/firmware/as102/as102_data2_st.hex
```

The Elgato stick with the 3.4 kernel driver must be plugged into the USB port while the operation system is running. After plugging this stick in the Banana Pro USB port, the kernel messages (`dmesg`) will be as follows. For better readability, I deleted the time stamps:

```
as10x_usb: device has been detected
cma: dma_alloc_from_contiguous(cma ef0ab1c0, count 4, align 2)
cma: dma_alloc_from_contiguous(): returned d3078c80
DVB: registering new adapter (Elgato EyeTV DTT Deluxe)
DVB: registering adapter 1 frontend 0 (Elgato EyeTV DTT Deluxe)...
as10x_usb: firmware: as102_data1_st.hex loaded with success
as10x_usb: firmware: as102_data2_st.hex loaded with success
Registered device Elgato EyeTV DTT Deluxe
```

The Elgato stick is recognized automatically, and the firmware is uploaded to the stick. If autodetect does not work for you, include the `dvb-as102` in the `/etc/modules` module. After the initialization of the stick, the kernel adds `dvb` devices to the Linux device tree. The `ls -l /dev/dvb/adapter*` command shows this tree:

```
/dev/dvb/adapter1:
total 0
crw-rw---T+ 1 root video 212, 4 Mär 29 16:14 demux0
crw-rw---T+ 1 root video 212, 5 Mär 29 16:14 dvr0
crw-rw---T+ 1 root video 212, 6 Mär 29 16:14 frontend0
```

It will later on be used by VDR. A standard LeMaker kernel can make use of up to eight DVB USB sticks.

As a second example, we will demonstrate the usage of the Tevii DVB-S2 box S660.

Figure 9: The Tevii DVB-S2 USB box (source: dvbshop.net)

In the LeMaker kernel (the LeMedia branch), the driver for this DVB-S2 box is already activated. Only the firmware is missing. The firmware files are available from Tevii and can be installed by following these steps:

```
cd ~
wget http://www.tevii.com/s2_liplianin_1.tar
tar xvf s2_liplianin_1.tar
cd tevii*
cd linux/firmware/
sudo cp *.fw /lib/firmware/
```

After a reboot, you will see the following kernel messages (dmesg):

```
dvb-usb: found a 'TeVii S660 USB' in cold state, will try to load a
firmware
dvb-usb: downloading firmware from file 'dvb-usb-s660.fw'
dvb-usb: found a 'TeVii S660 USB' in warm state.
dvb-usb: will pass the complete MPEG2 transport stream to the software
demuxer.
dvb-usb: MAC address: 00:18:bd:5c:54:cc
dvb-usb: schedule remote query interval to 150 msecs.
dvb-usb: TeVii S660 USB successfully initialized and connected.
```

 Contrary to how the Elgato driver works, Tevii S660 will be reinitialized after reboot. The Elgato stick must be replugged after rebooting in order to upload the firmware files again.

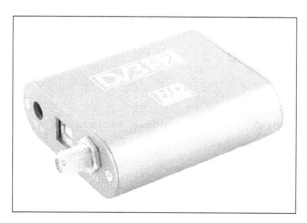

Figure 10: The DVB-SKY S960 USB receiver

The DVB-SKY USB box (*Figure 10*) also needs the correct firmware files in order to work.

The firmware itself is provided on DVB-SKY's website. The installation process is simple:

```
cd ~
wget http://www.dvbsky.net/download/linux/dvbsky-firmware.tar.gz
tar xvfz dvbsky-firmware.tar.gz
sudo cp *.fw /lib/firmware
```

The DVB userspace driver

Sundtek, Germany, does not provide a kernel source code driver. For its DVB-S2 USB stick, Sundtek also provides userspace drivers.

Figure 11: Sundtek SkyTV Ultimate IV 2015. (source: Sundtek)

The driver can be downloaded and installed from the Sundtek web page:

```
su
cd /tmp
wget http://www.sundtek.de/media/sundtek_netinst.sh
chmod 777 sundtek_netinst.sh
./sundtek_netinst.sh
```

The driver installation output is in German. So, of left at a [J/N] prompt, insert J for *Yes* (in German *Ja* means *Yes*).

After these steps, the driver is installed, and the stick can already be used for VDR. The kernel itself does not show any messages during the driver installation because the driver is a userspace driver.

VDR scripts

Before VDR can be started for the first time, we need to supply start and stop scripts and implement remote control codes into the VDR configuration setup. The VDR start script will be located in the /usr/local/bin directory and is called runvdr. Edit this new file (sudo nano /usr/local/bin/runvdr) and fill it with the following content:

```
#!/bin/sh

sudo pkill irexec

export VDPAU_DRIVER=sunxi;
export DISPLAY=:0.0;
export VDPAU_OSD=1;
export VDPAU_DEINT=1;

chmod 0777 /dev/disp;
chmod 0777 /dev/cedar_dev;
chmod 0777 /dev/g2d;

/usr/local/bin/vdr -l 0 --lirc=/dev/lircd -v /video -s /usr/local/bin/
vdrshutdown.sh \
  -P'softhddevice -f -a hw:3,0'

sudo pkill irexec
sudo irexec -d
```

Afterwards, change the rights of this script using this command:

`sudo chmod 775 /usr/local/bin/runvdr`

Within this script, `irexec` is killed first. This is required because we will start VDR using the power button of the remote control and we only want to start it once. The next remote control power button push shall end VDR. In the `export` section of the preceding script, system variables are set for display and VDPAU. Within the VDPAU section, `de-interlacer` is also switched on. In the `chmod` section of the preceding script, executable rights are set for the display, video acceleration, and the on-screen display. VDR itself is started without any logging (`-1 0`), the `/video` video directory, and the `/usr/local/bin/vdrshutdown.sh` shutdown script. In addition to VDR itself, we start the `softhddevice` output plugin, which is started in the (`-f`) fullscreen mode and uses the (`-a hw:3,0`) HDMI output. Refer to the *Defining a sound device* section on how to change audio output from HDMI to analog or SPDIF. For example, use –a `hw:0,0` for analog the audio output.

In the next step, we will add the VDR shutdown script. Edit the new `/usr/local/bin/vdrshutdown.sh` file, and add the following content:

```
#!/bin/sh
# VDR shutdown script

TIMER=$((($2-300)/60))
#echo "/usr/local/bin/runvdr" | at now + $TIMER min
for i in $(atq | cut -f 1); do atrm $i; done
/usr/bin/at -f /usr/local/bin/runvdr now + $TIMER min

svdrpsend HITK Menu
svdrpsend HITK Right
svdrpsend HITK Right
svdrpsend HITK Up
svdrpsend HITK OK
svdrpsend HITK Right
svdrpsend HITK OK
svdrpsend HITK OK
exit 1
```

Make this file executable and install at-daemon. This daemon is required for the wake-up on timer. In addition to this, the script calls several `svdrpsend` daemon actions, which close VDR:

```
sudo chmod 775 /usr/local/bin/vdrshutdown.sh
sudo apt-get install at
```

The VDR shutdown script provides the next timer to the at-daemon. This daemon will start VDR again 5 minutes before the actual recording.

Finally, we need to add the `lirc` remote control keys to the `/var/lib/vdr/remote.conf` file. These lines can be added at the end of this file:

```
LIRC.Up           KEY_UP
LIRC.Down         KEY_DOWN
LIRC.Menu         KEY_MENU
LIRC.Ok           KEY_OK
LIRC.Back         KEY_BACK
LIRC.Left         KEY_LEFT
LIRC.Right        KEY_RIGHT
LIRC.Red          KEY_RED
LIRC.Green        KEY_GREEN
LIRC.Yellow       KEY_YELLOW
LIRC.Blue         KEY_BLUE
LIRC.0            KEY_0
LIRC.1            KEY_1
LIRC.2            KEY_2
LIRC.3            KEY_3
LIRC.4            KEY_4
LIRC.5            KEY_5
LIRC.6            KEY_6
LIRC.7            KEY_7
LIRC.8            KEY_8
LIRC.9            KEY_9
LIRC.Info         KEY_INFO
LIRC.Play/Pause   KEY_PLAY
LIRC.Record       KEY_RECORD
LIRC.FastFwd      KEY_F5
LIRC.FastRew      KEY_F4
LIRC.Power        KEY_POWER
LIRC.Channel+     KEY_CHANNELUP
LIRC.Channel-     KEY_CHANNELDOWN
LIRC.Volume+      KEY_VOLUMEUP
LIRC.Volume-      KEY_VOLUMEDOWN
LIRC.Mute         KEY_MUTE
LIRC.Audio        KEY_AUDIO
```

After reboot (`sudo reboot`), VDR can be started by pushing the power button of the remote control.

> If VDR does not start correctly, it can be started manually from a terminal using the following command:
>
> `sudo /usr/local/bin/runvdr`
>
> If no `remote.conf` file is provided and any remote control key is pressed after starting VDR, it will recognize the remote control and guide the user through a setup procedure. The same applies to the keyboard.

VDR, including OSD, will look similar to what is shown in this screenshot:

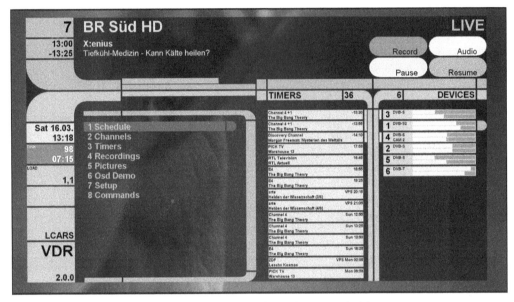

Figure 12: A screenshot of VDR (source: tvdr.de)

Adding plugins to VDR

In this section, we will install a few plugins for VDR. These plugins can be used in order to watch DVDs, listen to audio CDs, watch teletext, and much more. A complete overview regarding the VDR plugins are available at `http://www.vdr-wiki.de/wiki/index.php/Plugins`. The principal installation for all VDR plugins is identical: the source code of the plugins must be placed in the `/usr/local/src/vdr-2.2.0/PLUGINS/src` directory. Compilation and installation are started in the main VDR directory with this command:

```
sudo make plugins
sudo make install
```

Watching DVDs

In order to watch DVDs with Banana Pro, a USB DVD player must be connected to the embedded board. Before the VDR DVD plugin can be installed, some additional packages must be installed first:

```
sudo apt-get install cvs a52dec-dev libdvdnav-dev libdvdread-dev
```

Watching commercial DVDs requires the installation of the libdvdcss2 package. From a legal point of view, the installation of libdvdcss2 is controversial. The installation itself can be realized using this command:

```
sudo apt-get install libdvdcss2
```

The DVD plugin can be installed using the **Concurrent Version System** (**CVS**):

```
su
cd /usr/local/src/vdr-2.2.0/PLUGINS/src
cvs -d:pserver:anonymous@dvdplugin.cvs.sourceforge.net:/cvsroot/dvdplugin
login
cvs -z3 -d:pserver:anonymous@dvdplugin.cvs.sourceforge.net:/cvsroot/
dvdplugin co -P dvd
```

Before the compilation process is started, Makefile of the video output plugin (softhddevice) must be changed. This file is located in the /usr/local/src/vdr-2.2.0/PLUGINS/softhddevice directory.

Uncomment the following line within this file:

```
CONFIG += -DUSE_VDR_SPU       # use VDR SPU decoder.
```

Before the compilation process is started, two source code changes need to be applied to the DVD plugin. Note line 284 in the /usr/include/dvdnav/dvdnav.h file:

```
dvdnav_status_t dvdnav_program_play(dvdnav_t *this, int32_t title,
int32_t pgcn, int32_t pgn);
```

It needs to be replaced with the following:

```
dvdnav_status_t dvdnav_program_play(dvdnav_t *self, int32_t title,
int32_t pgcn, int32_t pgn);
```

Additionally, change line 378 in the /usr/local/src/vdr-2.2.0/PLUGINS/src/dvd/player-dvd.c file from DeviceTrickSpeed(sp); to DeviceTrickSpeed(sp, false);.

Now, start the compilation process:

```
su
cd /usr/local/src/vdr-2.2.0
sudo make plugins
sudo make install
```

Finally, add the DVD plugin in /usr/local/bin/runvdr:

```
/usr/local/bin/vdr -l 0 --lirc=/dev/lircd -v /video -s /usr/local/bin/
vdrshutdow
n.sh \
-P'softhddevice -f -a hw:3,0' \
 -Pdvd
```

After the next reboot, the dvd plugin will be available.

Listening to audio CDs

What would a Multimedia Center be without the option to play audio CDs? The VDR cdplayer plugin can be installed from a mercurial repository. Therefore, we install mercurial together with the developer packages of libcdoi and libcddb. Later, the library can check the CD database (CD db) and provide CD text:

```
sudo apt-get install mercurial
sudo apt-et install libcdio-dev
sudo apt-get install libcddb-dev
```

The installation of cdplayer can be done using these commands:

```
su
cd /usr/local/src/vdr-2.2.0/PLUGINS/src/
hg clone http://hg.uli-eckhardt.de/cdplayer
```

The cdplayer plugin requires the installation of one additional file into the VDR plugin of the configuration directory:

```
sudo mkdir /var/lib/vdr/plugins/cdplayer
sudo cp /usr/local/src/vdr-2.2.0/PLUGINS/src/cdplayer/contrib/cd.mpg /
var/lib/vdr /plugins/cdplayer
```

The compilation process has already been described previously. Also, the `cdplayer` plugin must be added to `/usr/local/bin/runvdr`:

```
/usr/local/bin/vdr -l 0 --lirc=/dev/lircd -v /video -s /usr/local/bin/
vdrshutdow

n.sh \
 -P'softhddevice -f -a hw:3,0' \
 -Pdvd \
 -Pcdplayer
```

 Make sure that the line with the last plugin in the `runvdr` file is not terminated by a backslash. In addition to this, there must be no empty space after a line termination when pressing the *Backspace* button.

Watching teletext

Teletext delivers quick information on different topics while you watch TV. The VDR `teletext` plugin does this job even in the on-screen display:

Figure 13: The VDR teletext plugin. (source: VDR wiki)

The VDR `teletext` plugin will be checked out from GitHub:

```
cd /usr/local/src/vdr-2.2.0/PLUGINS/src
git clone git://projects.vdr-developer.org/vdr-plugin-osdteletext.git
```

It is compiled and installed in the same way as described previously. The associated line in `runvdr` is:

```
-P'osdteletext --directory=/dev/shm --cache-system=packed --max-
cache=128'
```

Changing VDR's skin

In this section, we will provide a new skin for VDR. We will install the `nOpacity` skin and a scraper, which provides pictures and additional content information to **Electronic Program Guide** (**EPG**) and recordings. The look of the `nOpacity` plugin can be seen in the following screenshot:

Figure 14: The skin of VDR nOpacity (source. http://projects.vdr-developer.org/projects/skin-nopacity/wiki)

The `nOpacity` skin can be installed from GitHub:

```
su
cd /usr/local/src/vdr-2.2.0/PLUGINS/src
git clone git://projects.vdr-developer.org/skin-nopacity.git
```

The `nOpacity` skin itself requires `ImageMagick` or `GraphicsMagick` to display icons, channel logos, and EPG images. Install `ImageMagick` as follows:

```
sudo apt-get install imagemagick-common
```

After the *normal* plugin installation, we must take care of the paths used for icons, logos, and EPG images. The following paths can be set at startup:

```
-i path, --iconpath=path

    Path to the icons (Default: /var/lib/vdr/plugins/skinnopacity/icons/)
```

```
-l path, --logopath=path

    Path to the logos (Default: /var/lib/plugins/skinnopacity/logos/)
```

```
-e path, --epgimages=path

    Path to the epgimages (Default: /var/lib/vdr/plugins/skinnopacity/
epgimages/)
```

During a "make install", all icons and theme files are automatically copied. For channel logos, you can use logos from `https://github.com/3PO/Senderlogos`. To download them, just make a change in the directory you want to place the logos in:

```
su

cd /urr/local/src/vdr-2.2.0/PLUGINS/src

git clone https://github.com/3PO/Senderlogos.git logos
```

The VDR tvscraper plugins support the display of posters, banners, and actor thumbs in combination with the `nOPacity` skin. It can be installed as follows:

```
sudo apt-get install libsqlite3-dev libcurl4-gnutls-dev libXML2-dev
libjansson-dev
```

To clone the Git repository, use this command:

```
su

cd /usr/local/src/vdr-2.2.0/PLUGINS/src

git clone git://projects.vdr-developer.org/vdr-plugin-tvscraper.git
tvscraper-git
```

I added the following lines to `/usr/local/bin/runvdr` in order to start nOpacity together with `tvscraper`:

```
-P'skinnopacity -l /var/lib/vdr/plugins/skinflat/logos' \
-P'tvscraper -d /root/cache'
```

The `tvscraper` plugin uses the `/root/cache` directory as the cache directory. Generate this directory as follows:

```
sudo mkdir /root/cache
```

Streaming TV to mobile devices

In this section, we will install a streaming server for VDR. This streaming server can stream even on an HD TV and wirelessly to mobile devices. The `streamdev` plugin is installed as follows:

```
sudu su
cd /usr/local/src/vdr-2.2.0/PLUGINS/src
git clone git://projects.vdr-developer.org/vdr-plugin-streamdev.git
```

For all the VDR plugins, compile this add-on as follows:

```
sudo su
cd /usr/local/src/vdr-2.2.0
make
make plugins
make install
```

The compiling process generates both `streamdev-server` as well as `streamdev-client`. The latter can be used in order to connect to another VDR acting as the `streamdev-server`. A file called `streamdevhosts.conf` grants access to the streaming server. Copy this file into the plugin configuration directory:

```
sudo cp /usr/local/src/vdr-2.2.0/PLUGINS/src/streamdev/streamdevhosts.
conf.example /var/lib/vdr/plugins/streamdevhosts.conf
```

My `streamdevhosts.conf` file includes the following content:

```
#
# streamdevhosts   This file describes a number of host addresses that
#                  are allowed to connect to the streamdev server
running
#                  with the Video Disk Recorder (VDR) on this system.
# Syntax:
#
# IP-Address[/Netmask]
#

127.0.0.1            # always accept localhost
192.168.178.0/24     # any host on the local net
```

These settings grant access to the local (`192.168.178.x`) network. Replace this IP address with yours.

The `/usr/local/bin/runvdr` file must include the following line in order to activate the streaming:

```
-P streamdev-server
```

On an Android mobile phone, you can download VLC media player in order to start the streaming process. Be sure to be logged into the same network (for example, `192.168.178.x`), and call the following address in order to start the streaming of the first TV channel:

```
http://IP-address_of_VDR_Server:3000/TS/1
```

Replace `IP-address_of_VDR_server` with the IP address of the VDR server running `streamdev-server`. Replace `1` with the channel you want to stream.

Switching to external players

The last plugin I would like to describe allows you to switch between external players and VDR. This plugin can, for example, be used in order to start the XBMX media center. The `externalplayer` plugin is installed using `mercurial`:

```
su
apt-get install mercurial
cd /usr/local/src/vdr-2.2.0/PLUGINS/src
hg clone http://hg.uli-eckhardt.de/externalplayer
```

Afterwards, we create a new directory in the VDR configuration directory and copy the `externalplayer` example configuration file into this directory:

```
su
mkdir -p /var/lib/vdr/plugins/externalplayer
cp /usr/local/src/vdr-2.2.0/PLUGINS/src/externalplayer/examples/
externalplayer.conf /var/lib/vdr/plugins/externalplayer
```

Edit the file as follows:

```
    {
      MenuEntry = "XBMC";
      Command = "/usr/local/bin/start_xbmc.sh";
      OutputMode = extern;
      InputMode = normal; # XBMC should be configured for LIRC.
    }
```

The `/usr/local/bin/start_xbmc.sh` file contains the following lines:

```
cd /root
LD_LIBRARY_PATH=/usr/local/lib DISPLAY=:0.0 /allwinner/xbmc-pvr-binhf/
lib/xbmc/xbmc.bin -l /dev/lirc0
```

Additional plugins

There are more than 100 different plugins for VDR that are available. Some plugins show the telephone number of a caller, others automatically cut out an advertisement or provide the OSD of another VDR server. Now that you know how plugins can be installed principally, I invite you to test more of them. The procedure is always the same: download the plugin into the VDR plugin source directory (`/usr/local/src/VDR/PLUGINS/src`), execute the `make plugins` and `make install` commands in the VDR main directory and add the plugin via its plugin name to `/usr/local/bin/runvdr`.

Remote controlling the VDR

Wouldn't it be nice to program TV recording timers while travelling? Using `vdradmin-am`, it's now possible to do this:

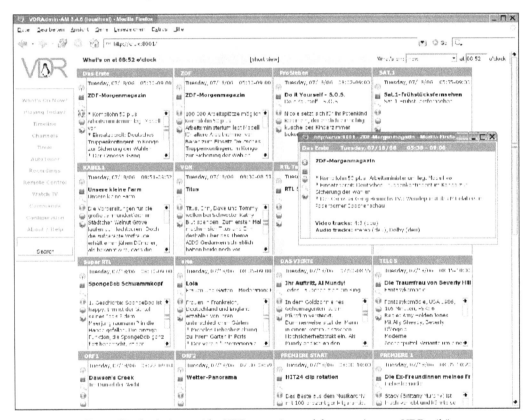

Figure 15: vdradmin provides VDR access in a web browser (source: VDR wiki)

- Follow these steps in order to install `vdradmin-am`:

```
su

apt-get install libauthen-sasl-perl libdigest-hmac-perl libio-
socket-inet6-perl

cd /usr/local/src

git clone http://projects.vdr-developer.org/git/vdradmin-am.git

cd vdradmin-am

./make.sh install

./make.sh cvs

./make.sh po
```

  During installation, the user will be prompted with a few questions. It is safe to provide default answers and simply press the *Enter* key on each question.

- The `vdradmin-am` configuration is now started with the following command:

```
vdradmind.pl --config
```

- The `vdradmind.pl` command will start the `vdradmin-am-daemon`. By default, the daemon runs on port `8001` unless otherwise stated during the configuration.

- The VDR configuration can be accessed by an external browser by typing `http://<ip/hostname>:8001/` in the browser.

  Replace `<ip/hostname>` with the IP address or the hostname of VDR Banana Pro.

Troubleshooting

This section provides some solutions to troubleshooting, which may arise.

Device permissions

The default permissions of `/dev/ump` and `/dev/mali` make these unusable for normal users. Add a file to `/etc/udev/rules.d/`, for example, called `50-mali.rules`, with the following content:

```
KERNEL=="mali", MODE="0660", GROUP="video"
KERNEL=="ump", MODE="0660", GROUP="video"
```

This should give a user belonging to the group video the right permissions to use `mali` successfully.

Changing libvdpau version

The installation of libvdpau, as described previously, works very well with VDR: the TV picture is scaled properly. However, this VDPAU library version does not work correctly with mplayer. mplayer itself works perfectly using Jens Kuske's branch of libvdpau, which can be checked out as follows:

```
git clone https://github.com/linux-sunxi/libvdpau-sunxi

cd libvdpau-sunxi

make

sudo make install
```

The mplayer itself can be used to play movies as follows:

```
mplayer -vo vdpau -vc ffmpeg12vdpau,ffh264vdpau, filename
```

Replace filename with the name of the movie to be played.

The Xbox Multimedia Center (XBMC) installation

Although Kodi (formerly known as XBMC) is not (yet) perfectly suited to use on Banana Pro, this section will describe the installation of Kodi from sources.

The only available implementation of Kodi for Banana Pro makes use of an Android library called CedarX. This is a library for the Allwinner CedarX **Video Processor Unit** (**VPU**) that's used for audio and video decoding and encoding. Additionally, libve will be used in the following description. This library provides the core of the CedarX video decoding functionality.

In order to use these libraries for Linux, a wrapper library called libhybris will be installed:

```
su

cd /

wget http://people.freedesktop.org/~siamashka/files/20130509/system.tar.
gz

tar -xzf system.tar.gz

cd /system/lib

wget https://github.com/allwinner-dev-team/android_external_cedarx/raw/
ef36cd760e9d76a2/CedarAndroidLib/LIB_JB_F23/libcedarv_adapter.so
```

```
wget https://github.com/allwinner-dev-team/android_external_cedarx/raw/
ef36cd760e9d76a2/CedarAndroidLib/LIB_JB_F23/libcedarv_base.so
```

```
wget https://github.com/allwinner-dev-team/android_external_cedarx/raw/
ef36cd760e9d76a2/CedarAndroidLib/LIB_JB_F23/libcedarxosal.so
```

```
wget https://github.com/allwinner-dev-team/android_external_cedarx/raw/
ef36cd760e9d76a2/CedarAndroidLib/LIB_JB_F23/libve.so
```

Then, we need to compile and install libhybris with the CedarX libve patches (to some directory of your choice, but not into /usr because it would clash with the GLESv2 Mali libraries):

```
git clone -b cedarx git://github.com/ssvb/libhybris.git
cd libhybris/hybris
./autogen.sh --prefix=/usr/local/hybris
make
make install
```

> Accelerated Kodi on Banana Pro currently only works with the mali driver version r3p0.

In order to install XBMC, we will first install all the required dependencies:

```
sudo apt-get update
sudo apt-get upgrade
sudo apt-get build-dep xbmc
```

In addition to this, some more packages need to be installed:

```
sudo apt-get install swig default-jre libgtk2.0-bin libssh-4 libssh-dev
```

Now, we set the hardware acceleration:

```
su
echo -e "\nA10HWR=1" >> /etc/environment
```

Native compilation of XBMC on Banana Pro requires a swap file. This fill will provide enough memory for the XBMC compilation and linking. Without a swap file, the compilation process will terminate with an out of memory message:

```
su
dd if=/dev/zero of=/swap bs=1M count=384
mkswap -c /swap
swapon /swap
```

Now, create the workspace directory and check out the XBMC source code:

```
su
cd /
mkdir melehacking
cd melehacking
git clone git://github.com/rellla/xbmca10.git
cd xbmca10
git checkout stage/Frodo
```

During the build process, the following external libraries and repositories are used or downloaded:

- `taglib`: https://github.com/downloads/taglib/taglib/taglib-1.8.tar.gz
- `cedarx`: https://github.com/linux-sunxi/cedarx-libs/tree/master/libcedarv/linux-armhf
- `libmad`: ftp://ftp.mars.org/pub/mpeg/libmad-0.15.1b.tar.gz.
- `mali`: https://github.com/linux-sunxi/sunxi-mali-proprietary/tree/master/r3p0/armhf
- `mali-dev`: https://github.com/linux-sunxi/sunxi-mali/tree/master/include

The XBMC build process is started as follows:

```
cd tools/a10/depends
make
make -C xbmc
cd ../../../
make install
```

Before we can start XBMC, we need to replace `libvecore.so` with a `symlink` to the `libhybris` wrapper:

```
cd /allwinner/xbmc-pvr-binhf/lib
mv libvecore.so libvecore.so.old_native_linux_blob
ln -s /usr/local/hybris/lib/libvecore.so libvecore.so
```

Finally, we can start XBMC, as follows:

```
cd /allwinner/xbmc-pvr-bin/lib/xbmc
/allwinner/xbmc-pvr-bin/lib/xbmc# ./xbmc.bin
```

Summary

In this chapter, we built a multimedia center, which we can use to watch TV, DVDs, or listen to audio CDs. The multimedia center can be controlled by a remote control. You learned how additional plugins can be added to the multimedia center in order to, for example, change its skin or add additional functionality such as teletext.

Finally, Kodi was installed from sources.

6
Remote Controlling a Smart Monitor Car

As this is now the dawn of the IoT age, and we see a smart home for the first time, people are increasingly paying attention to security. The IP camera is the main product that monitors an environment. However, most IP cameras are placed in the corners of a house and can't be removed. So, we can now put this IP camera in a mobile car. Banana Pro acts as a single board computer has the camera and GPIO interfaces, respectively, so it will be a very good choice to make a movable IP camera—a smart monitor car with the IP camera and remote control.

In this chapter, I will introduce you to the setup of the IP camera based on Banana Pro, and then describe what we need to set up a small mobile car. In order to realize the remote control function, I will then describe how to control the Banana Pro GPIO status via the Internet.

We will firstly install `ffmpeg` as the video streaming tool and then install `nginx` as the webserver so that we can see the video from some other Internet device. Then, we will learn how to set up the Banana Pro camera module. After the IP camera is working, we will set up a small car and use `webiopi` to remote control the car. Finally, we will combine the two functions together by modifying some part of the code of the IP camera. This chapter contains the following in detail:

- Implementing an IP camera
- Setting up the hardware of a small car
- Remote controlling a small car

Implementing the IP camera

First, download and install the `Raspbian_For_BananaPro` image from
`http://www.lemaker.org/product-bananapro-download-16.html`.

At the time of writing this chapter, I've used the `Raspbian_For_BananaPro_v1412`
version as the base kernel image.

After installing Raspbian for the Banana Pro image, we'd better use the `bpi-config`
tools to expand the root filesystem:

```
sudo bpi-config
```

Select the first item to expand the filesystem. Then, finish rebooting the system.

Make sure that your Banana Pro can connect to your router network, regardless of
whether it's via Ethernet or the wireless connection.

We create a directory as the workspace for this project:

```
cd ~
mkdir remote_monitor_car
```

So, `remote_monitor_car` would be the workspace for all the source code.

Installing ffmpeg

The `ffmpeg` is the leading multimedia framework, and it is able to decode, encode,
transcode, mux, demux, stream, filter, and plays pretty much anything that humans
and machines have created. It supports all kinds of formats, ranging from the most
obscure and ancient to the cutting edge.

It contains `libavcodec`, `libavutil`, `libavformat`, `libavfilter`, `libavdevice`,
`libswscale`, and `libswresample`, which can be used by applications. It also contains
`ffmpeg`, `ffserver`, `ffplay`, and `ffprobe`, which can be used by end users for the
purposes of transcoding, streaming, and playing.

You can get more information on `ffmpeg` by visiting `http://ffmpeg.org/`.

Later, we will use *v4l2* to get the video from camera, and *x264* to encode the video.
Then, we'll stream the video via the **Real Time Message Protocol** (**RTMP**). So, in
order to build `ffmpeg` with these functions, we first need to the install `libx264`,
`libv4l`, and `librtmp` developing packages:

```
sudo apt-get install libx264-dev libmp3lame-dev libpulse-dev libv4l-dev
libtheora-dev libvorbis-dev libopencore-amrnb-dev libopencore-amrwb-dev
libvo-amrwbenc-dev librtmp-dev
```

After this, we need to download and build the `ffmpeg` source code:

```
cd ~/remote_monitor_car
git clone git://source.ffmpeg.org/ffmpeg.git
cd ffmpeg
./configure --prefix=/usr --enable-nonfree --enable-gpl --enable-
version3 --enable-vdpau --enable-libx264 --enable-libmp3lame --enable-
libpulse --enable-libv4l2 --enable-libtheora --enable-libvorbis --enable-
libopencore-amrnb --enable-libopencore-amrwb --enable-libvo-amrwbenc
--enable-librtmp
make -j2
```

This would take about 1.5 hours to finish compiling. After it's finished, we need install `ffmepg`:

```
sudo make install
```

Installing nginx

The **nginx** (**engine x**) is an HTTP and reverse proxy server, a mail proxy server, and a generic TCP proxy server. To watch the video captured by the camera, we need to host an `nginx` web server on Banana Pro. Here, we download `ngx_openresty` because it is a full-fledged web application server that bundles the standard `nginx` core, lots of third-party `nginx` modules, and most of their external dependencies. The `ngx_openresty` project provides convenience when compiling and installing `nginx` based applications.

Download `nginx_openresty` from a fork:

```
cd ~/remote_monitor_car
git clone https://github.com/Tony-HIT/bananapro_ipcamera.git
cd bananapro_ipcamera
```

Before compiling OpenResty, we need to install some necessary packages:

```
sudo apt-get install libpcre3 libpcre3-dev openssl libssl-dev
```

Then, we can build the `nginx` webserver with the RTMP module:

```
sudo rm -f -R /usr/local/live
./configure  --prefix=/usr/local/live  \
        --add-module=bundle/nginx-rtmp-module  \
        --with-http_ssl_module  \
```

```
    --with-http_mp4_module  \
    --with-pcre-jit
make -j2
```

It would take about half an hour to finish the compiling; after this, we need install `nginx`:

```
sudo make install
```

Configuring the nginx server

In order to use the `nginx` server normally, we need to configure and make some modifications after installing the preceding `nginx` server.

Starting the nginx server

Initially, enter the following command to start the `nginx` server:

```
sudo /usr/local/live/nginx/sbin/nginx
```

You will see the following **1936.error.log** error:

```
bananapi@lemaker ~/remote_monitor_car/bananapro_ipcamera $ sudo /usr/local/live/nginx/sbin/nginx
nginx: [emerg] open() "/home/logs/nginx-rtmp/1936.error.log" failed (2: No such file or directory)
```

We can solve this using following three steps:

1. Edit the `/usr/local/live/nginx/conf/nginx.conf` configuration file to change the log file location (at line 95 and line 103):

    ```
    error_log /usr/local/live/nginx/logs/nginx-rtmp/1936.error.log;

    rtmp {
            log_format access_log_rtmp
            '$remote_addr,[$time_local],$command,$app,$name,"$args",'
            '$bytes_received,$bytes_sent,"$flashver",$session_
    time,$session_readable_time,'
            '"$pageurl","$tcurl","$swfurl",$connection';

            access_log /usr/local/live/nginx/logs/nginx-rtmp/1936.
    access.log access_log_rtmp;
    ```

2. Add a new directory:

    ```
    sudo mkdir /usr/local/live/nginx/logs/nginx-rtmp
    ```

3. Start the `nginx` server again. Then, we can use the following command to check whether the `nginx-rtmp` port has opened:

```
sudo /usr/local/live/nginx/sbin/nginx
netstat  -an | grep 1936
```

Accessing the nginx server

To access the Banana Pro `nginx` server, enter Banana Pro's IP address in a web browser on your PC or smart phone. You can get this IP address of Banana Pro using this command:

```
ifconfig
```

After you enter the IP address, you will see this error:

This error is caused by the access permission to the `nginx` files; we should change the permission of some files, as follows:

```
sudo chmod 755 /usr/local/live/ngix/html
sudo chmod 755 /usr/local/live/ngix/html/js
```

Then, we can reboot the `nginx` server like this:

```
sudo /usr/local/live/nginx/sbin/nginx -s reload
```

Next, refresh the Banana Pro `nginx` web page on your PC or smart phone; you will see this page:

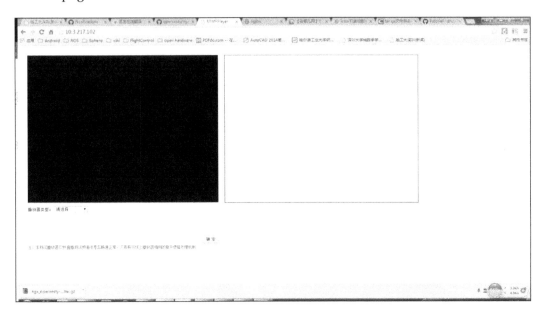

Autostarting the nginx server at system boot

Create the `/etc/init.d/nginx` file, and fill in the following content:

```
#! /bin/sh

PATH=/usr/local/sbin:/usr/local/bin:/sbin:/bin:/usr/sbin:/usr/bin

DESC="nginx daemon"
NAME=nginx
DAEMON=/usr/local/live/nginx/sbin/$NAME
CONFIGFILE=/usr/local/live/nginx/conf/$NAME.conf
PIDFILE=/usr/local/live/nginx/logs/$NAME.pid
SCRIPTNAME=/etc/init.d/$NAME

set -e
[ -x "$DAEMON" ] || exit 0

do_start() {
$DAEMON -c $CONFIGFILE || echo -n "nginx already running"
}
```

```
do_stop() {
kill -INT `cat $PIDFILE` || echo -n "nginx not running"
}

do_reload() {
kill -HUP `cat $PIDFILE` || echo -n "nginx can't reload"
}

case "$1" in
start)
echo -n "Starting $DESC: $NAME"
do_start
echo "."
;;
stop)
echo -n "Stopping $DESC: $NAME"
do_stop
echo "."
;;
reload|graceful)
echo -n "Reloading $DESC configuration..."
do_reload
echo "."
;;
restart)
echo -n "Restarting $DESC: $NAME"
do_stop
do_start
echo "."
;;
*)
echo "Usage: $SCRIPTNAME {start|stop|reload|restart}" >&2
exit 3
;;
esac

exit 0
```

After editing the /etc/init.d/nginx file, we should change the permission of the file and give it the right running level:

```
sudo chmod 755 etc/init.d/nginx file
sudo apt-get install chkconfig
```

```
sudo chkconfig -add nginx
sudo chkconfig -level nginx 2345 on
```

Then, when rebooting the system, the `nginx` sever will autostart so that we don't have to enter any command.

Setting up a camera

You can use a USB camera or the Banana Pro camera module, which can be connected to the CSI connector on the Banana Pro. The Banana Pro camera module can be bought from an online shop. Here, we will describe how to use the Banana Pro camera module as it is designed for Banana Pro:

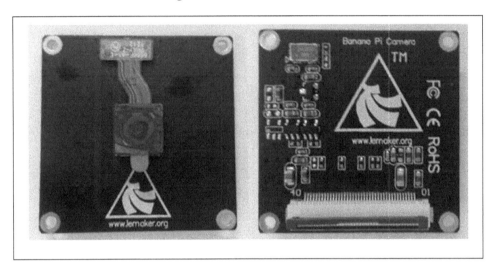

Camera specifications

The Banana Pro camera module uses the OV5640 CMOS sensor and it can capture a 500W image. You can find more details on this in the following table:

Size	8.5mm × 8.5mm × 7.0mm
Sensor type	OV5640(1/4")
Still resolution	5 megapixels
Active array size	2592 × 1944
Video mode	1080p 720p 640 x 480p
Video stabilization	No
F/No	2.8

EFL			3.37 mm
BFL(optical)			0.58 mm
Optical FOV			70°
TV distortion	Horizontal		56.3°
	Diagonal		67.4°
	<1.0%		TV distortion
IR filter			650±10nm
Object distance			20cm-180 cm
Resolution			≥200lW/PH(Center)
Image area			3673.6μm x 2738.4 μm
Pixel size			1.4μm x 1.4μm
Temperature range	Operating temperature		-30°C to 70°C
	Stable temperature		0°C to 50°C
Output formats			An 8-bit/10-bit RGB RAW output
Max frame rate			30fps@720P and VGA
IC assembly			CSP
Substrate			FPC
Assembly technique			Glue
Chief Ray Angle Correction			Yes
Automatic exposure control (AEC)			Yes
Automatic white balance (AWB)			Yes
Automatic black level calibration			Yes
Automatic black level calibration (ABLC)			Yes
Automatic 50/60 Hz luminance detection			Yes
Mirror and flip			Yes
Cropping			Yes
Lens correction			Yes
Support for LED and the flash strobe mode			Yes
On-chip phase lock loop (PLL)			Yes
The standard serial SCCB interface			Yes
Digital video port (DVP) parallel output interface			Yes
One-time programmable (OTP) memory			Yes

Connecting the camera module

When we connect the camera module to the Banana Pro, we'd better power off the Banana Pro in case of damage done to Banana Pro or the camera module.

On the camera module itself, use the very edge of your fingernail to *gently* raise the black section of the connector backward. It will swing open to a maximum of 90 degrees (similar to how a RAM module fits into a motherboard, although this is only typically 30-45 degrees of movement).

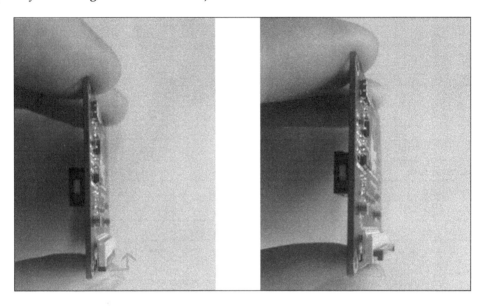

Taking the ribbon cable, we see that on each end, there is a silvered end (with the cables exposed), and on the reverse of this is a blue band The other end of the ribbon has these switched around so that the silvered parts are on opposite sides of the ribbon at each end.

With one end of the blue band facing you (this is done so that the metal ends of the ribbon meet the metal receiving pins inside the connector; use a magnifying glass to check this if you want), insert the end of the ribbon into the connector of the camera module. There are two little guides to help you do this. Don't rush it, and make sure it is seated properly and fully (otherwise, you run the risk of crimping and squashing, and potentially, damaging/ruining it) before pushing the black hinge back into position with a very satisfying *soft click*. A light tug on the ribbon will tell you if it is secure:

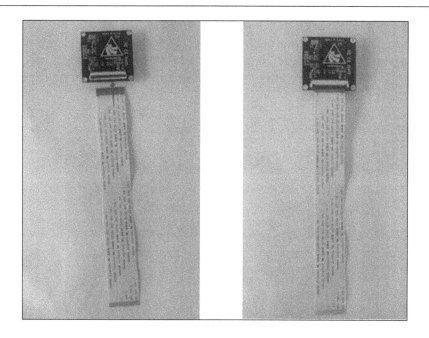

On the Banana Pro, locate `cameraconnector`. It is on the same edge of the board as the microSD card, but it is located on top.

Do not even think of trying to use the other CON2 connector, even though it looks the same. That one (it is positioned behind the Ethernet socket) is for LVDS (LCD modules, touch screens, and similar devices) and the pin definitions are VERY different.

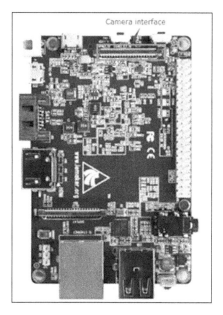

Beware! This connector for CON1 works in a different way compared to the camera module. It has a black T-bar that pushes up and down and in and out of the white part of the connector, which is fixed to the board (but it only moves by about 1 mm); it then swings back (but again, only by a small amount of about 10 degrees). Do not force it back any further!

Like you saw earlier, insert the ribbon into the slot carefully and fully and at 90 degrees (in both orientations, do this front to back *AND* from side to side) using the inner guides to assist you. Then, swing the black T-bar back and push it down.

Testing the camera module on Banana Pro

After connecting the camera module to Banana Pro correctly, we need to switch on the Banana Pro again. To use the camera module on Banana Pro, we need to load two drivers to enable the camera:

```
sudo modprobe sun4i_csi0
```

```
sudo modprobe ov5640
```

Then, we can use `mplayer` to test the camera:

```
mplayer tv://
```

If the camera has been installed properly, `mplayer` will show the image in real time:

Streaming a video via the Internet

After `nginx` and the camera module have been set up correctly, we can stream the video via the Internet using `ffmpeg` and view it on another device by following these steps:

1. Start streaming the video on the Banana Pro:

    ```
    ffmpeg -f video4linux2 -i /dev/video0 -s 640x480 -r 30 -an -g 1
    -pix_fmt yuv420p -f flv "rtmp://127.0.0.1:1936/publish/bb"
    ```

    ```
    frame=13056 fps= 15 q=24.8 size=  102470kB time=00:14:29.66 bitrate= 965.2kbits/
    frame=13064 fps= 15 q=24.8 size=  102532kB time=00:14:30.20 bitrate= 965.2kbits/
    frame=13072 fps= 15 q=24.8 size=  102594kB time=00:14:30.73 bitrate= 965.2kbits/
    frame=13080 fps= 15 q=24.8 size=  102657kB time=00:14:31.26 bitrate= 965.2kbits/
    frame=13088 fps= 15 q=24.8 size=  102719kB time=00:14:31.80 bitrate= 965.2kbits/
    frame=13096 fps= 15 q=24.8 size=  102781kB time=00:14:32.30 bitrate= 965.2kbits/
    frame=13104 fps= 15 q=24.8 size=  102844kB time=00:14:32.83 bitrate= 965.2kbits/
    frame=13112 fps= 15 q=24.8 size=  102906kB time=00:14:33.36 bitrate= 965.2kbits/
    frame=13120 fps= 15 q=24.8 size=  102968kB time=00:14:33.90 bitrate= 965.2kbits/
    frame=13128 fps= 15 q=24.8 size=  103031kB time=00:14:34.43 bitrate= 965.2kbits/
    frame=13136 fps= 15 q=24.8 size=  103093kB time=00:14:34.96 bitrate= 965.2kbits/
    frame=13144 fps= 15 q=24.8 size=  103155kB time=00:14:35.50 bitrate= 965.2kbits/
    frame=13152 fps= 15 q=24.8 size=  103218kB time=00:14:36.03 bitrate= 965.2kbits/
    frame=13160 fps= 15 q=24.8 size=  103280kB time=00:14:36.56 bitrate= 965.2kbits/
    frame=13168 fps= 15 q=24.8 size=  103342kB time=00:14:37.10 bitrate= 965.2kbits/
    frame=13176 fps= 15 q=24.8 size=  103405kB time=00:14:37.63 bitrate= 965.2kbits/
    frame=13184 fps= 15 q=24.8 size=  103467kB time=00:14:38.16 bitrate= 965.2kbits/
    frame=13192 fps= 15 q=24.8 size=  103529kB time=00:14:38.70 bitrate= 965.2kbits/
    frame=13200 fps= 15 q=24.8 size=  103591kB time=00:14:39.23 bitrate= 965.2kbits/
    frame=13208 fps= 15 q=24.8 size=  103654kB time=00:14:39.76 bitrate= 965.2kbits/
    frame=13216 fps= 15 q=24.8 size=  103716kB time=00:14:40.30 bitrate= 965.2kbits/
    frame=13224 fps= 15 q=24.8 size=  103778kB time=00:14:40.83 bitrate= 965.2kbits/
    frame=13232 fps= 15 q=24.8 size=  103841kB time=00:14:41.36 bitrate= 965.2kbits/
    frame=13240 fps= 15 q=24.8 size=  103903kB time=00:14:41.90 bitrate= 965.2kbits/
    ```

2. View the camera video on some other device, such as a PC or mobile phone. You will need to have Adobe flash player installed on your PC or mobile phone. For example, open the Chrome browser on your PC, and enter the IP address of the Banana Pro in the address bar. Then, you'll see this interface:

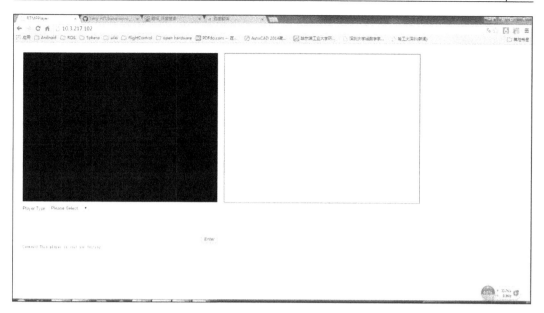

3. Use the drop-down menu on the web page to select **RTMP Player**:

4. Fill in **RTMP Address** and **FileName**. These two parameters should be identical to the `ffmpeg` streaming command. Here, the IP address of the Banana Pro is `10.3.217.102` and the file name is `bb`, so after we fill in the blanks, it should look like this:

5. Finally, we need to press the *Enter* button, and we'll see the camera video:

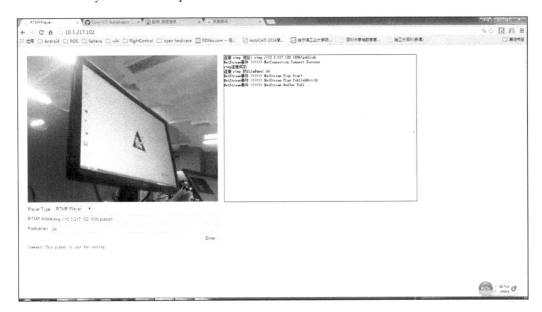

Setting up the hardware of a smart monitor car

In the preceding sections, we learned how to stream video from a camera. Now, we hope to use a mobile car to carry the camera so that we can monitor a larger environment.

Preparing the materials

To set up a small car, we need many different components, such as a car frame, DC motor, batteries, and so on.

A car suite

We can buy many different car suites from online shops. For our purposes, we will use this car suite:

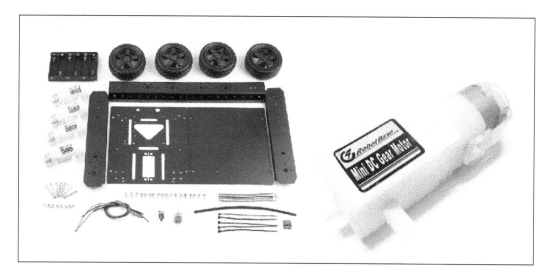

This car suite includes a car frame, four wheels, four DC motors, some cables, and screws. The most important part here is the DC motor. The DC motor only has two control pins. When the voltage difference between the two pins as well as the current is enough, the motor will rotate in two different directions according to the polarity of the voltage difference. The wheels will be connected to the motors and they will rotate together.

The L289N motor drive board

Driving the DC motor needs a high current, but the output current from the Banana Pro pins is not enough. So, we need a motor drive adapter board to make the drive current enough. The most commonly drive board consists of the ST L289N dual H bridge DC motor drive IC. There are many such L298N driver boards that can be used to drive the DC motor.

Do not connect a motor; no matter how small it is compared to the Banana Pro, it will damage Banana Pro.

Battery

Although preceding the car suit provides a battery case for you to put an AA sized battery, it is not very a good choice because the capacity is too small. We can use two 3.7V/6000mAh Li batteries for a serial connection to provide the power.

A 5 inch LCD

We also need a small LCD so that we can operate the car without the HDMI display when we make the car move on the floor:

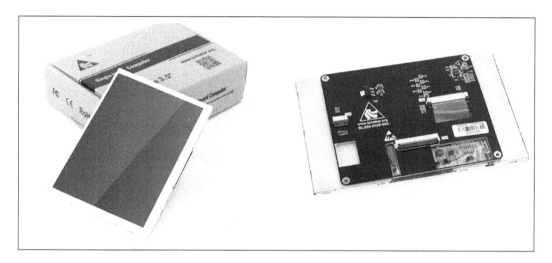

Assembly

First, we need to assemble the car frame and DC motor. We need solder two cables in each motor before we fix the motor onto the frame.

Then, we will fix the L298N motor drive board and batteries at the bottom of the car frame.

Finally, we'll connect the motor and batteries to the right connectors of the L298N motor drive board.

We can see the details of the assembly of the car in the following pictures. In order to make the wheels on the same side be controlled in the same way, we need to pay special attention to the connections between the motor and motor drive board. So, pay attention to the motor cable color and the connections between the cables and the motor drive board. Also, the negative side of the battery is connected to the GND on the motor drive board, while the positive side of the battery is connected to one of the terminals of the switch on the car frame. The other terminal of the switch is connected to the VMS on the motor drive board.

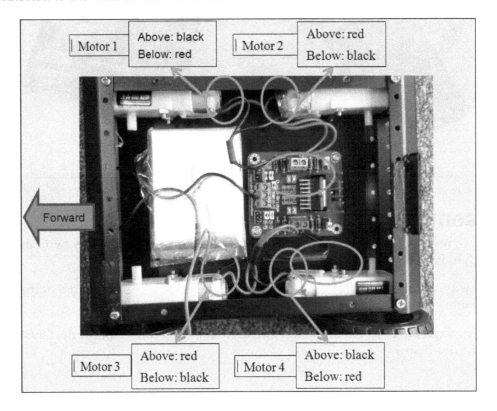

Then, we need to connect the Banana Pro to the motor drive board. The relationship between the connections can be seen in the following table:

The connection between Banana Pro and the L298N motor drive board	
Pins on Banana Pro	**Pins on the L298N motor drive board**
Pin 1	EA
Pin 13	I1
Pin 15	I2
Pin 17	EB
Pin 7	I3
Pin 11	I4
Pin 9	GND

We should remember that we need to connect the **ground** (**GND**) on Banana Pro to the GND on the motor drive board so that the reference voltage is the same.

After this, we can fix the Banana Pro to the top of the car frame. Next, we'll put the 5 inch LCD on top of the Banana Pro:

Configuring the display output for the 5 inch LCD

Firstly, download the 5 inch configuration file for Banana Pro:

```
cd /home/bananapi/remote_monitor_car
wget https://raw.githubusercontent.com/LeMaker/fex_configuration/master/
bin/banana_pro_5lcd.bin
```

Then, replace it with the old configuration file:

```
sudo cp /boot/script.bin /boot/script.bin.bak
sudo cp banana_pro_5lcd.bin /boot/script.bin
```

Finally, we can reboot the system, and we will see the display on the 5 inch LCD.

Controlling a smart monitor car using a remote

To remote control the car, we need to select the right gpio library so that we can change the IO state on the Banana Pro via the Internet. The webiopi will be the best choice. To control the movements of the car, we also need to know the control logic of the motor.

Webiopi for Banana Pro

Webiopi is originally developed for the Raspberry Pi, but it was ported to Banana Pro by LeMaker, and it is called webio-lemaker on the LeMaker GitHub account. The webiopi is a web application that allows us to control Banana Pro with the help of a browser. All the tutorials and examples for the Raspberry Pi version of webiopi can be directly used for the Banana Pro version of webiopi. As webiopi allows us to control our Banana Pro over the Internet, it's a good starting point for remote controlling from home.

Installing webiopi for Banana Pro

First, we need to download the webiopi library for Banana Pro and build it:

```
cd ~/remote_monitor_car
git clone https://github.com/LeMaker/webio-lemaker.git
cd webiopi-lemaker
sudo ./setup.sh
```

Testing webiopi on Banana Pro

After installing the Banana Pro version of `webiopi`, we can use a very easy example to test it. To create a `webiopi` project, we need three category files: the Python script, the HTML file, and the config file:

- **The Python script**: It is used to communicate with the low-level GPIO on Banana Pro; it will be loaded and executed by the `webiopi` server.

- **The HTML file**: It is used to create the web page UI. The `index.html` file is composed of a few HTML tags, including a little JavaScript part and CSS lines.

- **The config file**: It is put in the `/etc/webiopi/config` directory by default; it states the path and part of the `gpio` configuration.

Here, we use a single GPIO control function to explain the details of the basic usage of `webiopi`. Firstly, create a project folder:

```
cd ~
mkdir myproject
cd myproject
mkdir python
mkdir html
```

Secondly, create the `script.py` file in the Python folder, for example, `~/myproject/python/script.py`, and edit the file with the following content:

```
import webiopi
import datetime

GPIO = webiopi.GPIO

LIGHT = 17 # GPIO pin using BCM numbering

HOUR_ON  = 8  # Turn Light ON at 08:00
HOUR_OFF = 18 # Turn Light OFF at 18:00

# setup function is automatically called at webio-lemaker startup
def setup():
    # set the GPIO used by the light to output
    GPIO.setFunction(LIGHT, GPIO.OUT)

    # retrieve current datetime
    now = datetime.datetime.now()
```

```
    # test if we are between ON time and tun the light ON
    if ((now.hour >= HOUR_ON) and (now.hour < HOUR_OFF)):
        GPIO.digitalWrite(LIGHT, GPIO.HIGH)

# loop function is repeatedly called by webio-lemaker
def loop():
    # retrieve current datetime
    now = datetime.datetime.now()

    # toggle light ON all days at the correct time
    if ((now.hour == HOUR_ON) and (now.minute == 0) and (now.second ==
0)):
        if (GPIO.digitalRead(LIGHT) == GPIO.LOW):
            GPIO.digitalWrite(LIGHT, GPIO.HIGH)

    # toggle light OFF
    if ((now.hour == HOUR_OFF) and (now.minute == 0) and (now.second
== 0)):
        if (GPIO.digitalRead(LIGHT) == GPIO.HIGH):
            GPIO.digitalWrite(LIGHT, GPIO.LOW)

    # gives CPU some time before looping again
    webiopi.sleep(1)

# destroy function is called at WebIOPi shutdown
def destroy():
    GPIO.digitalWrite(LIGHT, GPIO.LOW)
```

Thirdly, create the index.html file in the HTML folder, for example, ~/myproject/html/index.html. The webiopi JavaScript library allows you to make your own interface easily with buttons that are bound to GPIO. You only need a single <script> tag to include /webiopi.js. It will then automatically load jQuery, which is a nice JS library. You don't need to put webiopi.js and jquery.js in your project HTML folder. You just need the <script> tag in your index.html. The webiopo server filters browser requests to serve both the webiopi.js and jquery.js files from the default webiopi resource folder. The index.html file is composed of a few HTML tags, including a little JavaScript part and a few CSS lines. The most important thing to take care of here is the anonymous JS function passed to the webiopi JS library with webiopi().ready(). This ensures that the webiopi and jQuery libraries are loaded before modifying the UI. Also, take take of the parenthesis when prefixing function calls with webiopi(). After the creation of the button, we use a jQuery function to append it to an HTML element, which is declared later in the <body> tag.

The `index.html` file content is as follows:

```
<!DOCTYPE html PUBLIC "-//W3C//DTD HTML 4.01 Transitional//EN"
"http://www.w3.org/TR/html4/loose.dtd">
<html>
<head>
        <meta http-equiv="Content-Type" content="text/html;
charset=UTF-8">
        <title>WebIOPi | Light Control</title>
        <script type="text/javascript" src="/webiopi.js"></script>
        <script type="text/javascript">
        webiopi().ready(function() {
                // Create a "Light" labeled button for GPIO 17
                var button = webiopi().createGPIOButton(17, "Light");

                // Append button to HTML element with ID="controls"
using jQuery
                $("#controls").append(button);

                // Refresh GPIO buttons
                // pass true to refresh repeatedly of false to refresh
once
                webiopi().refreshGPIO(true);
        });

        </script>
        <style type="text/css">
                button {
                        display: block;
                        margin: 5px 5px 5px 5px;
                        width: 160px;
                        height: 45px;
                        font-size: 24pt;
                        font-weight: bold;
                        color: white;
                }

                #gpio17.LOW {
                        background-color: Black;
                }

                #gpio17.HIGH {
                        background-color: Blue;
                }
```

```
        </style>
</head>
<body>
        <div id="controls" align="center"></div>
</body>
</html>
```

Then, edit `/etc/webiopi/config` as follows:

- Locate the [SCRIPTS] section, and add following line to load the Python script:

```
...
[SCRIPTS]
myproject = /home/bananapi/myproject/python/script.py
...
```

- Locate the [HTTP] section, and add following line to tell webiopi where to find your HTML resources:

```
...
[HTTP]
doc-root = /home/bananapi/myproject/html
...
```

The preceding two steps are enough to run our app, but we want to limit the GPIO to control the light only. By default, we can remotely change the functions and values of all GPIO.

- Locate the [REST] section, and add the following lines:

```
...
[REST]
gpio-export = 17
gpio-post-value = true
gpio-post-function = false
...
```

Finally, we can run `webiopi` foreground before using the daemon service:

```
sudo webiopi -d -c /etc/webiopi/config
```

We can now open the browser in our Banana Pro IP at port 8000 (10.3.217.102:8000), and we will see the following HTML interface:

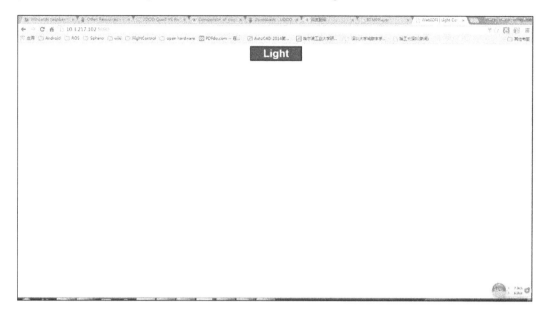

The first time you open the webiopi control interface, it will require the username and password (these are webiopi/bananapi by default).

We can click on the **Light** button to change the output state of pin 17 (this is the same as the physical pin 11 on the board).

Using webiopi to control the car

The previous section has showed us how to control the IO on the Banana Pro with the help of the webiopi library; now, we will use webiopi to control the car.

The control logic

We set motor 1 and motor 2 to the motor A group, while motor 3 and motor 4 are assigned to the motor B group. As the EA and EB control pins are directly connected to the 3.3V and 5V pins on Banana Pro, we do not need to enable EA and EB when we write the control code. We just need to control the state of **I1**, **I2**, **I3**, and **I4** pins so that we can control the motors. The control logic is shown as follows:

Control logic and car direction						
I1(13)	**I2(15)**	**I3**	**I4**	**A group**	**B group**	**Car direction**
1	0	0	1	Clockwise	Anticlockwise	Forward
0	1	1	0	Anticlockwise	Clockwise	Reverse
1	0	1	0	Clockwise	Clockwise	Left
1	0	1	0	Anticlockwise	Anticlockwise	Right
0	0	0	0	X	X	Stop

Writing the webiopi controlling code

Like the preceding testing example that we just looked at, we also need three files including the `index.html`, `script.py`, and config files.

To do this, first create a webiopi project directory for the car control code:

cd ~/remote_monitor_car

mkdir car_control

cd car_control

mkdir python

mkdir html

To realize the control via the web page, we need to use the webiopi macro mechanism as follows:

1. Firstly, we need to write the `~/remote_car_monitor/car_control/python/script.py file` according to the preceding control logic table:

```
import webiopi
import time
import sys

GPIO = webiopi.GPIO

pin7  = 4
```

```
pin11 = 17
pin13 = 27
pin15 = 22

# setup function is automatically called at WebIOPi startup
def setup():
    GPIO.setFunction(pin7,  GPIO.OUT)#all 10 --> 7
    GPIO.setFunction(pin11, GPIO.OUT)
    GPIO.setFunction(pin13, GPIO.OUT)
    GPIO.setFunction(pin15, GPIO.OUT)

    GPIO.digitalWrite(pin7,  GPIO.LOW)
    GPIO.digitalWrite(pin11, GPIO.LOW)
    GPIO.digitalWrite(pin13, GPIO.LOW)
    GPIO.digitalWrite(pin15, GPIO.LOW)



# loop function is repeatedly called by WebIOPi
def loop():
    # gives CPU some time before looping again
    webiopi.sleep(1)



# destroy function is called at WebIOPi shutdown
def destroy():
    GPIO.digitalWrite(pin7,  GPIO.LOW)
    GPIO.digitalWrite(pin11, GPIO.LOW)
    GPIO.digitalWrite(pin13, GPIO.LOW)
    GPIO.digitalWrite(pin15, GPIO.LOW)

@webiopi.macro
def stop():
    GPIO.digitalWrite(pin7,  GPIO.LOW)
    GPIO.digitalWrite(pin11, GPIO.LOW)
    GPIO.digitalWrite(pin13, GPIO.LOW)
    GPIO.digitalWrite(pin15, GPIO.LOW)



@webiopi.macro
def forward(dl):
    GPIO.digitalWrite(pin7,  GPIO.LOW)
```

```
        GPIO.digitalWrite(pin11, GPIO.HIGH)
        GPIO.digitalWrite(pin13, GPIO.HIGH)
        GPIO.digitalWrite(pin15, GPIO.LOW)
        time.sleep(dl)
        #replace GPIO.cleanup()
        GPIO.digitalWrite(pin11, GPIO.LOW)
        GPIO.digitalWrite(pin13, GPIO.LOW)


    @webiopi.macro
    def reverse(dl):
        GPIO.digitalWrite(pin7,  GPIO.HIGH)
        GPIO.digitalWrite(pin11, GPIO.LOW)
        GPIO.digitalWrite(pin13, GPIO.LOW)
        GPIO.digitalWrite(pin15, GPIO.HIGH)
        time.sleep(dl)
        #replace GPIO.cleanup()
        GPIO.digitalWrite(pin7,  GPIO.LOW)
        GPIO.digitalWrite(pin15, GPIO.LOW)


    @webiopi.macro
    def turn_left(dl):
        GPIO.digitalWrite(pin7,  GPIO.HIGH)
        GPIO.digitalWrite(pin11, GPIO.LOW)
        GPIO.digitalWrite(pin13, GPIO.HIGH)
        GPIO.digitalWrite(pin15, GPIO.LOW)
        time.sleep(dl)
        #replace GPIO.cleanup()
        GPIO.digitalWrite(pin7,  GPIO.LOW)
        GPIO.digitalWrite(pin13, GPIO.LOW)


    @webiopi.macro
    def turn_right(dl):
        GPIO.digitalWrite(pin7,  GPIO.LOW)
        GPIO.digitalWrite(pin11, GPIO.HIGH)
        GPIO.digitalWrite(pin13, GPIO.LOW)
        GPIO.digitalWrite(pin15, GPIO.HIGH)
        time.sleep(dl)
        #replace GPIO.cleanup()
        GPIO.digitalWrite(pin11, GPIO.LOW)
        GPIO.digitalWrite(pin15, GPIO.LOW)
```

2. Secondly, write the ~/remote_car_monitor/car_control/html/index. html file to create the web page with five control buttons: stop, forward, reverse, left, and right:

```
<!DOCTYPE html PUBLIC "-//W3C//DTD HTML 4.01 Transitional//EN"
"http://www.w3.org/TR/html4/loose.dtd">
<html>
<head>
        <meta http-equiv="Content-Type" content="text/html;
charset=UTF-8">
        <title>WebIOPi | Car Control</title>
        <link type="text/css" href="index.css" charset="utf-8"
rel="stylesheet">

        <script type="text/javascript" src="/webiopi.js"></script>
        <script type="text/javascript">
        webiopi().ready(function() {
        delay_time=0.03
        accel_time=0.05
        slow_time=0.01


                // Create a button to call forward macro
                var forwardBtn = webiopi().
createButton("forwardBtn", "forward", function() { //id, label,
callback
                // Call the macro
                webiopi().callMacro("forward", delay_time);
                });

                var reverseBtn = webiopi().
createButton("reverseBtn", "reverse", function() {
                        webiopi().callMacro("reverse", delay_time);
                });

                var leftBtn = webiopi().createButton("leftBtn",
"left", function() {
                        webiopi().callMacro("turn_left", delay_time);
                });

                var rightBtn = webiopi().createButton("rightBtn",
"right", function() {
                        webiopi().callMacro("turn_right", delay_time);
                });
```

```
                var stopBtn = webiopi().createButton("stopBtn",
    "stop", function() {
                    // Call the macro
                    webiopi().callMacro("stop", []);
                });

                // Append the button to the controls box using a
    jQuery function
                $("#controls").append(forwardBtn);
                $("#controls").append(reverseBtn);
                $("#controls").append(leftBtn);
                $("#controls").append(rightBtn);
                $("#controls").append(stopBtn);



                // Refresh GPIO buttons
                // pass true to refresh repeatedly of false to
    refresh once
                webiopi().refreshGPIO(true);
        });

        </script>
    </head>
    <body>
    <div>
    <h2>Remote Control By webio-lemaker</h2>
    <div id="controls"></div>
    </div>
    </body>
    </html>
```

3. Thirdly, we need to create a file, called ~/remote_car_monitor/car_
control/html/index.css, to describe the elements of the control buttons on
the web page:

```
#stopBtn {
  position:absolute;
  left:160px;
  top:60px;

  display: block;
  margin: 5px 5px 5px 5px;
  width: 150px;
  height: 50px;
```

```
    font-size: 24pt;
    font-weight: bold;
    color: white;
}

#forwardBtn {
  position:absolute;
  left:160px;
  top:150px;

  display: block;
  margin: 5px 5px 5px 5px;
  width: 150px;
  height: 50px;
  font-size: 24pt;
  font-weight: bold;
  color: white;
}

#reverseBtn {
  position:absolute;
  left:160px;
  top:300px;

  display: block;
  margin: 5px 5px 5px 5px;
  width: 150px;
  height: 50px;
  font-size: 24pt;
  font-weight: bold;
  color: white;
}

#leftBtn {
  position:absolute;
  left:10px;
  top:225px;

  display: block;
  margin: 5px 5px 5px 5px;
  width: 150px;
  height: 50px;
  font-size: 24pt;
  font-weight: bold;
```

```
        color: white;

    }

#rightBtn {
    position:absolute;
    left:310px;
    top:225px;

    display: block;
    margin: 5px 5px 5px 5px;
    width: 150px;
    height: 50px;
    font-size: 24pt;
    font-weight: bold;
    color: white;
}
```

4. Finally, we need to edit the `/etc/webiopi/config` file:

   ○ Locate the `[SCRIPTS]` section, and add the following line to load the Python script:

   ```
   ...
   [SCRIPTS]
   myscript = /home/bananapi/remote_monitor_car/
   car_control/python/script.py
   ...
   ```

   ○ Locate the `[HTTP]` section, and add following line to tell `webiopi` where to find your HTML resources:

   ```
   ...
   [HTTP]
   doc-root = /home/bananapi/remote_monitor_car/
   car_control/html
   ...
   ```

The preceding two steps are enough to run our app, but we want to limit the GPIO pins to control the car only. By default, we can remotely change the functions and values of all GPIO:

○ Locate the [REST] section, and add following lines:

```
...
[REST]
gpio-export = 4,17,27,22
gpio-post-value = true
gpio-post-function = false
...
```

Then, we can test whether the web page has the correct functions by running the following:

```
sudo webiopi -d -c /etc/webiopi/config
```

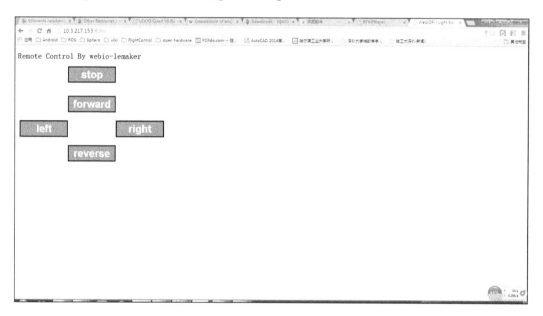

We then can switch the motor power on, and click the five buttons to see whether the car can run forward, backward, turn left, right, and finally, stop. If the direction is wrong, you need to change the control signal logic.

Adding the car controls to the IP camera web page

Previously in the *Implementing the IP camera* section, we have realized that the IP camera and car remote control function independently; now, we can add the car controlling function into the IP camera monitoring web page to remote control the car more freely. Then, we can use the device to monitor our home or explore some narrow space.

Open the `/usr/local/live/nginx/html/index.html` file and replace all the content in the file with the content which is available at `https://raw.githubusercontent.com/Tony-HIT/monitor_car_control_webiopi/master/ip_patch/index.html`.

After replacing the content of the `index.html` file, we can run the following command to start controlling the car and IP camera together.

Firstly, open a terminal and run the command as follows:

```
sudo webiopi -d -c /etc/webiopi/config
```

This is done to start the `webiopi` service.

Then, open another terminal and run this command to start the IP camera service:

```
ffmpeg -f video4linux2 -i /dev/video0 -s 640x480 -r 30 -an -g 1 -pix_fmt
yuv420p -f flv "rtmp://127.0.0.1:1936/publish/bb"
```

Now, we can open the web browser on our PC to see the new web page; it combines the IP camera video display and the `webiopi` control together:

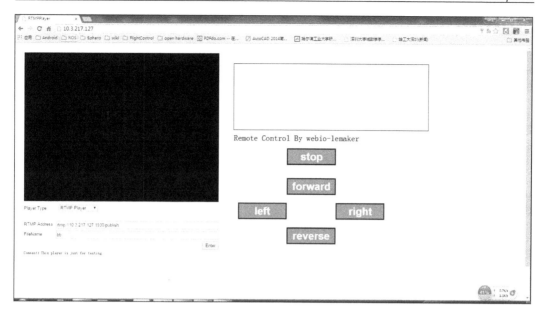

The output will look similar to what is shown in the following screenshot:

We then can click the buttons to drive the car and also see the camera video on the web page.

Summary

In this chapter, we first installed `ffmpeg` and `nginx` to make Banana Pro the IP camera server. The `ffmpeg` is used to capture videos and send them out. The `Nginx` is used to host the web server function.

Then, we learned how to connect the Banana Pro camera and run the driver of the Banana Pro camera. Then, we combined `ffmpeg`, `nginx` and the camera together to stream videos via the Internet.

Next, we set up a small mobile car that had four wheels, and we also learned how to install a 5 inch LCD on the Banana Pro so that we could operate it from anywhere directly using this LCD.

Then, we used the `webiopi` library for Banana Pro to realize the remote control of the Banana Pro GPIO so that we could drive the car using some other Internet device.

Finally, we combined the IP camera and remote car controls together to realize the whole remote monitor car system.

After the chapter, you learned how to setup a remote monitor car system, then you can also extend the application by adding some motion detection or face detection to get more powerful function.

7
A Laser Engraver

When we take a look at a laser machine, it seems very expensive and technical to use. However, with the help of open source hardware, we can make a laser machine prototype using open source software. A laser engraving machine is a kind of photoelectric combination of **numerical control** (**NC**) machine tools. It can be widely used in all kinds of nonmetal materials for fine carving.

In this chapter, we will introduce you to how you can make a small laser engraving machine using Banana Pro and a motor adapter board. Unlike other tools, a very small area of laser beam is focused on the material to make it gasify quickly and is similar to using the rays of the sun to focus on something with a magnifying glass. Compared with other lasers, in terms of easy operation and safety considerations, the laser engraving machine is not too powerful.

This machine is faster and more efficient than a mechanical engraving machine. When cutting three-dimensional words through a small aperture, you'll notice that the font is not deformed, and there are no burrs while cutting organic glass words. There is also no need for the polishing processing. Compared with other machines, it is more precise and can carve complex image designs. It can also carve or cut glass, leather, rubber, and other special materials. The carved objects don't need to be fixed during the time when laser engraving machine is working.

We first need to know what is required in order to set up this laser engraving machine. After this, we will set up a laser engraving frame with acrylic materials and 3D print components. Later on, we will figure out how to install the `GrbController` software on Banana Pro and load a driver on the motor adapter board.

This chapter explains the following topics in detail:

- Setting up the frame for laser engraving
- Configuring the Banana Pro software
- Installing the Banana Pro software on a PC
- Loading a program into the laser CPU
- Using a laser engraver

Setting up the frame for laser engraving

To set up the right frame for laser engraving, we first need to prepare all the requisite materials, and follow the required steps to assemble this frame.

Preparing materials

Since you will need many different and special materials, except the basic Banana Pro, I will explain them to you and give you a short description of each component. All the original design files of the laser engraver packages can be found on GitHub at `https://github.com/Tony-HIT/laser_engraver.git`.

This GitHub repo includes the laser CPU hardware and frame mechanism designs. Other components, such as laser emitters, power adapters, and motors, can be found at online shops such as Amazon.com.

- **The laser Central Processing Unit (CPU)**: This is used to drive the motors and provide power to other components such as the Banana Pro. It is AVR micro controller-based and can load code with the help of the Arduino IDE. The schematic and PCB design files can be found on GitHub, mentioned at the beginning of the chapter:

- **USBtinyISP**: This is used to connect to the laser CPU in order to load the code from a PC or other main device:

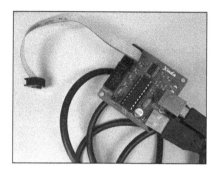

- **DC 12V power adapter**: This is used to supply power to the entire system. It will be connected to the laser CPU:

- **Laser emitter**: This is the core component that is used to engrave objects. It is connected to the laser CPU:

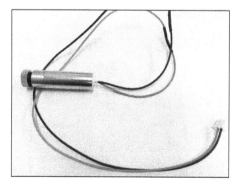

- **Laser radiator**: This is used to fix the laser emitter and decrease the amount of heat when the system works:

- **Power switch**: This is used to switch the system on and off:

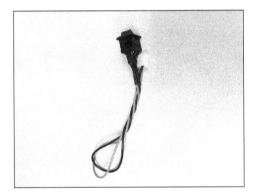

- **The X/Y motor**: There are two motors, one for the x axis and the other for the y axis. Using the plane movements of the x and y axes, we can engrave different shapes into materials:

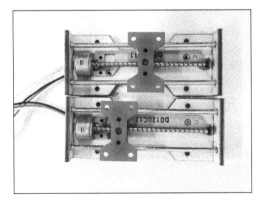

- **Micro USB cable**: This is used to connect to the Banana Pro and laser CPU:

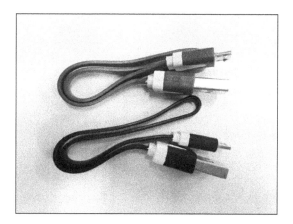

- **Protective glasses**: You will need protective glasses to protect your eyes when you observe the laser engraving process:

- **5 inch LCD**: This is used to monitor the system because we cannot use a large display monitor:

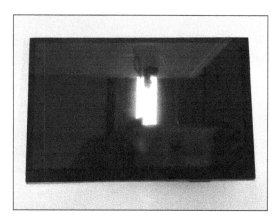

- **Acrylic frame**: This is used to fix all the components. The acrylic frame design file can be found on GitHub, which was mentioned at the beginning of the chapter.

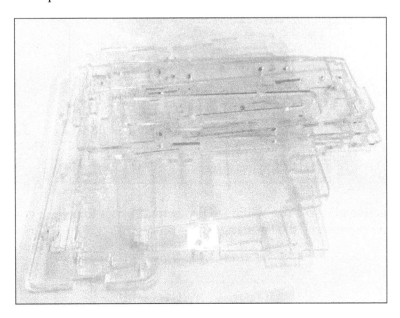

Setting up the laser engraving machine hardware

Setting up the hardware of the laser engraving machine is a little complex. So, an installation guide has been written and uploaded on to the GitHub repo, which you may have downloaded at the beginning of the chapter. You can find it at https:// github.com/Tony-HIT/laser_engraver/installation_guide.

In this installation guide, you will be provided with all the help you need to learn about 3D designs so that you understand each step.

Firstly, note that a screw, nut, and copper cylinder should be used in all the steps provided in the installation guide, as shown in this screenshot:

In the installation guide, we use a tabular representation to present the installation process of the laser engraver frame. Each step shows you the parts you need and the resulting parts you get after performing the steps. The left-hand side of the tabular is the part we need, while the last right-hand side column is the result. We also use a red square to highlight the connector we need to use in each step.

After we've followed the installation guide to complete all the steps, we will get a laser engraver that looks like this:

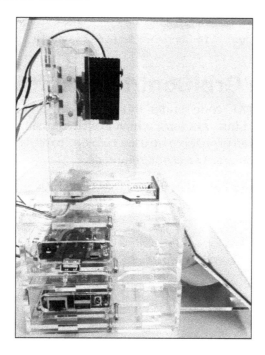

Configuring software on Banana Pro

We will configure software under the Lubuntu operating system; you can download it from `http://www.lemaker.org/product-bananapro-resource.html`.

Installing dependencies

Firstly, we need to make sure that all the software on Banana Pro is of the latest version. The following command will update all the software:

```
sudo apt-get update
```

The output of the preceding command should be similar to what is shown in this screenshot:

Then, we can install all the packages we need, as follows:

```
sudo apt-get install git libudev-dev build-essential qt4-dev-tools
```

Installing the GrblController software

The `GrblController` is a G code sender and monitoring and homing tool for GRBL for Mac, Windows, and Linux systems, which is written using the Qt Desktop Framework in C++. We can probably also use `linuxCNC` to replace `GrblController`, but here we will use `GrblController` as the reference.

Firstly, we need to create a new directory as the workspace into which we will download all the packages we need for `GrblController`:

```
cd ~
```

```
mkdir cncWorkspace
```

Then, we can download the GrblController source code from GitHub:

```
cd ~/cncWorkspace
git clone https://github.com/zapmaker/GrblHoming
```

To build the source code, we need create a new folder that will contain all the built files:

```
mkdir GrblHoming-build
cd GrblHoming-build
```

Now, you are working in the ~/ cncWorkspace/ GrblHoming-build directory.

Next, let's compile the source code:

```
qmake ../GrblHoming/GcodeSenderGUIthreads.pro
sudo make
```

Then, you need to wait for a moment before this is done so that no errors occur during the process.

When it's finished, the output should be similar to what is shown in this screenshot:

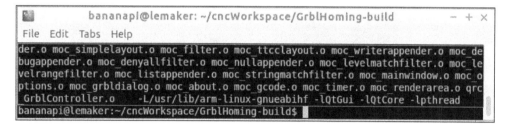

Now, you will get an executable file named GrblHoming-build.

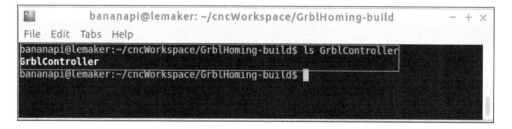

In order to operate conveniently, we need to generate a desktop shortcut:

```
cd /home/bananapi/Desktop/
touch GrblController.desktop
nano GrblController.desktop
```

After this, fill the following content in the `GrblController.desktop` file:

```
[Desktop Entry]
Type=Application
Name=GrblController
Icon=/home/bananapi/ cncWorkspace//GrblHoming/grbl.ico
Exec=/home/bananapi/ cncWorkspace GrblHoming-build/GrblController
```

Then, save the file. You will find a shortcut named `GrblController` on the desktop. Next, you can double-click the shortcut to open `GrblController`:

Installing software on a PC

To make sure that Banana Pro can control the X/Y motor, we need the G code as the controlling reference. A very easy-to-use software called Inkscape for PCs can be used as our G code generator without the need for any compiling process. After configuring the Banana Pro, we will move to our PC to install some necessary software so that we can generate the G code and load the driving code into the laser CPU. Since all the software to be installed, explained in the following sections, has multiple OS versions, here, we will showcase only the Windows version. However, if you're using the Mac OS X or a Linux version, it is also acceptable.

Installing Inkscape

Download Inkscape at `https://inkscape.org/en/download/windows/` and choose the corresponding version according to your own Windows operating system version.

After downloading it, we will get an `.exe` file named `Inkscape-XXXXXXX.exe`. Then, we can double-click the installing file and follow the installing wizard to complete the installation.

After the installation of Inkscape, you will find its icon on your desktop:

Then, we need to download and install the laser printer G code plugin (the laser engraver extension) for Inkscape. The download link is `http://www.slackersdelight.com/instructables/laserengraver.zip`.

After downloading the plugin, you will find a `.zip` file named `laserengraver.zip` in your download path. Unzip it to the Inkscape installation directory, for example, `C:\Program Files(X86)\Inkscape\share\extensions`.

The unzipped files should include the following files:

- `Dxf_input.inx`
- `Dxf_input.py`
- `Laserengraver.py`
- `Laserengraver_laser.inx`

Now, as you can see, we have finished the installation of Inkscape.

Installing Arduino

Download Arduino from `https://www.arduino.cc/en/Main/Software`. Since we've used the Windows OS as the reference so far, we will select the **Windows ZIP file for non admin install**:

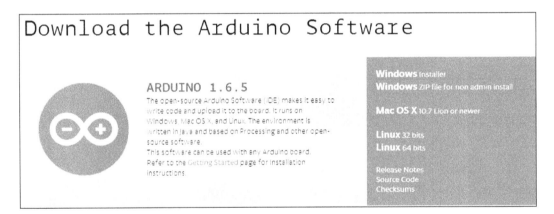

Now, unzip the `.zip` file and direct it to the unzip folder; you will find the `arduino.exe` program, as follows:

Loading a program into the laser CPU

In order to establish communication between laser CPU and Banana Pro, we should first load the bootloader and driving programs into the laser CPU.

Loading bootloader

Follow these steps to load the bootloader:

1. Connect the laser CPU to the USBtinyISP, and then, connect the USBtinyISP to the PC, as follows:

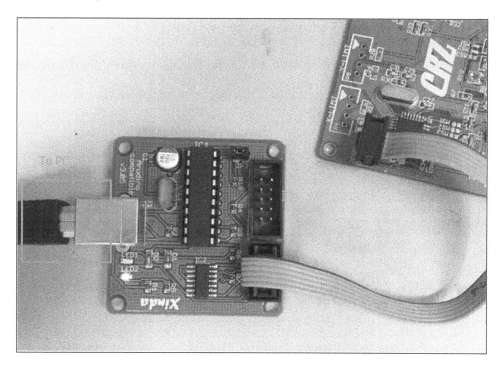

2. After connecting USBtinyISP to the PC, we can verify whether the connection is successful by checking the Windows device manager (by navigating to **My Computer** | **Property** | **Manager**):

3. Double-click the Arduino program and be ready to configure the **Tools** setting:

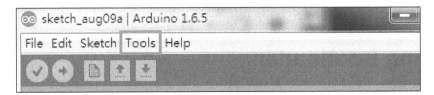

4. Select the **Arduino Nano** boards configuration by navigating to **Tools | Board | Arduino Nano**.

5. Select the **USBtinyISP** programmer by navigating to **Tools | Programmer | USBtinyISP**.

6. To select **Burn Bootloader**, click on **Tools**, then select **Burn Bootloader**.

   Then, wait for a few minutes until the the burning process has been completed. We will see the following output if it is burned successfully:

Loading the driving code

Please follow these steps to load the driving code into the laser CPU:

1. Download the GRBL_CRZ open source by GIT.

2. In your Windows system, download the source code, which will hypothetically be on the desktop. The download link of GRBL_CRZ is https://github.com/Jevonsz/GRBL_CRZ. We can download the ZIP package directly from the right-hand side of the download page.

3. Then, you will see a folder named GRBL_CRZ. Inside the folder, there are a lot of files, such as config.h, coolant_control.cpp, and so on.

4. Connect the laser CPU to your PC via a USB cable:

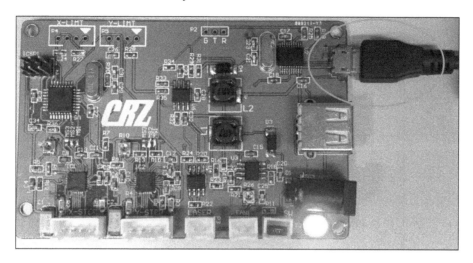

5. To make sure the connection between the laser CPU and your PC has been successfully set up, right-click on **My Computer** | **Property** | **Manager** , and check the information shown in this screenshot:

6. Load the GRBL_CRZ code to the laser CPU.
7. Copy the GRRZ source code file to the libraries directory of Arduino:

8. Then, start Arduino, and select **File** | **Sketchbook** | **libraries** | **GRBL_CRZ** | **GRBL**:

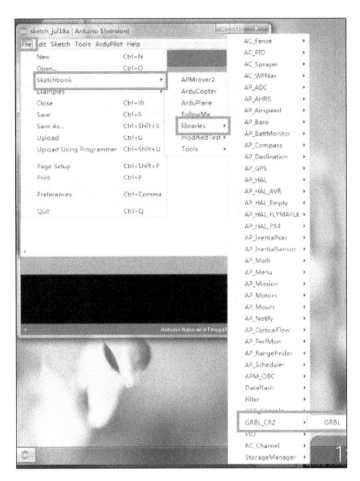

9. Compile the GRBL_CRZ code by clicking on the correct tick icon in the top-left corner of the window. If it's been compiled successfully, you'll see the following successful output:

Done compiling.

10. Choose the right COM port according to step 2. Then, click the right arrow icon to load the compiled hex code to the laser CPU. If it's been loaded successfully, the output should succeed.

Until now, we have finished all the processes that are required to set up the software and hardware.

How to use a laser engraver

In order to engrave different drawings on materials, we need to first generate the code of the drawing and then use the code to drive the motor.

Generate the G code

Please follow these steps to generate the G code:

1. Start the Inkscape software on your PC.

2. Press *Ctrl* + *Shift* + *D*, and set the parameters according to the following figure:

3. Press *Enter* to save the changes made.

4. Press *Ctrl + I* to load the picture that you want to engrave. Here, we'll use a picture of a Chinese dragon for our example:

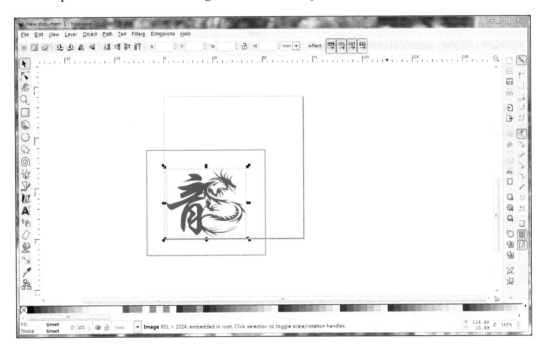

5. Press *Shift + Alt + B*, and select **Edge detection**. Then, click on **Update** and then, click on **OK**:

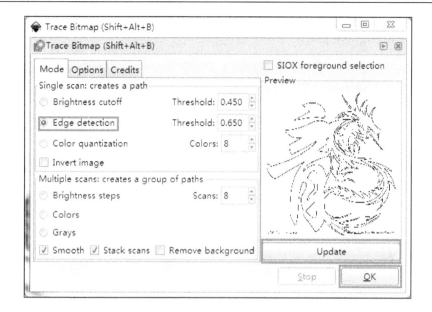

Now, you will find the edge of the picture on the 70x70 board:

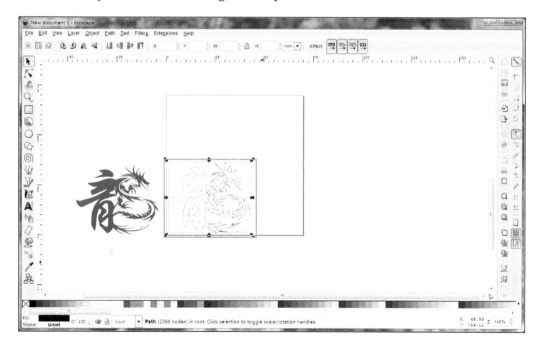

6. Navigate to **Path | Object to path** in the menu bar to transform the words into the engrave path:

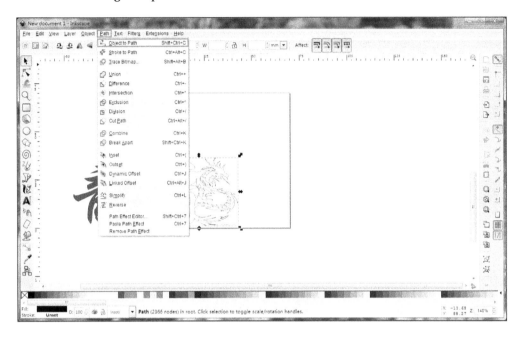

7. Navigate to **Extensions | Laserengraver | Laser…**:

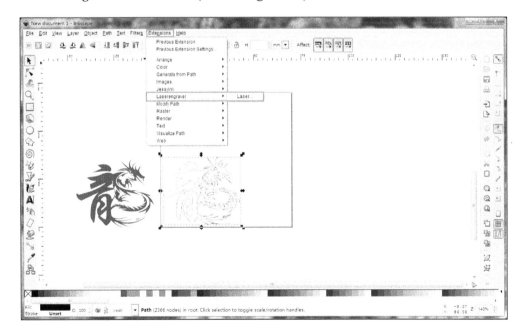

In the interface of **Laser**, set the **Laser engraving speed** to **70** and input the **dragon.nc** filename:

In the interface of **Preferences**, you can set the **Directory** path where you want to save the crz.nc file according to your own preference:

8. Next, click on **Apply** to generate the file. We will get the Gcode.nc file that's under the saving directory.

Beginning the engraving process

You can use hard cardboard from useless cartons to act as the engraving material. Use the following steps to engrave the desired shape on the cardboard:

1. Copy the generated `.nc` file to Banana Pro.

2. Start the GrbController software in the Banana Pro Lubuntu operating system.

3. Configure the settings according to what is shown in this screenshot:

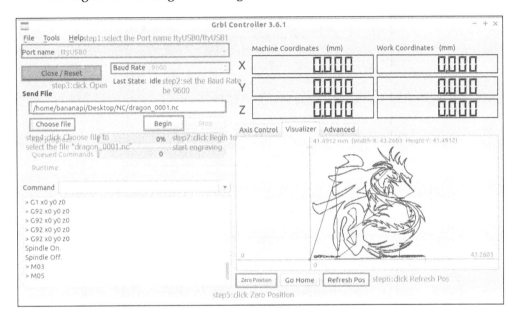

4. When the process is about to start, the laser engrave machine will execute a command according to the G code.

5. The results would be similar to what is shown here:

Summary

In this chapter, we built a frame for a laser engraver machine using acrylic that can mount Banana Pro, a laser, motor, and other necessary components.

Secondly, we installed the GrbController controller software on Banana Pro, which can execute the G code to drive the X/Y motor.

Thirdly, we installed the Inkscape software that can transform a picture to G code, and we also installed the Arduino software that is used to load the drive code into the laser CPU.

Then, we configured the laser CPU using the GRBL_CRZ open source package.

Finally, we explained an example of how to use the laser engraver.

8
Scratch – Building a Smart House

Scratch is designed keeping learning and education in mind. A wide variety of educators have been supporting Scratch's creators since 2007. Scratch is a programming language that makes it easy to create interactive art, stories, simulations, and games—and share these creations online. Scratch is designed especially for ages 8 to 16, but is used by people of all ages. Millions of people create Scratch projects in a wide variety of settings, including homes, schools, museums, libraries, and community centers.

LeScratch is a Scratch message handler that runs in the background to let a Scratch client communicate with hardware. For educational purposes, people of any age can earn easy access to the principles of microcomputers. When people learn to code in Scratch, they learn important strategies to solve problems, design projects, and share ideas. In combination with LeScratch, people also get extended functions to control sensors that contain the original Scratch functions, which makes it more fun and applicable.

The powerful microcomputer, Banana Pro, offers a wealth of hardware interfaces and communication buses. In this chapter, I will firstly introduce you to how you can install and configure the LeScratch package, and then, I will explain the details of how we extend the functionalities of Scratch 1.4 to control the hardware peripherals and sensors of Banana Pro. Finally, I will show you a demonstration that uses most of the sensor modules, such as LeScratch Smart House, which is built with the help of the LeScratch handler, running in cooperation with the Scratch 1.4 client on Banana Pro.

This chapter contains the following in detail:

- Configuring LeScratch
- Controlling the LeScratch peripherals
- Building the LeScratch smart house

Configuring LeScratch

The Scratch 1.4 education software runs in cooperation with LeScratch to let people earn easy access to the principles of microcomputers. Before starting, system configurations should be set to support the LeScratch functionalities in order to send and receive messages among peripherals. In this chapter, we'll use the Raspbian for BananaPro v1412 system image version, which can be downloaded at http://www.lemaker.org/article-17-1.html. Now, let's declare the my_LeScratch project directory under the home directory: all the operations in the following sections are based on this directory:

```
cd ~
mkdir my_LeScratch
```

Installing the prerequisites

LeScratch needs to preinstall some packages, such as python-dev, python-setuptools, i2c-tools, and python-smbus:

```
sudo apt-get install python-dev
sudo apt-get install python-setuptools python-smbus i2c-tools
```

Since the I2C driver is installed and enabled by default, you only have to install the SPI drivers; now open the terminal and write the following commands to install py-spidev:

```
cd ~/my_LeScratch
git clone https://github.com/doceme/py-spidev
cd py-spidev
sudo python setup.py install
```

Also, remember to download the latest version of RPi.GPIO for Banana Pro, shown as follows, before installing the new version. When you do this delete the old version first:

```
cd /usr/local/lib/python2.7/dist-packages
ls
sudo rm -rf RPi
sudo rm RPi.*
```

Then, open the terminal and write the following commands to install the RPi.GPIO library:

```
sudo apt-get update
cd ~/my_LeScratch
git clone https://github.com/LeMaker/RPi.GPIO_BP -b bananapro
cd RPi.GPIO_BP
python setup.py install
sudo python setup.py install
```

LeScratch communicates with some sensors using the wiringPi library. By default, the Banana Pro image file we're using is preinstalled with the wiringPi library, so you don't need to set it up again. In case you don't have the package, use the following commands to install it:

```
cd ~/my_LeScratch
git clone https://github.com/LeMaker/WiringBP.git -b bananapro
cd WiringBP
chmod +x ./build
sudo ./build
```

Setting up the system

Extension boards communicate with Banana Pro through various communication interfaces. The I2C module is included in the latest Banana Pro distributions and is enabled by default. However, the SPI driver should be enabled manually:

```
sudo modprobe spi-sun7i
```

The preceding command only temporarily enables the SPI module. Also, you can permanently enable it by commenting out `blacklist spi-sun7i` line in `/etc/modprobe.d/bpi-blacklist.conf`. In the latest system image, the blacklist file is removed, which means that this command can be skipped:

```
sudo nano /etc/modprobe.d/bpi-blacklist.conf
```

Then, you will still have to load the SPI modules by adding `spi-sun7i` and `spidev` to `/etc/modules`:

```
sudo nano /etc/modules
```

Setting up Scratch Mesh

To modify Scratch Mesh and save it permanently, you need to run Scratch with the `sudo` permission:

```
sudo scratch
```

Refer to `http://wiki.scratch.mit.edu/wiki/Mesh` (*1.3 Mesh by Modification of Scratch*) for detailed steps on this (note, you may find that in step 7, you need to right-click on the **System Browser** and select **accept**). Reboot after setting you've completed the preceding instructions.

Running LeScratch

Before starting the LeScratch program, it is suggested that you start Scratch 1.4 (saved in the Mesh mode) first, such that the connections can be built once the LeScratch script is run. You will find the LeScratch folder under the home directory. The `LeScratch.py` file that is implemented with Python can be run easily:

```
cd ~/LeScratch
```

```
sudo python LeScratch.py
```

If the following phenomenon occurs, it means the connection between LeScratch and Scratch has failed, thus sending or receiving messages is not possible:

The solution for this is simple: you need to find the **Sensing** block as shown in this screenshot:

Then, right-click on the **slider sensor** block value, and select **disable remote sensor connections**:

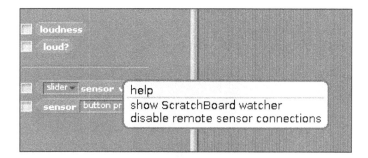

Again, you will have to right-click on the **slider sensor** block value, and select **enable remote sensor connections**:

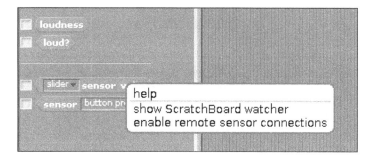

Then, you will receive a message, as shown in the following screenshot, which means the remote sensor connection has been built:

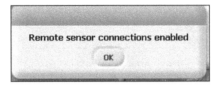

When you have already run the LeScratch handler, and you load a new demo of Scratch, you usually need to wait a bit until the connection between LeScratch and Scratch is built, as shown in the following image, which means the communication is successful. Otherwise, you need to restart the LeScratch handler.

When the LeScratch handler is similar to what is shown in this terminal, it means that it's running well.

Controlling the LeScratch peripherals

We can now run the LeScratch Python program and Scratch 1.4 to try all the sensor modules one by one. In this section, we're going to parse the details of each extension. Then, we're going to introduce you to the demonstration which will be explained in the *Building the LeScratch smart house* section that uses most of our extension block: the LeScratch smart house. You can also create your own new applications and share them with LeScratch users in the LeMaker Forum at http://www.lemaker.org/forum-171-1.html.

General Purpose Input Output (GPIO)

GPIO is a generic pin on an integrated circuit whose behavior can be controlled by a user at runtime, regardless of whether it is an input or output pin.

Instructions

GPIO pins have no special purpose defined and go unused by default. A number out of the list defined by `RPi.BCM` [4, 5, 6, 12, 13, 16, 17, 18, 19, 20, 21, 22, 23, 24, 25, 26, 27] is usually available for GPIO controls. The GPIO board has 40 LEDs and 15 switches that can be used to indicate the status of all 40 pins on Banana Pro, and give digital input to its corresponding switch pins. You can purchase it at `http://www.lenovator.com/`.

In the first place, remember to declare which GPIO pins are going to be used by your program:

- `broadcast g[num]in` and `broadcast g[num]out`: The `in` value means input pin and value `out` value means output pin.

- `broadcast g[num]on` and `g[num]off`: The `on` value means set output to `1` or high and `off` means set to `0` or low.

Here are the different usages of GPIO controls:

Command	g[num]in	g[num]out	g[num]on	g[num]off
Function	This defines the input pin	This defines the output pin	This sets a pin to 1 or high	This sets a pin to 0 or low

Example: The GPIO board

In this example, we will put the GPIO board with LEDs on Banana Pro, as shown in the following image, in order to see whether there're any digital signal changes on the GPIO pins:

In the following image, you'll see many pieces of Scratch code and their corresponding explanations below the code. You'll be able to know how to use a GPIO pin as an input or output pin and how to read the GPIO input value by its named sensor value:

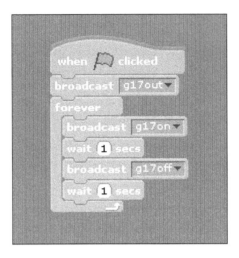

Click on the green flag to **run** and declare GPIO 17 as the output pin. In this **forever** loop, Set GPIO 17 to on or high and **wait** for 1 second. Then set **GPIO - 17** to off or low and **wait** for a second. Then continue to loop this process.:

When the spacebar is pressed, declare **GPIO 17** as input and GPIO 4 as output. In this **forever** loop, update the program for every loop. In each loop, check whether the GPIO-17 **sensor value** equals to 0; if yes, set GPIO 4 to on or high and then **wait** for 1 second. If not, set GPIO 4 to off or low, and then wait for 1 second.

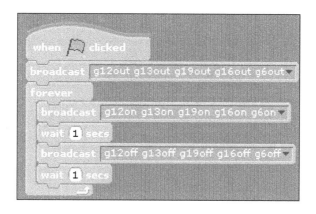

Click on the green flag to run and declare GPIO 12, 13, 19, 16, and 6 as output. In the **forever** loop, the process will be repeatedly executed until the code is stopped. Set the value of GPIO 12, 13, 19, 16, and 6 to true, that is on, wait for a second. Then, set GPIO 12, 13, 19, 16, and 6 to off and wait for a second

Note that, if you're trying to define your own GPIO input from the available list (4, 5, 6, 12, 13, 16, 17, 18, 19, 20, 21, 22, 23, 24, 25, 26, and 27), you will have to run LeScratch once to obtain the GPIO input list. For example, here, you add GPIO 5 as the input, but you will not find the GPIO-5 name in the sensor list.

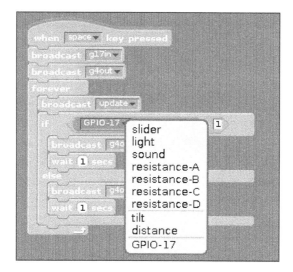

The operation to add a new GPIO control pin is as simple as what is shown in the following screenshot; you create a new `g5in` broadcast by clicking on a new item:

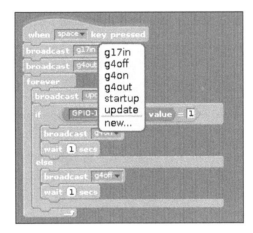

Then, enter `g5in` in words, as shown here:

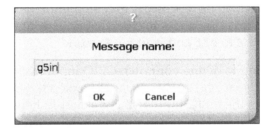

Next, run `LeScratch.py` to see if the terminal displays **Pin: 5** and so on:

```
Pin: 5 -> 1
Pin: 17 -> 0
4 set to OFF
Pin: 5 -> 1
Pin: 17 -> 0
4 set to OFF
Pin: 5 -> 1
Pin: 17 -> 0
```

If so, then it means that `GPIO-5` is successfully updated in the sensor list; you can now choose it from this block:

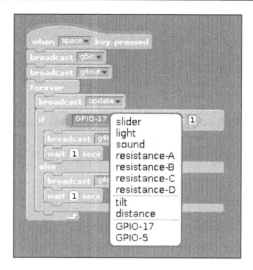

Inter-Integrated Circuit

Inter-Integrated Circuit (**I2C**) is a multimaster, multislave, single-ended serial bus, which is easy to control and has a high communication speed. The I2C bus has the SDA data line and the SCL clock line that control the sending and receiving of data. I2C has various addresses for extended devices once you attach an extension board to Banana Pro/Pi, open the terminal, and use the `i2c` tools to detect its address:

```
sudo i2cdetect -y 2
```

Instructions

The USB hub extension board , namely the LN-HUB-32IO board used as an example in this section, has a four-port USB hub and MCP23017 x2 32GPIO to communicate with Banana Pro/Pi, such that Scratch can control them with extended functions. You can purchase this extension board from `http://www.lenovator.com/`. The MCP23017 board is an I2C device.

We know that the chip MCP23017 can be used as two 8-bit ports, namely, port A and port B. To control its IO ports using LeScratch, specify the I2C address of MCP23017, using the following command formats:

- **I2C mode for port A**:

  `"i2"+ "address 0x(20-27)" + "a" +"bit (0 to 7)"`

- **I2C mode for port B**:

  `"i2"+ "address 0x(20-27)" + "b" +"bit (0 to 7)"`

- **The bit mode for port A**:

  ```
  "bit"+ "address 0x(20-27)" + "a" +"bit (7 to 0)"
  ```

- **The bit mode for port B**:

  ```
  "bit"+ "address 0x(20-27)" + "b" +"bit (7 to 0)"
  ```

The I2C mode only requires you to give decimal format number of bits (7 to 0), while the bit mode requires you to give a byte format number of bits (7 to 0). You'll find out exactly how to name the I2C address for controlling the I2C device in the following examples:

- `i221a1`: I2C address 0x21 port A bit 1 is ON
- `i222b4`: I2C address 0x22 Port B bit 4 is ON
- `bit22b01010101`: Address 0x22 port B from bit 7 to 0, output will be 0b01010101.
- `bit21a01010101`: Address 0x21 port A from bit 7 to 0, output will be 0b01010101
- `bit21aon`: Address 0x21 port A all ON, 0b11111111
- `bit21boff`: Address 0x21 port B all OFF or clear, 0b00000000
- `bit22aoff`: Address 0x22 port A all OFF or clear

Example – a LN-HUB-32IO USB hub

This is the LN-HUB-32IO device from Lenovator:

In the following example, you'll see many pieces of Scratch code and their corresponding explanations below the code. You'll learn how to use the I2C device by defining its address:

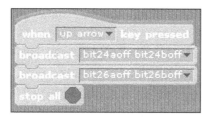

When the up arrow key is pressed (address 0x24, 0x26), clear port A and B:

When **A** is pressed on the keyboard (address 0x24, 0x26), clear port A and B. Next, in this forever loop, port A/B on the XXXX address will repeatedly set the port A on the 0x24 address to 0b10010111 and the 0x24 address on port B to 0b01101000:

When the up arrow is pressed (the 0x24 and 0x26 addresses), clear port A and B:

When **B** is pressed on the keyboard (the 0x24 and 0x26 addresses), clear port A and B. Then, in this **forever** loop, set address 0x24 port A bit 4 and bit 7 to 1, **wait** for 1 second and set address 0x24 port B to bit 1 and bit 6.

Serial Peripheral Interface (SPI)

The SPI bus is a synchronous serial communication interface specification that's used for short distance communication, which is in full duplex mode using the master-slave architecture with a single master. The master device originates from the frame for reading and writing. Multiple slave devices are supported through the selection of individual slave select lines (you can purchase these from http://www.lenovator.com/).There are typically four types of connections:

- **MOSI**: This is the master device output data and the slave device input data
- **MISO**: This is the master device input data and the slave device output data
- **SCLK**: This is the clock that's generated by the master device
- **CS**: This is the chip (slave device) select line that's controlled by the master device

For example, LN Digital has one 16-bit MCP23s17 that communicates with Banana Pro using SPI. MCP23s17 has eight different addresses that allow the extension of eight boards at the same time. LN Digital has been configured as an 8-bit port A and port B or a 16-bit port. Each port (A/B) can be configured as either input or output. By default, each is configured as the port A output (one to eight) and the port B input (one to eight) . In the following image, we put the SPI device LN Digital on Banana Pro; next we'll explain how to control a SPI device through its address:

Instructions

Similarly, we will define four kinds of commands to control SPI devices; also there is an SPI mode, which uses decimal format numbers and a bits mode, which uses byte format numbers:

- **The SPI mode for port A**:

  ```
  "sp"+ "address (0-7)" + "a" +"bit (0 to 7)"
  ```

- **The SPI mode for port B**:

  ```
  "sp"+ "address (0-7)" + "b" +"bit (0 to 7)"
  ```

- **The bits mode for port A**:

  ```
  "bits"+ "address (0-7)" + "a" +"bit (7 to 0)"
  ```

- **The bits mode for port B**:

  ```
  "bits"+ "address (0-7)" + "b" +"bit (7 to 0)"
  ```

The SPI mode requires you to provide a decimal format number of bit (7 to 0), while the bits mode requires you to provide a byte format number of bit (7 to 0). You'll find out exactly how to name the SPI address for controlling the SPI device in the following examples:

- `sp0a1`: SPI address 0x40 Port A bit 1 ON

- `sp1b4`: SPI address 0x42 Port B bit 4 ON

- `bits2b01010101`: Address 0x44 port B from bit 7 to 0, output will be 01010101

- `bits3a01010101`: Address 0x46 port A from bit 7 to 0, output will be 01010101

- `bits4aon`: Address 0x48 port A all ON, 0b11111111

- `bits5boff`: Address 0x4A port B all OFF/clear, 0b00000000

- `bits6aoff`: Address 0x4B port A all OFF/clear

Example – LN digital or SPI general

The Scratch code and explanation is shown as follows:

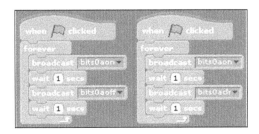

Click on the green flag to run. While true, set the SPI address 0x40 port A to all on, wait for 1 second, set SPI address 0x40 port A to all off and again wait for 1 second.

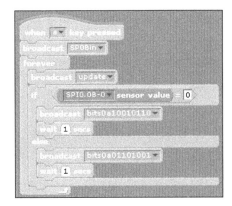

When **A** is pressed on the keyboard, declare the 0x40 address port B as input, in this **forever** loop, if the 0x40 SPI address port B bit 0 equals to 0, set SPI address 0x40 port A to 0b10010110 and **wait** for 1 second, otherwise, set SPI address 0x40 port A to 0b01101001 and **wait** for 1 second: second

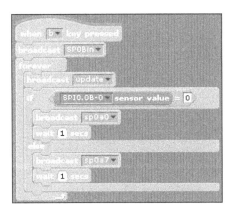

When **B** is pressed on the keyboard, declare address 0x40 port B as input. In this **forever** loop, if SPI address 0x40 port B bit *0 = 0*, set address 0x40 port A bit 0 to 1 and **wait** for 1 second, otherwise, set 0x40 port A bit7 to 1 and wait for 1 second.

Example: LN Digital (the LNDI commands)

The LN Digital extension board allows Scratch to access the following extra hardware:

- Eight open collector outputs
- Eight LED indicators
- Eight digital inputs
- Tactile switches (the interrupt event is set to listen on four input switches)
- Two changeover relays (port A output bit 1 — relay 1 and port A output bit 2 — relay 2)

Command	LNDI[num]in	LNDI[num]out	LNDI[num]on	LNDI[num]off
Function	This listens to the key input	This declares the output pin	This sets a pin to 1/high	This sets a pin to 0/low

In the following image, you'll see many pieces of Scratch code and its corresponding explanation below the code for this the SPI device: LN Digital. You'll learn how to use special commands for this device:

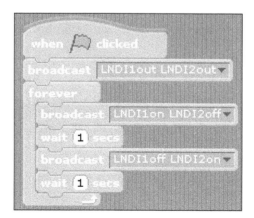

Click the green flag to run and declare **LNDI1, LNDI2** output. While true, set **LNDI1out** to on or high and **wait** for 1 second, otherwise, set **LNDI2out** to off or low and **wait** for 1 second

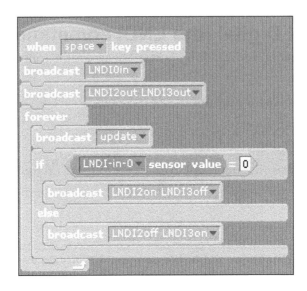

For this example, we will be using 0 to 3 input buttons for this device; for the other device, there can be 0 to 7 inputs. When spacebar is pressed, **LNDI1out, LNDI2out**, and **LNDI3out**, declare **LNDI1in** for input bit 1; in this **forever** loop, update the progress in every loop. In each loop, check if **LNDI-in-0** is 0. If yes, set **LNDI2** to on/high and **LNDI3** to off/low. Otherwise, set **LNDI2** to off/low and **LNDI3** to on/high.

- Set **LNDI1, 3** out to on/high
- Set **LNDI2out** to off/low
- Else (no input is detected)
- Set **LNDI1, 3** out to off/low
- Set **LNDI2** out to on/high

The step motor

Here, we will use the 29BYJ-48 stepper motor as the example to show you how to control motors using LeScrach.

Technical specifications

The 28BYJ-48 stepper motor is a so-called unipolar motor. A unipolar stepper motor has two or more windings, each with a center tap. Each section of winding is switched on in the direction of a magnetic field. Since in this arrangement, a magnetic pole can be reversed without switching the direction of the current, the commutation circuit can be made in a very simple manner (for example, a single transistor) for each winding. In this project, the ULN2803A integrated circuit is used.

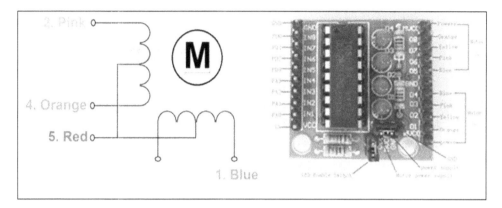

There are a number of ways to drive a stepper motor as follows:

- **Wave drive**: In this drive method, only a single phase is activated at a time. It is the fastest but is rarely used.

- **Full step drive**: This is the usual method for the full step driving of the motor. Two phases are always on so that the motor provides the maximum rated torque.

- **Half stepping**: When half stepping, the drive alternates between two phases: on and a single phase on. This increases the angular resolution, but the motor also has less torque.

- **Micro stepping**: Here, the windings are driven with the help of the sinusoidal AC waveform. This requires different hardware and isn't used in this project.

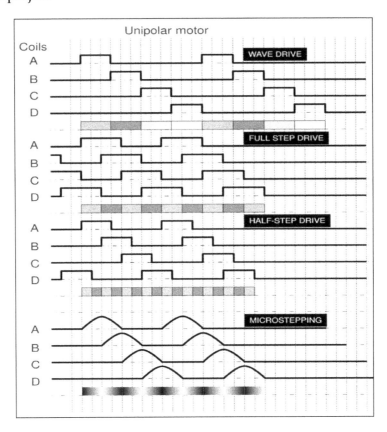

Example – the step motor

Note that in this example, the RPi.BCM pin definition is applied. Remember to firstly run LeScratch, and then, you can start the Scratch client; always remember to stop Scratch running blocks when you want to restart the LeScratch handler.

By default, two step motors are connected by the GPIO group motor (17, 18, 27, and 22) and motor (4, 25, 24, and 23), these two groups of numbers use the RPi.GPIO BCM definition. The connection from the motors to ULN2803A is by connecting red wires to VCC and then others (**IN1~IN8** and **GND**) are fixed. The IN1~IN8 input is connected to GPIO (17, 18, 27, 22) and (4, 25, 24, and 23), or equally, pin number (11, 12, 13, and 15) and (7, 22, 18, and 16).

The `stepM+ A/B + init` command for motor initialization, and the `stepM+ speed + A/B + steps + P/N` command gives speed, steps, and direction.

Here are some examples of this:

Following are the details of Scratch code:

- **A**: For motor **A**
- **5**: For speed 5/1000
- **256**: For steps, any numbers can be defined
- **P/N**: For directions, **P**: clockwise, **N**: anticlockwise

The scratch code and explanation is as follows:

Click on the green flag to run and initiate motor A (17, 18, 27, and 22) and motor B (4, 25, 24, and 23).While true, turn motor A at speed 5/1000 for 256 steps, in the direction clockwise (Positive P) and turn motor A at speed 5/1000 for 256 steps, in the direction anti-clockwise (Positive N). Repeat the same for step motor B:

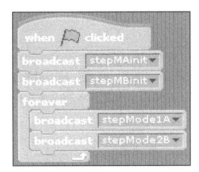

Click on the green flag to run and initiate motor A (17, 18, 27, and 22) and motor B (4, 25, 24, and 23).While true, set motor A working on **Mode1** to full step drive.

Set motor B working on **Mode2** to wave drive and **Mode1** speed 2.5, **Mode2** speed 2.5/3.

Real-time clock

Here, we will use the DS1307 **real-time clock (RTC)** as our example.

Technical specifications

The DS1307 serial RTC is a low-power, full **binary-coded decimal (BCD)** clock/
calendar. Its address and data is transferred serially through the I2C bidirectional
bus. The clock/calendar provides information on the seconds, minutes, hours,
day, date, month, and year. The end of the month date is automatically adjusted
for months with fewer than 31 days, including corrections for leap years. The clock
operates in either the 24-hour or the 12-hour format with the AM/PM indicator.
DS1307 has a built-in power-sense circuit that detects power failures and can switch
automatically to a backup supply.

Example – RTC

Note that in this example, the RPi.BCM pin definition is applied. Firstly, remember to
run LeScratch and only then can you start the Scratch client; also, always remember
to stop Scratch running blocks when you want to restart the LeScratch handler.

The RTC module simply provides Scratch with exactly the same date and time as the
Banana Pro system: the second, minute, hour, day, month, and year. This information
can also be displayed on the Scratch display screen if you choose the value from the
Sensor list in the sensing block. The RTC module use I2C connections for Banana Pro;
you can simply choose one of the I2C pins to connect with the RTC module:

VCC	SCLK	SDA	GND
Pin 4	Pin 5	Pin 3	Pin 6

Open the terminal and use i2c tools to detect the address of RTC module (it should
be 0x68):

```
sudo i2cdetect -y 2
```

The Scratch code and explanation is as follows:

The result is shown as follows:

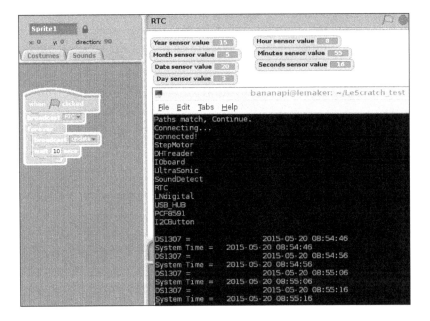

The ultrasonic sensor

The ultrasonic sensor can be used to detect the distance from the objects or obstacles.

Technical specifications

Working voltage	5 VDC
Static current	< 2 mA
Output signal	This is the electric frequency signal: a high-level signal is 5V, and a low-level signal is 0V
Sensor angle	< 15 degrees
Detection distance	2cm-450cm
Precision	~2 mm
Trigger signal	10us TTL impulse
Echo signal	output TTL PWL signal
Pins	VCC
	trig(T)
	echo(R)
	OUT
	GND

In short, the ultrasonic sensor works as follows:

1. Send a pulse signal to I/O TRIG, which is at least 10 µs long. This will activate the module so that it can start detecting if there are any objects in the front.

2. The ultrasonic module will automatically send eight 40 KHz square waves, and it will automatically detect when there is a reflecting signal.

3. When the reflect signal is sent back, the ECHO I/O will output a high-level signal, where the duration of this high-level signal is the time taken for the ultrasonic launch to return. As a result, *the measured distance = T (time of high-level output) * (340m/s)) / 2*. The reason for the division by two is that since this is an echo, it has traveled both to and from the object. Note that the speed of sound is dependent on the temperature, so keep this in mind if you need accuracy.

Example – the ultrasonic sensor

Note that in this example, the RPi.BCM pin definition is applied. Remember to firstly run LeScratch, and then, you can start the Scratch client; also, always remember to stop Scratch running blocks when you want to restart the LeScratch handler.

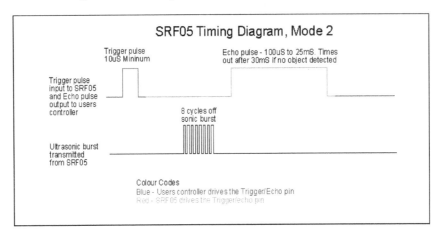

This module allows you to connect any digital pin to trigger and echo. The example for this is as follows.

VCC	Trigger	Echo	GND
Pin 1	Pin 16	Pin 18	Pin 6

The explanation is as follows:

When keyboard space is pressed, declare **Trigger Pin** on GPIO23. Declare **Echo Pin** on GPIO24. While true, update the distance calculation by ultrasonic sensor per every second (the frequency can be faster or slower as required). The result is as follows:

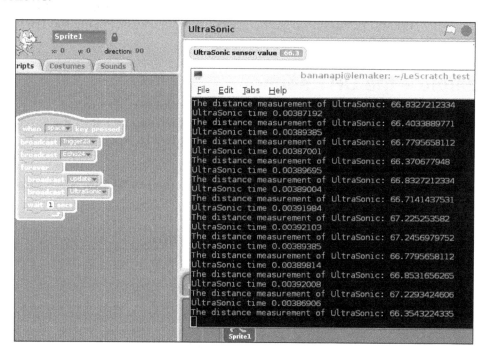

The humidity and temperature sensor

Here, we will use the DHT11 digital humidity and temperature sensor as an example of how to use LeScratch to control a humidity and temperature sensor.

Technical specifications

DHT11 is a basic digital humidity and temperature sensor. It uses a capacitive humidity sensor and a thermistor to measure the surrounding air, and spits out a digital signal on a data pin (no analog input pins are needed). It's fairly simple to use, but requires very careful timing to read data as follows:

- It requires 3 to 5V power and I/O
- It requires 2.5mA of current usage during conversion (while requesting for data)

- It is good for 20-90%RH humidity readings with ±5%RH accuracy

- It is good for 0 to 50°C temperature readings ±2°C accuracy

- It doesn't require more than 1 Hz of a sampling rate (once every 1 seconds), and the data pin connects to GPIO

Currently, the DHT extension block supports DHT11, DHT22, and AM2302, which use the wiringPi API and pin definitions and speed up data transfer using the 1-wire means of communication.

Example – the DHT sensor

Note that in this example, the wiringPiSetup() pin definition is applied. Remember, you have to first run LeScratch and only then can you start the Scratch client; also, always remember to stop Scratch running blocks when you want to restart the LeScratch handler.

This module allows you to connect any digital pins to the **DATA** pin. An example of this is as follows:

VCC	DATA	GND
Pin 1	Pin 7	Pin 6

In the following Scratch code, you'll see how to define the **DHT** sensor and its connections to Banana Pro. The explanation is after the Scratch code image:

Define DHT sensor use pin 7 (`wiringPiSetup()`). DHT11 means the sensor type and currently it supports `DHT11`, `DHT12`, `AM2302`. While true (constantly check and update the DHT sensor value DHT), update the temperature and humidity every 2 seconds

The result is shown of this is shown in the following screenshot. Note that sometimes, the read from sensors may fail due to the fact that the one-wire communication verification might go wrong, but this does not affect its function and usage.

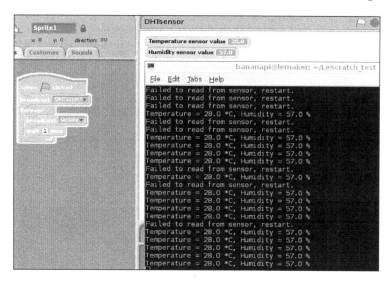

The sound detect sensor

The sound detection sensor can be used to detect the sound intensity of an environment, but note that it can only identify the existence of sound according to the vibration principle; it can't recognize specific loudness or sound frequencies. It's sensitive to sound intensity, and thus, it can check if any sound can be heard around.

Technical specifications

The details of the sensor are listed as follows:

- The working voltage should be between 3.3V-5V.
- The output of the digital switch is set at 0/low and 1/high. It can be connected to GPIO.
- The adjustable sensitivity to sound (digital potentiometer adjustment refers to the blue cube in the following image).
- With the fixed bolt hole and easy installation, the PCB size is 3.2cm x 1.7cm.

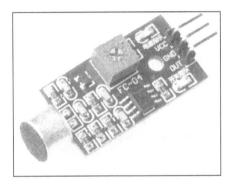

When the sound intensity from the environment is lower than the threshold given by the digital potentiometer adjustment, the **OUT** pin is 1/high; if the intensity is bigger than the threshold, the **OUT** pin is 0/low. By checking whether the **OUT** pin is high/low, we'll know if any sound has been produced. The digital **OUT** pin can drive the relay as a voice-activated switch.

Example – the sound detect sensor

Note that in this example, the RPi.BCM pin definition is applied. Remember to first run LeScratch, and then you can start the Scratch client; also, always remember to stop Scratch running blocks when you want to restart the LeScratch handler.

This module allows you to connect any digital pins to the **OUT** signal; the example for this is as follows:

VCC	OUT	GND
Pin 1	Pin 7	Pin 6

In this Scratch code, you'll see how to define the sound detect module and its connection to Banana Pro, the explanation is as below the code:

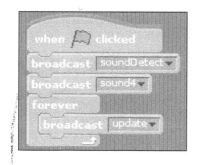

Click on the green flag to run and declare the sound detect sensor. Change the **OUT** pin connect to GPIO4. While true, constantly check for updates.

The result is shown as follows:

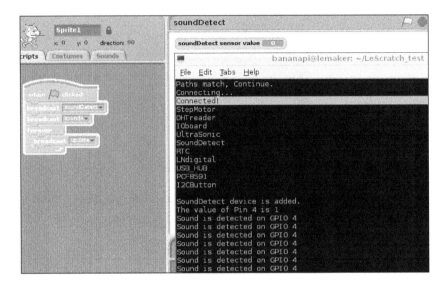

The AD/DA converter

Here, we use the PCF8591 AD/DA module as the example.

Technical specifications

PCF8591 is a single-chip, single-supply low-power 8-bit CMOS data acquisition device with four analog inputs, one analog output, and a serial I2C-bus interface. Three address pins, **A0**, **A1**, and **A2**, are used to program the hardware address, allowing the use of up to eight devices connected to the I2C-bus without additional hardware. The address, control, and data to and from the device are transferred serially via the two-line bidirectional I2C-bus. PCF8591 is featured as follows:

- It has a single power supply, operating supply voltage between 2.5 V and 6 V, and a low standby current
- The serial input/output is provided via I2C-bus
- The address is provided through three hardware address pins
- The sampling rate is given by the I2C-bus speed
- Four analog inputs are programmed as single or differential inputs such as AIN0~AIN3
- The analog voltage ranges from VSS to VDD
- It contains an on-chip track and hold circuit

- It has an 8-bit successive approximation A/D conversion
- The DAC can be multiplied with one analog output.

Example – the AD/DA convertor

Note that in this example, the `wiringPiSetup()` pin definition is applied. Remember, you first have to run LeScratch and only then can you start the Scratch client; also, always remember to stop Scratch running blocks when you want to restart the LeScratch handler.

This module simply use the I2C interface on the LN-IO board to connect with the AD/DA converter:

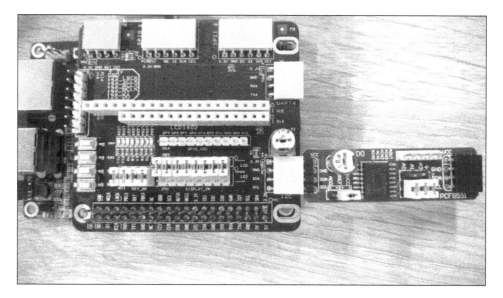

In the following DA conversion, the given digital value is 255 (DA255write and range 0~255); it is converted by the DA calculation. This then outputs the analog value from the AOUT pin; use a multimeter to measure the 0 ~3.3V range (here, it reads a voltage of 3.3V).

Click on the green flag to run and declare the PCF8591 AD/DA convertor. By default, the extension address would be *A2A1A0 = 000*. While true, set DA255 digital to analog, given digital number. The analog output equals to *255/255 *3.3* V.

The analog output formula is: *num/255 *3.3* V.

The result is shown as follows:

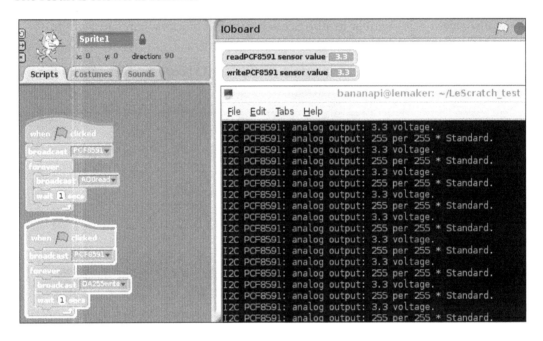

In the following AD conversion, we connect the analog channel 0, which connects to the VCC of 3.3V. After the AD calculation, it will be converted into the digital value of 255 (the digital range of 0~255).

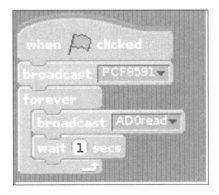

Click on the green flag to run; declare the PCF8591 AD/DA convertor. By default, the extension address would be *A2A1A0 = 000*. While true, **AD0** reads the 0 analog channel (connects to VCC 3.3V); the analog input is converted into a digital value and the analog input formula is: *num/255 *3.3* V.

The result is shown as follows:

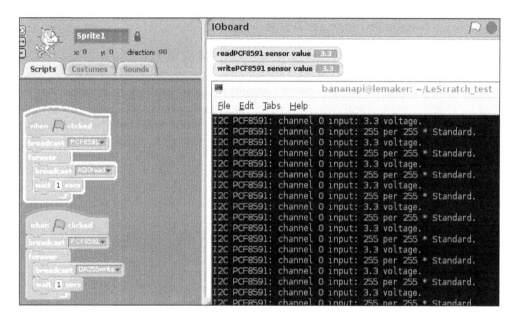

Photoresistor

The photoresistor module is sensitive to ambient light intensity, and is generally used to detect ambient brightness and intensity.

Technical specifications

Under the conditions that this light intensity module does not reach the threshold, the DO digital output port outputs a high level; when the ambient light intensity exceeds a set threshold, the module outputs a low DO; the DO can be directly connected to the control board. By detecting the high/low of the DO pin, we measure the changes in light intensity in the environment. If you connect the AO analog output to the AD modules and conduct the AD conversion, you can get a more accurate ambient light intensity value. The sensor sensitivity can be adjustable (through the digital potentiometer adjustment), and the following parameters are listed:

- The working voltage is 3.3V-5V

- There is a power indicator (red LED) and a digital switching output indicator (green LED)

- There is a digital potentiometer adjustment for sensor sensitivity (the blue cube on the board)

- The **AO** analog voltage output connects to the analog input channel **0** AIN0 of PCF8591, and the **DO** digital switching output (0 and 1) connects to GPIO pin on Banana Pro such as **GPIO4**

Example – a photoresistor

Note that in this example, the RPi.BCM pin definition is applied. Remember to first to run LeScratch and only then can you start the Scratch client; also, always remember to stop Scratch running blocks when you want to restart the LeScratch handler.

This module allows you to define your own **DO** pin; the **AO** signal is connected to the AIN0 AD/DA module for measurement of the voltage. The example of this is as follows:

VCC	DO	AO	GND
Pin 1	Pin 7	Ain0	Pin 6

Here is the Scratch code and comment:

Click on the green flag to run and declare a `Photoresistor` module. Then declare PCF8591 to read the analog value (sensor is light intensity sensitive). While true (constantly check for update per second).

 AIN0 read light intensity from channel 0 and **DO** gives digital indicator output.

The result is shown in the following screenshot (when the light intensity is low or the environment is dark, the voltage generated by the photoresistor is bigger. Complete darkness will generate 3.3V or a digital value of 255; if the environment is bright, the voltage is smaller, whereas total brightness equals to 0):

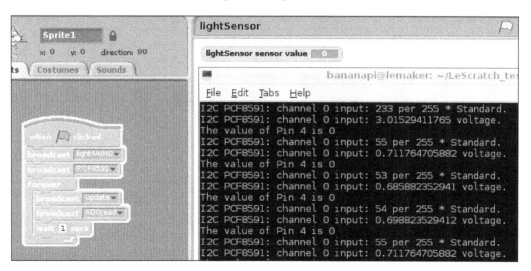

The touch sensor

The touch sensor is based on a touch-sensing IC (TTP223B), low-power capacitive touch switch module.

Technical specifications

Under normal touch conditions, the signal SIS pin outputs 0/low and the LED indicator lights off; when the corresponding sensing capacitor position is touched, the SIS signal outputs 1/high and the LED indicator lights up. If within 12 seconds no touch is detected, then the touch sensor will switch to low-power consumption. The parameters of the touch sensor are as follows:

- **Connections**: This refers to VCC (the power supply range is 3-5V and the current is 5mA), GND (ground), and SIS (touch signals)
- **Response time**: This is 220ms at a low-power state and 60ms at a touch state

Example – the touch sensor

Note that in this example, the RPi.BCM pin definition is applied. Remember to first run LeScratch, and only then can you start the Scratch client; also, always remember to stop Scratch running blocks when you want to restart the LeScratch handler.

This module allows you to connect any digital pins to the SIS pin; the example for this is as follows:

VCC	SIS	GND
Pin 1	Pin 29	Pin 6

Here is the Scratch code and comment:

Click on the green flag to run and declare the touch sensor; SIS will then connect to **GPIO5**. While true, constantly check for updates per second in the form of the SIS digital signal output. The result is shown as follows:

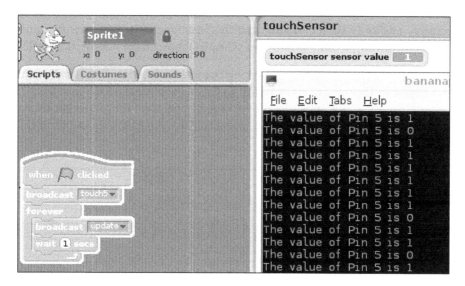

The tilt sensor

The tilt sensor can sense the change in the angles of objects.

Technical specifications

Level the module on the desktop and rotate it slowly in one direction, you will see the LED indicator light up; then, rotate it in the opposite direction (back to the original state), and the LED indicator will light off. Changing the angle of the object will trigger a digital switching signal (0/1) so that the LED indicator will light on or off. By monitoring the **DO** tilt sensor digital signal (low/high), the tilt status of the objects can be informed. The parameters are as follows:

- A working voltage of 5V

- A power LED (red) and digital switching output LED indicator (green)

- The lifetime of the tilt sensor is measured at room temperature and under normal use; however, the lifetime can be changed 1,00,000 times (/1sec).

- Its function is to sense the change in the angle of objects (with a precision of up to 15-45 degree)

- Adjustable sensitivity of the tilt sensor (the digital potentiometer can be adjusted with the blue cube on the board)

- Digital switching outputs **DO** (0 and 1)

Example – the tilt sensor

Note that in this example, the RPi.BCM pin definition is applied. Remember to first run LeScratch, and only then can you start the Scratch client; also, always remember to stop Scratch running blocks when you want to restart the LeScratch handler.

Note that the tilt sensor can easily go wrong (such as when the metal ball inside is stuck, and thus can't reach the right point; in this case both the **DO** signal and LED indicator won't work), This module allows connecting the **DO** pin to another pin in the [4,14,15,17,18,27,22,23,24,10,9,25,11,8,7] list; the example of this is as follows:

VCC	DO	GND
Pin 1	Pin 19	Pin 6

Here is the Scratch code and comment:

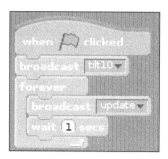

Click on the green flag to run and declare the tilt sensor module. While true, constantly check for updates per second in the form of the D0 digital signal output.

The result is shown as follows:

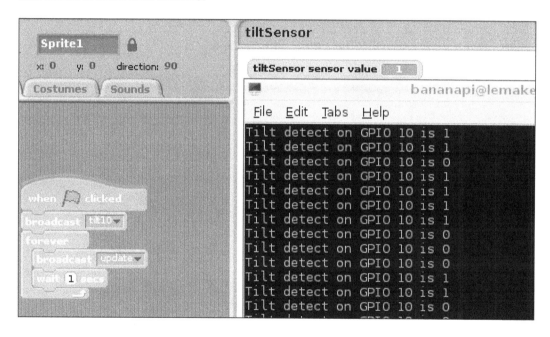

The LCD1602 display

A **Liquid Crystal Display** (**LCD**) screen is an electronic display module and has a wide range of applications. A 16 x 2 LCD display is very basic module and is very commonly used in various devices and circuits. LCDs are economical, easily programmable, and have no limitation of displaying special and even custom characters.

Technical specifications

LCDs have two registers, namely, command and data. The command register stores the command instructions given to an LCD. A command is an instruction given to the LCD to perform a predefined task, such as initializing itself, clearing its own screen, setting the cursor position, controlling the display, and so on. The data register stores the data to be displayed on the LCD. The data is the ASCII value of the character to be displayed on the LCD.

It's featured as follows:

- **Display Format**: This is in the form of 16 characters x two lines
- **Input Data**: A 4-bit or 8-bit interface is available
- **Display Font**: This is in the form of 5 x 8 dots
- **Power Supply**: A single power supply is available (5V±10%)

No.	Symbol	Level	Function	
1	Vss	--	0V	Power Supply
2	Vdd	--	+5V	
3	V0	--	for LCD	
4	RS	H/L	Register Select: H:Data Input L:Instruction Input	
5	R/W	H/L	H--Read L--Write	
6	E	H,H-L	Enable Signal	
7	DB0	H/L	Data bus used in 8 bit transfer	
8	DB1	H/L		
9	DB2	H/L		
10	DB3	H/L		
11	DB4	H/L	Data bus for both 4 and 8 bit transfer	
12	DB5	H/L		
13	DB6	H/L		
14	DB7	H/L		
15	BLA	--	BLACKLIGHT +5V	
16	BLK	--	BLACKLIGHT 0V-	

Example – the LCD1602 display

Note that in this example, the RPi.BCM pin definition is applied. Remember, you first have to run LeScratch, and only then can you start the Scratch client; also, always remember to stop Scratch running blocks when you want to restart the LeScratch handler.

This module simply uses the LCD1602 pins on IO board to connect with the LCD1602; the example for this is as follows:

Here is the Scratch code and comment:

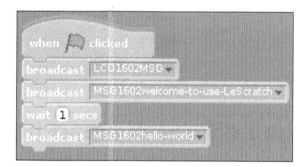

Click on the green flag to run and declare LCD1602 to display message.

- **Broadcast message**: `welcome-to-use-LeScratch`.
- **Broadcast message**: `hello-world`.

The result is shown as follows. Note that the last message will replace the previous one on the LCD screen:

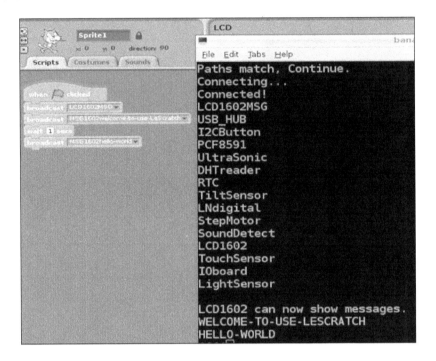

Building the LeScratch smart house

Imagine that you are still half awake on your sweet bed early in the morning. It's time to wake up but you expect something more interesting to replace the ringing of your alarm clock. What about this situation: you wake up to the singing of a gentle bird rather than the alarm clock, which might make you panic. Then, you touch a button on the wall and your favorite kind of music starts to play. Brushing your teeth, you glance at the LCD screen, showing the weather report and timetable; it gives you suggestions on what to wear and reminds you of your schedule for the day. After you get ready and head to the garage, the doors open by themselves when you get closer to them; lights in corridors turn on when there's a slight sound and switch off in intervals.

The LeScratch handler program is very simple to use and flexible when adding new extensions; apart from current realized sensor modules, it's easy to add more new modules as well. To implement all these intelligent and functional furniture mentioned previously in real house is a big job, but now you just need a Banana Pro to run the Scratch and LeScratch handler, some extra sensors and wires, and you're ready to make a little house model.

Download the 3D module file of the house, the LeScratch package, documentation, and the Scratch demo from `https://github.com/LeMaker/LeScratch/`. Now, let's start.

In the first place, prepare all the sensors, module parts, wires, and SD card and board; you can check the following list for more details:

LeScratch extensions	The smart house demonstration
The LED GPIO board	Step motor and motor driver
The MCP23017 USB hub	The RTC sensor
The MCP23s17 LN digital board	Ultrasonic sensor
Step motor and motor driver	Humidity and temperature sensor
The RTC sensor	Sound detection sensor
Ultrasonic sensor	The AD/DA Converter
Humidity and temperature sensor	Photoresistor
Sound detection sensor	Touch sensor
The AD/DA converter	Tilt sensor
Photoresistor	LCD
Touch sensor	Relays (this includes a 12V LED light and electromagnetic lock)
Tilt sensor	Speaker

The 3D design of the little house considers Banana Pro, which is set in the middle of the ground; all the currently supported sensors are fixed on the walls:

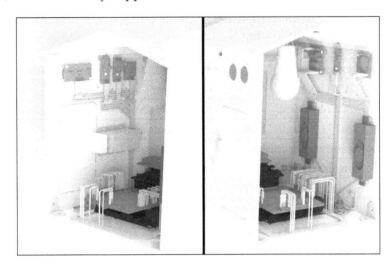

Below is the smart house from another perspective.

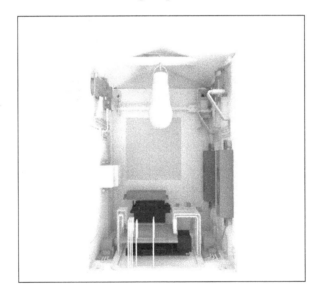

Shown below is the top view of the house.

Now you can start to build the house using pillars and screws to set the sensors, and the LCD and IO board are simple to connect to each other; you can connect each sensor to the board using Dupont lines. The pin assignments are listed in the following table; remember that we have left, right, and the front side of 40 pins. Apart from the VCC and GND, you can find other connections in each sensor section as follows:

Sensors	VCC	GND	Others
The step motor and motor driver	Pin 2 (right)	Pin 6 (right)	Pin 23, pin 26, pin 36, and pin 37
The RTC sensor	Pin 1 (right)	Pin 9 (right)	Pin 3 and Pin 5
Tilt sensor	Pin 4 (right)	Pin 14 (right)	Pin 19 (right)
Photoresistor	Pin 17 (right)	Pin 20 (right)	Pin 40 (right)
Ultrasonic sensor	Pin 1 (left)	Pin 6 (left)	Pin 8 and pin 10
Humidity and temperature sensor	Pin 17 (left)	Pin 34 (left)	Pin 35
Sound detection sensor	Pin 4 (left)	Pin 25 (left)	Pin 24
Touch sensor	Pin 2 (left)	Pin 30 (left)	Pin 31
Relay(from a 12V LED light)	Pin 2 (front)	Pin 6 (front)	Pin 21
Relay(electromagnetic lock)	Pin 4 (front)	Pin 9 (front)	Pin 38
The AD/DA converter	IO board	IO board	IO board
LCD	IO board	IO board	IO board

The complete house looks similar to what is shown in the following screenshot; each sensor has been highlighted with a name for you:

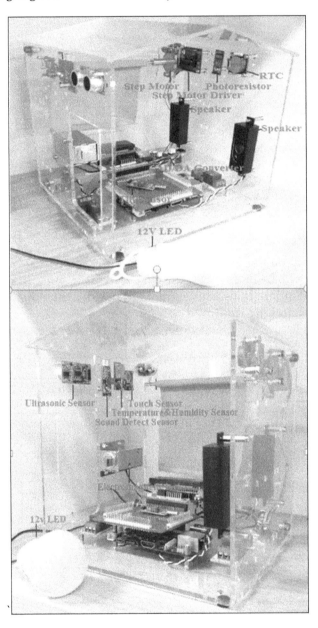

The Scratch program controlling all the sensors is divided into parts; now, we're going to explain each part:

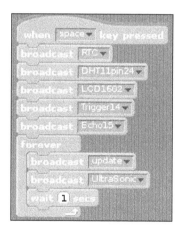

When the spacebar is pressed, the RTC sensor gives the exact time as the same as it is running on Banana Pro systems, displaying the time clock on the LCD screen per second. The temperature and humidity sensor measures environmental temperature and humidity, sending data to the LCD screen and displaying on it. Doors open according to the measured distance by the ultrasonic sensor, when people get close, the electromagnetic lock opens.

The LCD1602 command is to display RTC and DHT.

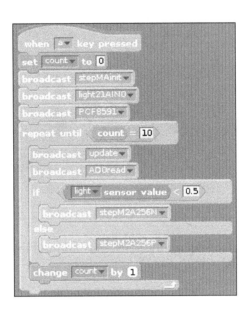

When the **A** key is pressed, initiate motor A and the light sensor. The photoresistor provides a threshold to control the opening and closing of the curtain, which is driven by a step motor; initiate PCF8591 reads the analog light intensity value, which is used as a threshold to control motor A. If the light intensity value < 0.5, motor A steps anticlockwise, else motor A steps clockwise.

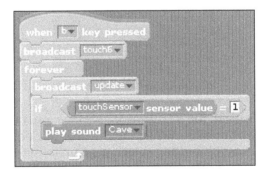

When B is pressed, the touch sensor is the switch to play music, which connects the speakers on the right wall. When the sensor is touched, play Cave sound:

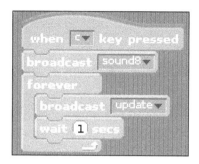

When C is pressed, the sound controlled LED light switches on if a sound has been detected and will switch off in delays of 1 minute.

Summary

In this chapter, we introduced you to how LeScratch works with the MIT Scratch education 1.4, and how hardware extensions can be used in real-life applications; LeScratch Smart House is an integrated example of currently supported peripherals. LeScratch is open source, and every user of Banana Pro is welcome to join the community in order to share new ideas and projects. You're also free to download source code from GitHub, and then modify or add more components in the LeScratch handler program using Python.

Index

A

AD/DA converter
 about 312
 example 313, 314
 technical specifications 312, 313
add-ons, Banana Pro
 about 27
 camera module 33
 GPIO add-ons 38
 LCD module 27
**Advanced Linux Sound Architecture
 (ALSA) 188**
AirPlay protocol
 about 101-103
 external USB SPDIF soundcard,
 using 103, 104
AirPrint
 about 104, 105
 CUPS, configuring 106-111
 printing, from Android and iOS 111, 112
Android 14, 15
arcade cabinet
 building 133
arcade cabinet, for Banana Pro
 assembling 157
 building 152
 frame, designing 156, 157
 joystick controller, configuring 164
 materials, preparing 152
 output, configuring to LCD 161-164
 playing 161, 166
Arduino
 download link 268
 installing 268

assembling, for Banana Pro arcade cabinet
 Banana Pro and joystick, assembling 158
 base frame, assembling 158
 LCD, mounting 159, 160
 top frame, assembling 160

B

Banana Pro
 about 1, 2
 add-ons 27
 cases 36-38
 connectors 4
 LEDs 9
 onboard microphone 39, 40
 operating systems 13
 specifications 3, 4
**basic principles, programming
 languages 42**
**basic requirements, programming
 languages**
 about 44
 nano editor 45
BCM_GPIO (Broadcom SOC channel) 55
BroadCom declaration Mode (BCM) 59

C

camera module
 about 33
 step-by-step guide 34, 35
camera setup
 about 226
 camera module, connecting 228-230
 camera module, testing 231
 specifications 226

CAN (Controller Area Network) 3
category files, webiopi project
config file 241
HTML file 241
Python script 241
C/C++
about 64, 65
C access, to onboard LEDs 67-72
debugger 73-76
WiringBP C code example 66
Chromium 58
components, laser engraving machine
5 inch LCD 261
acrylic frame 262
DC 12V power adapter 259
laser Central Processing Unit (CPU) 258
laser emitter 259
laser radiator 260
micro USB cable 261
power switch 260
protective glasses 261
USBtinyISP 259
X/Y motor 260
Concurrent Version System (CVS) 205
connectors, Banana Pro
40-pin GPIO header 6
AV output 6
camera interface 6
debug TTL UART 4
display interface 4
Ethernet interfaces 8
FEL button 8
HDMI 4
IR Receiver 8
microphone 6
microSD card slot 8
micro USB power 5
power button 6
reset button 6
SATA 2.0 interface 4
SATA/DC 5V 4
USB 8
USB OTG 6
Contao 112
contao content management system (CMS)
installing 116

Contiguous Memory Allocator (CMA)
mode 178
Coordinated Universal Time (UTC) 179
C programming 132
CSI (Camera Serial Interface) 3
Customized Style Sheets (CSS) file 131

D

dependencies
installing 264
dependencies, hardware accelerations
directory, installing 135
modules, installing 134
packages, installing 135
Digital Satellite Equipment Control
(DISEQC) settings 187
Digital Video Broadcast (DVB) 169
Domain Name Service (DNS) 98

E

Electronic Program Guide
(EPG) 179, 180, 208
engine x. See nginx

F

ffmpeg
about 220
installing 220
URL 220
flexible printed circuit (FPC) cable 29
FTDI/SPI control of devices
about 126
clock line 126
enable line 126
read line 127
write line 126
full binary-coded decimal (BCD) clock 303

G

games
iMAM4ALL games, playing 146
playing 146
playing, directly with command line 146

playing, from RetroArch menu
    interface 147, 148
SNES games, playing 146
gdb debugger commands 74
General Purpose Input Output (GPIO)
about 287
GPIO board example 289, 290
instructions 287
usages 287
GNU Compiler Collection (GCC) 64
GPIO add-ons 38
Graphics Processing Unit (GPU) 170
GrblController software
installing 264-266
gutenprint0-package
URL 104

H

hardware accelerations
dependencies, installing 134
device permission 138
installing 134
libdri2, installing 135
libump, installing 136
sunxi-mali driver, installing 136, 137
testing 139, 141
xf86-video-fbturbo, installing 137
hardware setup, of small car
5 inch LCD 237
5 inch LCD display output, configuring 240
about 234
assembly 237-239
battery 236
car suite 235
L289N motor drive board 236
materials, preparing 234
hostapd
URL 96
humidity and temperature sensor
about 307
example 308, 309
technical specifications 307, 308

I

Inkscape
download link 267
installing 267, 268
Integrated Development Environment
    (IDE) 76
Inter-Integrated Circuit (I²C)
about 291
instructions 291
USB Hub example 292, 294
IP camera 219
IP camera implementation
about 220
camera, setting up 226
ffmpeg, installing 220, 221
nginx, installing 221
nginx server, configuring 222
video, streaming via Internet 232-234

K

kernel preparation
about 170
accelerated mali driver, installing 176, 177
display driver brightness, correcting 175
display driver kernel logging,
    deactivating 173
DVB-SKY S960 USB box, adding 176
graphics memory, setting to maximum 172
I2S audio device, adding 170-172
IR driver key repetition, activating 174
sunxi lirc driver, activating 174
Kodi 14

L

laser CPU
bootloader, loading 269
driving code, loading 270-273
program, loading 269
laser engraving machine
about 257
engraving process 278
frame, setting up 258

G code, generating 273-277
  hardware, setting up 262, 263
  materials, prepraring 258
  using 273
LCD1602 display
  about 321
  example 322, 324
  technical specifications 322
LCD module
  7-inch LCD step-by-step guide 28-32
  about 27
LEDs
  about 9
  first boot 12
  programming 9-11
LeMaker Banana Pro camera module
  specifications 33, 34
LeScratch
  about 281
  running 284-286
LeScratch configuration
  performing 282
  prerequisites, installing 282, 283
  Scratch Mesh, setting up 284
  system, setting up 283, 284
LeScratch peripherals
  AD/DA converter 312
  controlling 286
  GPIO 287
  humidity and temperature sensor 307
  Inter-Integrated Circuit (I²C) 291
  LCD1602 display 321
  photoresistor 315
  real-time clock (RTC) 302
  Serial Peripheral Interface (SPI) 294
  sound detection sensor 309
  step motor 298
  tilt sensor 319
  touch sensor 318
  ultrasonic sensor 305
LeScratch smart house
  building 324-331
libdri2
  installing 135
libretro 142

libretro cores
  about 144
  iMAM4ALL libretro core, installing 144
  installing 144
  SNES libretro core, installing 144
libretro emulators
  configuration 145
  dependent packages, installing 142
  games, playing 146
  games, testing 149
  implementing 142
  libretro cores, installing 144
  libretro frontend, installing 142
libump
  installing 136
Linux
  about 15-18
  FEX file 18-22
  OS, transferring to hard disk 23, 24
Liquid Crystal Display (LCD) screen 321
Local Area Network (LAN) 106

M

materials, for Banana Pro arcade cabinet
  audio extended line 155
  joystick 153
  LCD display 155
  micro USB extended line 154
  mini keyboard 156
  preparing 152
  suitcase 152
  USB hub 154
measurement server
  about 125
  explanations 131
  FTDI/SPI control of devices 126-129
  web server 129, 130

N

Network Attached Storage (NAS) 88, 105
new kernels
  about 81
  compiling, on Banana Pro 82
  cross-compilation 83-85

nginx
 about 221
 installing 221
nginx server
 accessing 223
 autostarting, at system boot 224, 225
 configuring 222
 starting 222
numerical control (NC) machine tools 257

O

Omnivision 5640 CMOS image sensor 33
OpenVPN
 about 88-93
 connecting, from Android 93-95
 URL 88
operating systems, Banana Pro
 Android 14
 Linux 15-18

P

PCSX
 about 149
 building 149
 compiling 150, 151
 configuration 151
 dependent packages, installing 149
 installing 149-151
 patching 150
 PCSX ReARMed, downloading 149
PCSX games
 playing 151
 testing 152
photoresistor
 about 315
 example 316, 317
 technical specifications 315
Power Management Unit (PMU) 2
PPD (Postscript Printer Description)
 files 105
programming languages
 about 41
 basic principles 42
 basic requirements 44
 C/C++ 64

 Python 56
 remote connections 42
 Scratch 76
 shell programming 47
Pulse Width Modulation (PWM) 60
Putty
 about 42
 URL 42
Python
 about 56
 basics 56
 LEDs, setting 60-62
 Python window example 62, 63
 simple web server 57, 58
 using, for GPIO 58-60
Python/C interface 132
Python web server 131

R

real-time clock (RTC)
 about 8, 302
 example 303, 304
 technical specifications 303
Real Time Message Protocol (RTMP) 220
remote connections, programming
 languages
 about 42
 Secure Shell (SSH) 42, 43
 xrdp 43, 44
Remote Desktop Protocol (RDP) 43
RetroArch
 about 142
 building 142
 framebuffer version 143
 X11 version 143

S

Scratch
 about 76, 77
 LN Digital, using with 78-80
Scratch program 77
screen0_out_color_range mode 20
screen0_output_type mode 21
Serial Peripheral Interface (SPI)
 about 294

LN Digital extension 297
LN Digital or SPI general example 296
shell programming
about 47
Banana Pro LEDs, controlling
    from SSH 48, 49
Banana Pro temperature, reading 47
GPIOs, programming from shell 50, 51
shell example 52, 53
WiringBP 53-55
small car remote control
about 240
car controls, adding to IP camera
    web page 254, 255
webiopi, for Banana Pro 240
webiopi, using 245
software
configuring, on Banana Pro 264
installing, on PC 267
software development kit (SDK) 14
**Sony/Philips Digital Interface Format
    (SPDIF) 101**
sound detection sensor
about 309
example 310
technical specifications 310
step motor
about 298
example 300
full step drive 299
half stepping 299
micro stepping 300
technical specifications 299
wave drive 299
ways to drive 299
streamdev plugin 210
sunxi-mali driver
framebuffer version sunxi-mali 137
installing 136, 137
X11 version sunxi-mali 137

T

tilt sensor
about 319
example 320, 321
technical specifications 319, 320

touch sensor
about 318
example 318, 319
technical specifications 318
**troubleshooting, Video Disk Recorder
    (VDR)**
device permissions 213
libvdpau 214

U

U.FL connector 37
ultrasonic sensor
about 305
example 306, 307
technical specifications 305

V

**Video Decode and Presentation API for
    Unix (VDPAU) 169**
Video Disk Recorder (VDR)
about 81, 178
audio CDs, listening 206, 207
compiling 185-188
Debian multimedia packages, adding 180
default sound device, adding 188, 189
display settings 178, 179
DVB kernel driver 197-200
DVB userspace driver 200
DVDs, watching 205, 206
electrical SPDIF, using with Banana Pro 189
external players, switching to 211
FEX file, editing 181
irexec program 196
locales, setting 179
network address 180
plugins, adding 204
remote control, configuring 190-195
required modules, loading 180
scripts 201-203
skin, changing 208, 209
sound device, defining 188
teletext, watching 207
troubleshooting 213
TV, streaming to mobile devices 210
URL 178

USB DVB stick, adding 196
VDPAU, installing 183
VDPAU, patching 183
vdradmin-am 212, 213
Virtual Private Network (VPN) server 88

W

webiopi, for Banana Pro
  about 240
  installing 240
  testing 241-244
webiopi, for car remote control
  control logic 246
  webiopi controlling code, writing 246-253
web pages, serving
  about 112, 113
  contao, installing 116-124
  mysql, installing 114-116
  php, installing 113-116
WIN32 Disk Imager
  reference 9
wireless projects
  about 87
  AirPlay protocol 101-103
  AirPrint 104
  measurement server 125
  OpenVPN 88
  web pages, serving 112
  WLAN 95
WLAN
  about 95
  access point mode, setting up 96-100
  setting up 95, 96

X

XBMC 14
Xbox Media Centre 14
Xbox Multimedia Center (XBMC)
        installation 214-216
xf86-video-fbturbo
  installing 137

Thank you for buying
Banana Pro Blueprints

About Packt Publishing

Packt, pronounced 'packed', published its first book, *Mastering phpMyAdmin for Effective MySQL Management*, in April 2004, and subsequently continued to specialize in publishing highly focused books on specific technologies and solutions.

Our books and publications share the experiences of your fellow IT professionals in adapting and customizing today's systems, applications, and frameworks. Our solution-based books give you the knowledge and power to customize the software and technologies you're using to get the job done. Packt books are more specific and less general than the IT books you have seen in the past. Our unique business model allows us to bring you more focused information, giving you more of what you need to know, and less of what you don't.

Packt is a modern yet unique publishing company that focuses on producing quality, cutting-edge books for communities of developers, administrators, and newbies alike. For more information, please visit our website at www.packtpub.com.

About Packt Open Source

In 2010, Packt launched two new brands, Packt Open Source and Packt Enterprise, in order to continue its focus on specialization. This book is part of the Packt Open Source brand, home to books published on software built around open source licenses, and offering information to anybody from advanced developers to budding web designers. The Open Source brand also runs Packt's Open Source Royalty Scheme, by which Packt gives a royalty to each open source project about whose software a book is sold.

Writing for Packt

We welcome all inquiries from people who are interested in authoring. Book proposals should be sent to author@packtpub.com. If your book idea is still at an early stage and you would like to discuss it first before writing a formal book proposal, then please contact us; one of our commissioning editors will get in touch with you.

We're not just looking for published authors; if you have strong technical skills but no writing experience, our experienced editors can help you develop a writing career, or simply get some additional reward for your expertise.

Learning Banana Pi

ISBN: 978-1-78528-930-9   Paperback: 178 pages

Unleash the power of Banana Pi and use it for home automation, games, and various practical applications

1. Using Banana Pi, learn how to install and build basic projects from start to end.

2. Learn all the fundamentals and uses of Banana Pi to build projects in a short amount of time.

3. A step-by-step practical guide that teaches you how to get up and start running with Banana Pi to start working on your own projects.

Banana Pi Cookbook

ISBN: 978-1-78355-244-3   Paperback: 200 pages

Over 25 recipes to build projects and applications for multiple platforms with Banana Pi

1. Design, develop, and customize real-world applications and projects rapidly and easily using Banana Pi.

2. Quick solutions to the most common real-world problems on the amazing Banana Pi.

3. Step-by-step recipes to help you experience the vast possibilities of the device by setting up interesting applications.

Please check **www.PacktPub.com** for information on our titles

Raspberry Pi Cookbook for Python Programmers

ISBN: 978-1-84969-662-3   Paperback: 402 pages

Over 50 easy-to-comprehend tailor-made recipes to get the most out of the Raspberry Pi and unleash its huge potential using Python

1. Install your first operating system, share files over the network, and run programs remotely.

2. Unleash the hidden potential of the Raspberry Pi's powerful Video Core IV graphics processor with your own hardware accelerated 3D graphics.

3. Discover how to create your own electronic circuits to interact with the Raspberry Pi.

Learning Raspberry Pi

ISBN: 978-1-78398-282-0   Paperback: 258 pages

Unlock your creative programming potential by creating web technologies, image processing, electronics- and robotics-based projects using the Raspberry Pi

1. Learn how to create games, web, and desktop applications using the best features of the Raspberry Pi.

2. Discover the powerful development tools that allow you to cross-compile your software and build your own Linux distribution for maximum performance.

3. Step-by-step tutorials show you how to quickly develop real-world applications using the Raspberry Pi.

Please check **www.PacktPub.com** for information on our titles

www.ingramcontent.com/pod-product-compliance
Lightning Source LLC
Chambersburg PA
CBHW062051050326
40690CB00016B/3057